Organic Chemistry Laboratories

CHEM 2111 and CHEM 2112

John C. Gilbert | Stephen F. Martin

Australia • Brazil • Japan • Korea • Mexico • Singapore • Spain • United Kingdom • United States

Organic Chemistry Laboratories, CHEM 2111 and 2112

Experimental Organic Chemistry: A Miniscale & Microscale Approach, 6th Edition
John C. Gilbert | Stephen F. Martin

For product information and technology assistance, contact us at
Cengage Learning Customer & Sales Support, 1-800-354-9706
For permission to use material from this text or product,
submit all requests online at **cengage.com/permissions**
Further permissions questions can be emailed to
permissionrequest@cengage.com

This book contains select works from existing Cengage Learning resources and was produced by Cengage Learning Custom Solutions for collegiate use. As such, those adopting and/or contributing to this work are responsible for editorial content accuracy, continuity and completeness.

ISBN: 978-1-337-04263-5

Cengage Learning
20 Channel Center Street
Boston, MA 02210
USA

Cengage Learning is a leading provider of customized learning solutions with office locations around the globe, including Singapore, the United Kingdom, Australia, Mexico, Brazil, and Japan. Locate your local office at: **www.international.cengage.com/region.**

Cengage Learning products are represented in Canada by Nelson Education, Ltd.

For your lifelong learning solutions, visit **www.cengage.com/custom.**

Visit our corporate website at **www.cengage.com.**

Printed in Mexico

Brief Contents

CHAPTER 1

Introduction, Record Keeping, and Laboratory Safety

This chapter sets the stage as you undertake the adventure of experimental organic chemistry. Although we may be biased, we think that this laboratory experience is one of the most valuable you will have as an undergraduate student. There is much to be learned as you progress from the relatively structured format of your first laboratory course in organic chemistry to the much less defined experimental protocols of a scientific research environment. The laboratory practices described in the following sections should serve you well in the journey.

1.1 INTRODUCTION

The laboratory component of a course in organic chemistry has an important role in developing and augmenting your understanding of the subject matter. The theoretical concepts, functional groups, and reactions presented in the lecture part of the course may seem abstract at times, but they are more understandable as a result of the experiments you perform. The successes, challenges, and, yes, frustrations associated with the "hands-on" experience gained in the laboratory, as you gather and interpret data from a variety of reactions, provide a sense of organic chemistry that is nearly impossible to communicate in formal lectures. For example, it is one thing to be told that the addition of bromine (Br_2) across the π-bond of most alkenes is a rapid process at room temperature. It is quite another to personally observe the *immediate* decoloration of a reddish solution of bromine in dichloromethane (Br_2/CH_2Cl_2) as a few drops of it are added to cyclohexene. The principles developed in the lectures will help you to predict what reaction(s) should occur when various reagents are combined in experimental procedures and to understand the mechanistic course of the process(es). Performing reactions allows you to test and verify the principles presented in lecture. Moreover, careful and thoughtful analysis of the observations and results of the experiments will foster the skills in critical thinking that are a hallmark of successful scientists.

Of course, the laboratory experience in organic chemistry has another important function beyond reinforcing the concepts presented in lecture—to introduce you to the broad range of techniques and procedures that are important to the successful practice of experimental organic chemistry. You will learn how to handle a variety of chemicals safely and how to manipulate apparatus properly, talents that are critical to your success as a student of the chemical sciences. Along with becoming more skilled in the technical aspects of laboratory work, you should also develop a proper scientific approach to executing experiments and interpreting the results. By reading and, more importantly, *understanding* the concepts of this chapter, you will be better able to achieve these valuable goals.

1.2 PREPARING FOR THE LABORATORY

A common misconception students have about performing experiments is that it is much like cooking; that is, you merely follow the directions given—the "recipe"—and the desired product or data will result. Such students enter the laboratory expecting to follow the experimental procedure in a more or less rote manner. This unfortunate attitude can lead to inefficiencies, accidents, and minimal educational benefit and enjoyment from the laboratory experience.

To be sure, cooking is somewhat analogous to performing experiments. The successful scientist, just like a five-star chef, is a careful planner, a diligent worker, a keen observer, and, importantly, is fully prepared for failures! Experiments may not work despite your best efforts, just as a cake may fall even in the hands of a premier pastry chef.

The correct approach to being successful in the laboratory is *never* to begin any experiment until you understand its overall purpose and the reasons for each operation that you are to do. This means that you must *study*, not *just read*, the entire experiment *prior* to arriving at the laboratory. Rarely, if ever, can you complete the necessary preparation in 5 or 10 minutes, which means that you should not wait until just before the laboratory period begins to do the studying, thinking, and writing that are required. *Planning* how to spend your time in the laboratory is the key to efficient completion of the required experiments. Your performance in the laboratory will benefit enormously from proper advance work, and so will your grade!

The specific details of what you should do before coming to the laboratory will be provided by your instructor. However, to help you prepare in advance, we have developed a set of Pre-Lab Exercises for each of the experimental procedures we describe. These exercises are Web-based and are available online.

Your instructor may require you to submit answers to the Pre-Lab Exercises for approval before authorizing you to proceed with the assigned experiments. Even if you are not required to submit the exercises, though, you will find that answering them *prior* to the laboratory period will be a valuable educational tool to self-assess your understanding of the experiments to be performed.

You undoubtedly will be required to maintain a laboratory notebook, which will serve as a complete, accurate, and neat record of the experimental work that you do. Once more, your instructor will provide an outline of what specific information should appear in this notebook, but part of what is prescribed will probably necessitate advance preparation, which will further enhance your ability to complete the experiments successfully. The laboratory notebook is a *permanent record* of your accomplishments in the course, and you should take pride in the quality and completeness of its contents!

1.3 WORKING IN THE LABORATORY

You should be aware that experimental organic chemistry is *potentially* dangerous, because many of the chemicals used are toxic and/or highly flammable, and most of the procedures require the use of glassware that is easily broken. Careless handling of these chemicals and sloppy assembly of apparatus are sources of danger not only to you but also to those working near you. You *should* not be afraid of the chemicals and equipment that you will be using, but you should treat them with the respect and care associated with safe experimental practices. To facilitate this, there is an emphasis on the proper handling of chemicals and apparatus throughout the textbook, and the importance of paying particular attention to these subjects *cannot* be overemphasized. In a sense, laboratory safety is analogous to a chain that is only as strong as its weakest link: The possibility that an accident will occur is only as great as the extent to which unsafe practices are followed. In other words, if you and your labmates adhere to proper laboratory procedures, the risk of an accident will be minimized.

It is important that you follow the experimental procedures in this textbook closely. There is a good reason why each operation should be performed as it is described, although that reason may not be immediately obvious to you. Just as it is risky for a novice chef to be overly innovative when following a recipe, it is *dangerous* for a beginning experimentalist to be "creative" when it comes to modifying the protocol that we've specified. As you gain experience in the organic laboratory, you may wish to develop alternative procedures for performing a reaction or purifying a desired product, but *always* check with your instructor *before* trying any modifications.

Note that rather detailed experimental procedures are given early in the textbook, whereas somewhat less detailed instructions are provided later on. This is because many of the basic laboratory operations will have become familiar to you in time and need not be spelled out explicitly. It is hoped that this approach to the design of procedures will decrease your tendency to think that you are essentially following a recipe in a cookbook. Moreover, many of the experimental procedures given in the literature of organic chemistry are relatively brief and require the chemist to "fill in the blanks," so it is valuable to gain some initial experience in figuring out some details on your own.

Most of your previous experience in a chemistry laboratory has probably required that you measure quantities precisely, using analytical balances, burets, pipets, and other precise measuring devices (Secs. 2.5 and 2.6). Indeed, if you have done quantitative inorganic analysis, you know that it is often necessary to measure weights to the third or fourth decimal place and volumes to at least the first. Experiments in organic chemistry that are performed at the **microscale** level, that is, experiments in which less than about 1 mL of the principal reagents is used and the amounts of solvents are less than 2 or 3 mL, also require relatively precise measuring of quantities. For example, if you are to use 0.1 g of a reagent and your measuring device only allows measuring to the nearest 0.1 g, you could easily have as much as about 0.15 g or as little as 0.05 g of the reagent. Such deviations from the desired quantity represent significant *percentage* errors in measurement and can result in serious errors in the proportions of reagents involved in the reaction. Consequently, weights should be accurate to within about 0.01 g and volumes to within about 0.1 mL. This requires the use of appropriate analytical balances and graduated pipets.

Experiments being performed at the **miniscale** level, which we define as involving 1–5 g of reagents and usually less than about 25 mL of solvent, normally do not require such precise measuring. Weighing reagents to the nearest tenth of a gram is usually satisfactory, as is measuring out liquids in graduated cylinders, which are accurate to $\pm 10\%$. For example, if you are directed to use 20 mL of diethyl ether as solvent for a reaction, the volume need *not* be 20.0 mL. In fact, it probably will make little difference to the success of the reaction whether anywhere from

15 mL to 25 mL of the solvent is added. This is not to say that care need not be exercised in measuring out the amounts of materials that you use. Rather, it means that valuable time need not be invested in making these measurements highly precise.

We've inserted markers in the form of **stars** (★) in many of the experimental procedures in this textbook. These indicate places where the procedure can be interrupted without affecting the final outcome of the experiment. These markers are designed to help you make the most efficient use of your time in the laboratory. For example, you may be able to start a procedure at a point in the period when there is insufficient time to complete it but enough time to be able to work through to the location of a star; you can then safely store the reaction mixture and finish the sequence during the next laboratory period. We've *not* inserted stars at every possible stopping point but only at those where it is not necessarily obvious that interruption of the procedure will have no effect on the experimental results. Consult your instructor if in doubt about whether a proper stopping point has been reached.

As noted above, a *carefully* written **notebook** and *proper* **safety procedures** are important components of an experimental laboratory course. These aspects are discussed further in the following two sections.

1.4 THE LABORATORY NOTEBOOK

One of the most important characteristics of successful scientists is the habit of keeping a complete and understandable record of the experimental work that has been done. Did a precipitate form? Was there a color change during the course of the reaction? At what temperature was the reaction performed, and for how long did the reaction proceed? Was the reaction mixture homogeneous or heterogeneous? On what date(s) was the work performed? These are observations and data that may seem insignificant at the time but may later prove critical to the interpretation of an experimental result or to the ability of another person to reproduce your work. All of them belong in a properly kept laboratory notebook. We make suggestions for such a document in the following two sections. Your instructor may specify other items to be included, but the list we give is representative of a good notebook.

1.5 GENERAL PROTOCOL FOR THE LABORATORY NOTEBOOK

1. Use a *bound* notebook for your permanent laboratory record to minimize the possibility that pages will be lost. If a number has not been printed on each page, do so manually. Some laboratory notebooks are designed with pairs of identically numbered pages so that a carbon copy of all entries can be made. The duplicate page can then be removed and submitted to your instructor or put in a separate place for safekeeping. Many professional scientists use this type of notebook.
2. Reserve the first page of the notebook for use as a title page, and leave several additional pages blank for a Table of Contents.
3. Use as the main criterion for what should be entered in the notebook the rule that the record should be sufficiently complete so that anyone who reads it will know exactly what you did and will be able to repeat the work in precisely the way you originally did it.

4. Record all experimental observations and data in the notebook *as they are obtained*. Include the date and, if appropriate, the *time* when you did the work. In a legal sense, the information entered into the notebook *at the time of performance* constitutes the primary record of the work, and it is important for you to follow this principle. Many patent cases have been determined on the basis of dates and times recorded in a laboratory notebook. One such example is described in the Historical Highlight *The Importance of Record Keeping*, which is available online.
5. Make all entries in ink, and *do not delete anything you have written* in the notebook. If you make a mistake, cross it out and record the correct information. Using erasers or correction fluid to modify entries in your notebook is unacceptable scientific practice!

   Do not scribble notes on odd bits of paper with the intention of recording the information in your notebook later. Such bad habits only lead to problems, since the scraps of paper are easily lost or mixed up. They are also inefficient, since transcribing the information to your notebook means that you must write it a second time. This procedure can also result in errors if you miscopy the data.

   Finally, do not trust your memory with respect to observations that you have made. When the time comes to write down the information, you may have forgotten a key observation that is critical to the success of the experiment.
6. Unless instructed to do otherwise, do not copy *detailed* experimental procedures that you have already written elsewhere in your notebook; this consumes valuable time. Rather, provide a specific reference to the source of the detailed procedure and enter a *synopsis* of the written procedure that contains enough information that (1) you need not refer to the source while performing the procedure and (2) another chemist will be able to *duplicate* what you did. For example, when performing an experiment from this textbook, give a reference to the page number on which the procedure appears, and detail any *variations* made in the procedure along with the reason(s) for doing so.
7. Start the description of each experiment on a new page titled with the name of the experiment. The recording of data and observations from several different procedures on the same page can lead to confusion, both for yourself and for others who may read your notebook. If you are unable to complete the write-up of an experiment on sequential pages, be certain to specify the page(s) on which the continuation appears.

1.6 TYPES OF ORGANIC EXPERIMENTS AND NOTEBOOK FORMATS

There are two general classes of experiments, **investigative** and **preparative,** in this textbook. Investigative experiments normally involve making observations and learning techniques that are common to laboratory work in organic chemistry but do not entail conversion of one compound into another. Some examples are solubility tests, distillation, recrystallization, and qualitative organic analysis. In contrast, preparative experiments involve interconversion of different compounds. Most of the procedures described in this textbook fall into the latter category.

The format of the laboratory notebook is usually different for these two types of experiments. Once again, your instructor may have a particular style that is recommended, but we provide suggested formats below.

Notebook Format for Investigative Experiments

1. **Heading.** Use a new page of the notebook to start the entries for the experiment. Provide information that includes your name, the date, the title of the experiment, and a reference to the place in the laboratory textbook or other source where the procedure may be found.
2. **Introduction.** Give a brief introduction to the experiment in which you clearly state the purpose(s) of the procedure. This should require no more than one-fourth of a page.
3. **Summary of MSDS Data.** As directed by your instructor, either briefly summarize the Material Safety Data Sheet (MSDS) data (Sec. 1.10) for the solvents, reagents, and products encountered in the experiment or give a reference to where a printout of these data is located.
4. **Synopsis of and Notes on Experimental Procedure—Results.** Enter a one- or two-line statement for each part of an experiment. Reserve sufficient room to record results as they are obtained. As noted in Section 1.5 of "Notebook Format for Preparative Experiments," do *not* copy the experimental procedure from the textbook, but provide a synopsis of it.

   Much of this section of the write-up can be completed before coming to the laboratory, to ensure that you understand the experiment and that you will perform all parts of it.
5. **Interpretation of Instrumental Data.** If instructed to do so, discuss any instrumental data, such as gas-liquid chromatographic analyses and spectral data that you have obtained or are provided in the textbook.
6. **Conclusions.** Record the conclusions that can be reached, based on the results you have obtained in the experiment. If the procedure has involved identifying an unknown compound, summarize your findings in this section.
7. **Answers to Exercises.** Enter answers to any exercises for the experiment that have been assigned from the textbook.

A sample write-up of an investigative experiment is given in Figure 1.1.

Notebook Format for Preparative Experiments

1. **Heading.** Use a new page of the notebook to start the entries for the experiment. Provide information that includes your name, the date, the title of the experiment, and a reference to the place in the laboratory textbook or other source where the procedure may be found.
2. **Introduction.** Give a brief introduction to the experiment in which you clearly state the purpose(s) of the procedure. This should require no more than one-fourth of a page.
3. **Main Reaction(s) and Mechanism(s).** Write *balanced* equations giving the main reaction(s) for conversion of starting material(s) to product(s). The reason for balancing the equations is discussed in Part **4 Table of Reactants and Products**. Whenever possible, include the detailed mechanisms for the reactions that you have written.
4. **Table of Reactants and Products.** Set up a Table of Reactants and Products as an aid in summarizing the amounts and properties of reagents and catalysts being used and the product(s) being formed. Only those reactants, catalysts, and

1.

Your Name
Date

Separation of Green Leaf Pigments by TLC

Reference: *Experimental Organic Chemistry: A Miniscale and Microscale Approach,* 6th ed., by Gilbert and Martin, Section 6.2.

2. INTRODUCTION

The pigments in green leaves are to be extracted into an organic solvent, and the extract is to be analyzed by thin-layer chromatography (TLC). The presence of multiple spots on the developed TLC plate will indicate that more than a single pigment is contained in the leaves.

3. MSDS DATA

These data are available on the printouts inserted at the back of my lab book.

4. SYNOPSIS OF AND NOTES ON EXPERIMENTAL PROCEDURE—RESULTS

Procedure: Grind five stemless spinach leaves in mortar and pestle with 5 mL of 2:1 pet. ether and EtOH. Swirl soln. with 3 × 2-mL portions H_2O in sep. funnel; dry org. soln. for few min over anhyd. Na_2SO_4 in Erlenmeyer. Decant and concentrate soln. if not dark-colored. Spot 10-cm × 2-cm TLC plate about 1.5 mm from end with dried extract; spot should be less than 2 mm diam. Develop plate with $CHCl_3$. *Variances and observations:* Procedure followed exactly as described in reference. Org. soln. was dark green in color; aq. extracts were yellowish. Half of org. layer lost. TLC plate had five spots having colors and R_f-values shown on the drawing below.

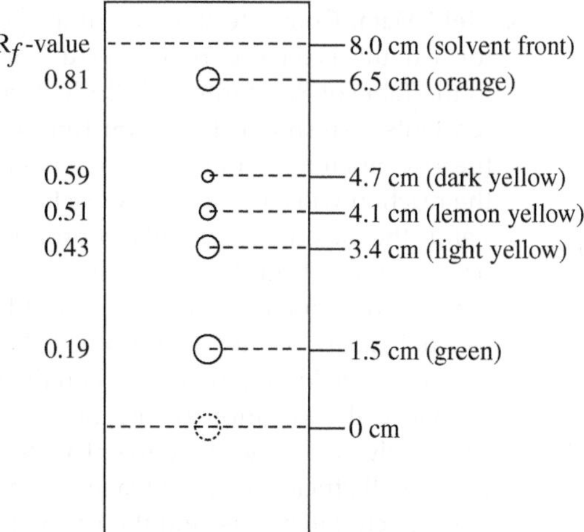

5. INTERPRETATION OF INSTRUMENTAL DATA

No data provided for this experiment.

6. CONCLUSIONS

Based on TLC analysis, the procedure used allows the extraction of at least five different pigments from the spinach leaves. Judging from colors, one of these is a carotene, three are xanthophylls, and the last is chlorophyll *b*.

7. ANSWERS TO EXERCISES

(Answers intentionally omitted.)

Figure 1.1
Sample notebook format for investigative experiments.

products that appear in the main reaction(s) should be listed in the table; many other reagents may be used in the work-up and purification of the reaction mixture, but these should *not* be entered in the table.

Your instructor will have specific recommendations about what should appear in the table, but the following items are illustrative.

a. The name and/or structure of each reactant, catalyst, and product.

b. The molar mass of each compound.

c. The weight used, in grams, of each reactant and the volume of any liquid reactant. We recommend that the weight and/or volume of any catalysts used be entered for purposes of completeness.

d. The molar amount of each reactant used; this can be calculated from the data in Parts **b** and **c.**

e. The theoretical mole ratio, expressed in whole numbers, for the reactants and products; this ratio is determined by the *balanced* equation for the reaction, as given in Part **3**, Main Reaction(s) and Mechanism(s).

f. Physical properties of the reactants and products. This entry might include data such as boiling and/or melting point, density, solubility, color, and odor.

g. As directed by your instructor, either briefly summarize the MSDS data (Sec. 1.10) for the solvents, reagents, and products encountered in the experiment or give a reference to where a printout of these data is located.

5. Yield Data. Compute the maximum possible amount of product that can be formed; this is the **theoretical yield.** This can easily be calculated from the data in the Table of Reactants and Products as follows. First determine which of the reactants corresponds to the **limiting reagent.** This is the reagent that is used in the *least* molar amount relative to what is required theoretically. In other words, the reaction will stop once this reactant is consumed, so its molar quantity will define the maximum quantity of product that can be produced. From the number of moles of limiting reagent involved and the balanced equation for the reaction, determine the theoretical yield, in moles (written as "mol" when used as a unit, as in "g/mol"), of product. This value can then be converted into the theoretical yield in grams, based on the molar mass of the product.

Once the isolation of the desired product(s) has been completed, you should also calculate the **percent yield,** which is a convenient way to express the overall efficiency of the reaction. This is done by obtaining the **actual yield** of product(s) in grams, and then applying the expression in Equation 1.1. Generally, the calculated value of percent yield is rounded to the nearest whole number. As points of reference, most organic chemists consider yields of 90% or greater as being "excellent," and those below 20% as "poor."

$$\text{Percent yield} = \frac{\text{Actual yield (g)}}{\text{Theoretical yield (g)}} \times 100 \qquad (1.1)$$

6. Synopsis of and Notes on Experimental Procedure. Provide an outline of the experimental procedure that contains enough detail so that you do not have to refer to the textbook repeatedly while performing the experiment. Note any variations that you use, as compared to the referenced procedure, and observations that you make while carrying out the formation and isolation of the product(s).

7. **Observed Properties of Product.** Record the physical properties of the product that you have isolated in the experiment. Appropriate data under this heading might include boiling and/or melting point, odor, color, and crystalline form, if the product is a solid. Compare your observations with those available on the compound in various reference books (e.g., the *CRC Handbook of Chemistry and Physics* or *Lange's Handbook of Chemistry*).
8. **Side Reactions.** If instructed to do so, list possible side reactions (those reactions leading to undesired products) that are likely to occur in the experiment. It is important to consider such processes because the by-products that are formed must be removed by the procedure used to purify the desired product. You may need to consult your lecture notes and textbook to predict what side reactions might be occurring.
9. **Other Methods of Preparation.** If instructed to do so, suggest alternative methods for preparing the desired compound. Such methods may involve using entirely different reagents and reaction conditions. Your lecture notes and textbook can serve as valuable resources for providing possible entries for this section.
10. **Method of Purification.** Develop a flowchart that summarizes the sequence of operations that will be used to purify the desired product. The chart will show at what stages of the work-up procedure unchanged starting materials and unwanted by-products are removed. By understanding the logic of the purification process, you will know why each of the various operations specified in the purification process is performed.

    Purifying the final product of a reaction can be the most challenging part of an experimental procedure. Professional organic chemists are constantly required to develop work-up sequences that allow isolation of a pure product, free from starting materials and other contaminants. They do this by considering the chemical and physical properties of both the desired and undesired substances, and it is important for you to gain experience in devising such schemes as well.
11. **Interpretation of Instrumental Data.** If instructed to do so, discuss any instrumental data, such as gas-liquid chromatographic analyses and spectral data you have obtained or that are provided in the textbook.
12. **Answers to Exercises.** Enter answers to any exercises for the experiment that have been assigned from the textbook.

A detailed example of the write-up for a preparative experiment involving the dehydration of cyclohexanol (Sec. 10.3) is given in Figure 1.2. You may not actually perform this reaction; nevertheless, you should carefully study the example to see how to prepare specific entries for the first eight items listed. The various entries in Figure 1.2 are labeled with circled, **boldface** numbers and are discussed further in the following paragraphs. It is assumed for illustrative purposes that an actual yield of 2.7 g is obtained.

1 Use a new page of the notebook to start the entries for the experiment. Provide information that includes your name, the date, the title of the experiment, and a reference to the place in the laboratory textbook or other source where the procedure can be found.

2 Self-explanatory.

① **1.** **Your Name**
Date

Dehydration of Cyclohexanol

Reference: *Experimental Organic Chemistry: A Miniscale and Microscale Approach,* 6th ed., by Gilbert and Martin, Section 10.3.

② **2.** INTRODUCTION

Cyclohexene is to be prepared by the acid-catalyzed dehydration of cyclohexanol.

③ **3.** MAIN REACTION(S) AND MECHANISM(S)

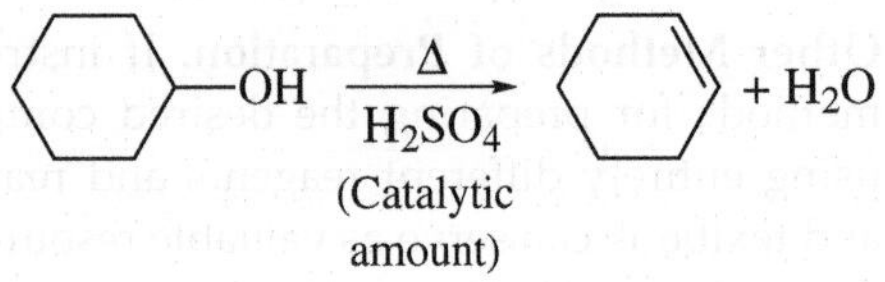

$$\text{Cyclohexanol-OH } (\mathbf{1}) \xrightarrow[\text{H}_2\text{SO}_4 \text{ (Catalytic amount)}]{\Delta} \text{Cyclohexene } (\mathbf{2}) + H_2O$$

(Mechanism intentionally omitted.)

④ **4.** TABLE OF REACTANTS AND PRODUCTS

⑤ Compound	⑥ M.M.	⑦a Volume Used (mL)	⑦b Weight Used (g)	⑧ Moles Used	⑨ Moles Required	⑩ Other Data
Cyclohexanol	100.2	5.2	5	0.05	1	bp 161 °C (760 torr), mp 25.1 °C, d 0.962 g/mL, colorless
Sulfuric acid (9 *M*)	98.1	2.5	#	#	0	d 1.84 (18 *M* H_2SO_4)
Cyclohexene	82.2	*	*	*	1	bp 83 °C (760 torr), mp 103.5 °C, d 0.810, colorless

#Entry left blank because this row is for the catalyst.

*Entry left blank because this row is for the product.

⑪ LIMITING REAGENT: Cyclohexanol

⑫ MSDS DATA

These data are available on the printouts inserted at the back of my lab book.

⑬ **5.** YIELD DATA

Theoretical yield of cyclohexene = moles of limiting reagent (cyclohexanol) × M.W. of cyclohexene

= 0.05 mol × 82.2 g/mol

= 4.1 g

Actual yield = 2.7 g

(Continued)

Figure 1.2
Sample notebook format for investigative experiments.

Percent yield = [Actual yield (g)/theoretical yield (g)] × 100
= [2.7/4.1] × 100 = 66%

(14) **6.** SYNOPSIS OF AND NOTES ON EXPERIMENTAL PROCEDURE—RESULTS

Procedure: Put alcohol in 25-mL rb flask and add H_2SO_4. Mix, add stirbar, attach to fractional dist. apparatus. Heat with oil bath; heating rate such that head temp. stays below 90 °C. Stop when 2.5 mL remain in rxn. flask. Put distillate in 25-mL Erlenmeyer and add 1–2 g K_2CO_3.* Occasionally swirl mix. for 15 min and transfer liquid to 10-mL rb by decantation or pipet. Add stirbar and do simple distillation (no flames!); receiver must be close to drip tip of adapter to minimize losses by evaporation. Collect product at 80–85 °C (760 torr).
Variances and observations: Procedure followed exactly as described in reference. Distillate cloudy throughout dehydration step; formed two layers in receiver. Head temperature never exceeded 77 °C. Liquid in stillpot darkened as reaction proceeded. Addition of carbonate (1 g) to distillate caused evolution of a few bubbles of gas (CO_2?). Had to add about 0.5 g more of carbonate to get rid of cloudiness. Left solution over drying agent for one week (next lab period). Used pipet to transfer dried liquid to distillation flask. Collected cyclohexene in ice-cooled 10-mL rb flask attached to vacuum adapter protected with $CaCl_2$ tube. Stopped distillation when about 1 mL of yellowish liquid remained in stillpot.

(15) **7.** OBSERVED PROPERTIES OF PRODUCT

bp 80–84 °C (760 torr); colorless liquid; insoluble in water; decolorizes Br_2/CH_2Cl_2 solution and produces brown precipitate upon treatment with $KMnO_4/H_2O$.

(16) **8.** SIDE REACTIONS

2 [cyclohexanol]—OH $\xrightarrow[\text{H}_2\text{SO}_4 \text{ (Catalytic amount)}]{\Delta}$ [dicyclohexyl ether] **3**

[cyclohexanol]—OH + $HOSO_3H$ ⟶ [cyclohexyl]—OSO_3H **4**

2 [cyclohexene] $\xrightarrow[\text{H}_2\text{SO}_4 \text{ (Catalytic amount)}]{\Delta}$ [cyclohexylcyclohexene] **5** ⟶ Polymeric hydrocarbons **6**

(Continued)

Figure 1.2 *(Continued)*

(17) **9.** OTHER METHODS OF PREPARATION

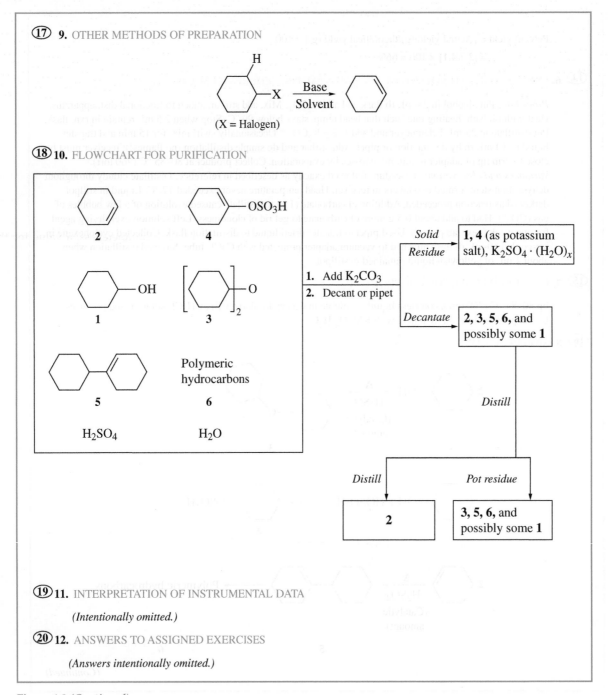

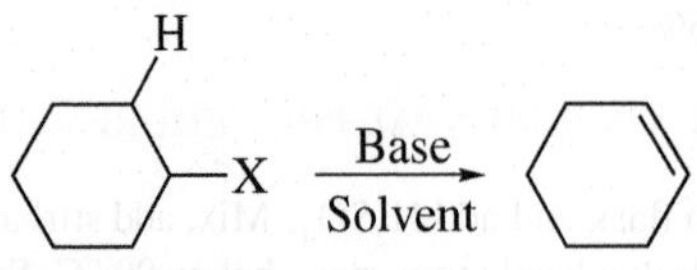

H
X
Base
Solvent
(X = Halogen)

(18) **10.** FLOWCHART FOR PURIFICATION

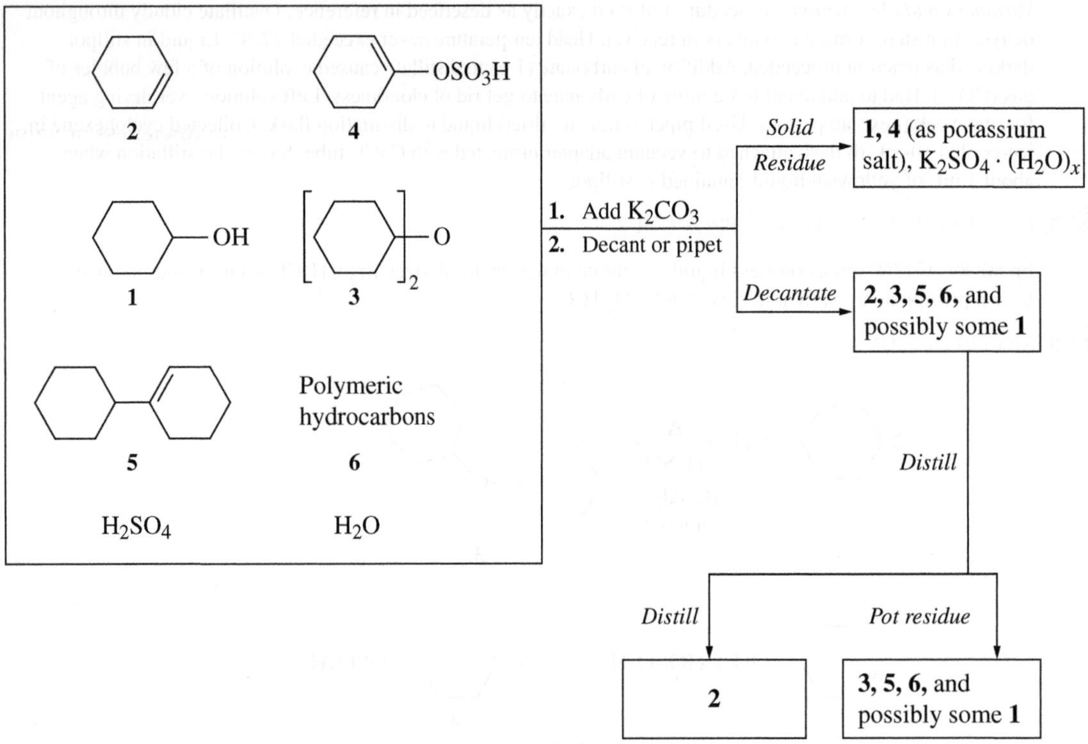

OSO_3H
2
4
OH
O
1
3
2
5
Polymeric hydrocarbons
6
H_2SO_4
H_2O

1. Add K_2CO_3
2. Decant or pipet

Solid Residue → **1, 4** (as potassium salt), $K_2SO_4 \cdot (H_2O)_x$

Decantate → **2, 3, 5, 6,** and possibly some **1**

Distill

Distill → **2**

Pot residue → **3, 5, 6,** and possibly some **1**

(19) **11.** INTERPRETATION OF INSTRUMENTAL DATA

(Intentionally omitted.)

(20) **12.** ANSWERS TO ASSIGNED EXERCISES

(Answers intentionally omitted.)

Figure 1.2 *(Continued)*

3 There is only a single reaction in our example, but in many cases more than one step is involved; write equations for *all* of the main reactions. A mechanism for the reaction is intentionally omitted in our example.

4 Use the illustrated format for the Table of Reactants and Products unless instructed to do otherwise.

5 Enter the name or structure of each reactant catalyst, if any, and desired product.

6 Record the molar mass (M.M.) of each reactant and desired product. For completeness, make an entry for any catalyst used, although this may be optional.

7a Give the volume, in milliliters (mL) or microliters (μL), of each *liquid* reactant and catalyst.

7b Record the weight, in grams (g) or milligrams (mg), of each reactant. This entry is optional for liquid catalysts but should be provided for reference purposes.

8 Calculate the moles used of each reactant. For completeness, a value for the catalyst is computed in our example.

9 Obtain the **theoretical ratio** for reactant(s) and product(s) by referring to the *balanced* main equation(s) for the reaction.

10 List selected physical properties of reactant(s) and product(s). The information needed is generally available in reference books.

11 Determine the **limiting reagent** in the following way. Compare the actual ratio of reactants used to that theoretically required. The reagent that is used in the least molar amount, relative to the theoretical amount, is the limiting reagent. In our example, there is only a single reagent, cyclohexanol, so it obviously must be the limiting reagent.

12 Self-explanatory. However, if you are instructed to provide MSDS data in the form of printouts from the online resources, be sure to read them. Ignorance is *not* bliss when it comes to handling chemicals!

13 Calculate the **theoretical yield** of the desired product both in moles and in grams. Knowing in our case that the limiting reagent is cyclohexanol and, from the main equation, that 1 mole of alcohol yields 1 mole of cyclohexene, it is clear that no more than 0.05 mole of the alkene can be formed.

Assuming that you were able to isolate 2.7 g of pure cyclohexene in the experiment, the **percent yield** would be calculated according to Equation 1.1.

14 Self-explanatory.

15 Self-explanatory.

16 Self-explanatory.

17 Self-explanatory.

18 Develop this diagram by considering what components, in addition to the desired product, may be present in the reaction mixture *after* the main reaction is complete. The chart shows how and where each of the inorganic and organic contaminants of the product is removed by the various steps of the work-up procedure. Ideally, pure cyclohexene results.

19 Self-explanatory.

20 Self-explanatory.

1.7 SAMPLE CALCULATIONS FOR NOTEBOOK RECORDS

Students frequently have difficulty in setting up Tables of Reactants and Products and calculating theoretical yields, so two hypothetical examples are provided for your reference.

Example 1

Problem Consider the reaction shown in Equation 1.2. Assume that you are to use 5 g (7.8 mL) of 1-pentene and 25 mL of concentrated HBr solution. Prepare a Table of Reactants and Products, determine the limiting reagent, and calculate the theoretical yield for the reaction.

$$CH_2=CHCH_2CH_2CH_3 + HBr \longrightarrow CH_3CH(Br)CH_2CH_2CH_3 \quad (1.2)$$

Answer First of all, note that the equation is balanced, because the "1" that signifies that 1 mole of each reactant will react to produce 1 mole of product is omitted by convention. Because an aqueous solution of HBr, rather than the pure acid, is being used, the amount of HBr present must be determined. Concentrated HBr is 47% by weight in the acid, and its density, d, is 1.49 g/mL, a value that would be recorded in the column headed "Other Data." Consequently, 25 mL of this solution contains 17.5 g of HBr (25 mL × 1.49 g/mL × 0.47). The needed data can then be entered into Table 1.1.

The limiting reagent is 1-pentene because theory requires that it and HBr react in a 1:1 molar ratio, yet they have been used in a ratio of 0.07:0.22. This means that no more than 0.07 mole of product can be formed, since theory dictates that the ratio between 2-bromopentane and 1-pentene also be 1:1. The calculation of the theoretical yield is then straightforward.

You may find it convenient to use units of milligrams (mg), microliters (μL), and millimoles (mmol) instead of grams, milliliters, and moles, respectively, in performing measurements and calculations when small quantities of reagents are used, as is the case for microscale reactions. For example, let's consider how Table 1.1 would be modified if 0.1 g of 1-pentene and 0.5 mL of concentrated HBr solution were used. If the calculations were done in grams and moles, the entries

Table 1.1 *Table of Reactants and Products for Preparation of 2-Bromopentane*

Compound	*M.M.*	*Volume Used (mL)*	*Weight Used (g)*	*Moles Used*	*Moles Required*	*Other Data*
1-Pentene	70.14	7.8	5	0.07	1	*
HBr	80.91	25	17.5	0.22	1	*
2-Bromopentane	151.05	†	†	†	1	*

*These entries have been intentionally omitted in this example.
†These entries are left blank because this line is for the product.
Limiting reagent: 1-pentene
Theoretical yield: 151.05 g/mol × 0.07 mol = 10.5 g

Table 1.2 *Table of Reactants and Products for Preparation of 2-Bromopentane*

Compound	*M.M.*	*Volume Used (mL)*	*Weight Used (g)*	*Mmols Used*	*Mmols Required*	*Other Data*
1-Pentene	70.14	0.16	100	1.4	1	*
HBr	80.91	0.5	358	4.4	1	*
2-Bromopentane	151.05	†	†	†	1	*

*These entries have been intentionally omitted in this example.
†These entries are left blank because this line is for the product.
Limiting reagent: 1-pentene
Theoretical yield: 151.05 g/mol × 1.4 mol × 211 mg

under "Moles Used" would be 0.0014 and 0.4, respectively. Errors can arise when making such entries, because a zero may inadvertently be added or dropped.

This potential problem is less likely if you enter the data as milligrams and millimoles. If you recognize that 0.1 g of alkene is 100 mg and 0.5 mL of HBr solution contains 358 mg of HBr (0.5 mL × 1490 mg/mL × 0.48), the entries would be those shown in Table 1.2. You may then determine the limiting reagent and calculate the theoretical yield as in Example 1. Note that the necessary cancellation of units occurs when the molar mass is expressed in mg/mmol.

Although the volume of 1-pentene to be used is expressed in milliliters, you may be measuring out this amount with a device that is calibrated in microliters (μL, 1 μL $= 10^{-3}$ mL). Thus, in the present example, you would be using 160 μL of 1-pentene (0.16 mL × 10^3 μL/mL).

Example 2

Problem Now consider the transformation illustrated in Equation 1.3. Assume that you are to use 7 mL of ethanol and 0.1 mL of concentrated H_2SO_4 as the catalyst. Prepare a Table of Reactants and Products, determine the limiting reagent, and calculate the theoretical yield for the reaction.

$$2\,CH_3CH_2OH \xrightarrow[\text{(Catalytic amount)}]{H_2SO_4} CH_3CH_2OCH_2CH_3 + H_2O \quad (1.3)$$

Answer As in the previous example, a volumetric measurement must first be converted to a weight. The density of ethanol is 0.789 g/mL, information that would be entered under the column headed "Other Data," so that means 5.5 g is being used. Table 1.3 can then be completed. Note that the catalyst, although recorded in the table, is not used in any of the calculations because, by definition, it is not consumed during the reaction. Including it should help remind the experimentalist that it is indeed required to make the reaction occur!

Calculation of the theoretical yield is performed as in Example 1, with the important exception that a factor of 0.5 is incorporated to adjust for the fact that only one-half mole of diethyl ether would be produced for each mole of ethanol that is used.

Table 1.3 *Table of Reactants and Products for Preparation of Diethyl Ether*

Compound	*M.M.*	*Volume Used (mL)*	*Weight Used (g)*	*Moles Used*	*Moles Required*	*Other Data*
Ethanol	46.07	7	5.5	0.12	2	*
Sulfuric acid	†	0.1	†	†	†	*
Diethyl ether	74.12	‡	‡	‡	1	*

*These entries have been intentionally omitted in this example.
†These entries are left blank for reactants that serve only as catalysts.
‡These entries are left blank because this line is for the product.
Limiting reagent: ethanol
Theoretical yield: 74.12 g/mol × 0.12 mol · 0.5 = 4.4 g

1.8 SAFE LABORATORY PRACTICE: OVERVIEW

There is little question that one of the most important abilities that you, the aspiring organic chemist, can bring to the laboratory is a sound knowledge of how to perform experimental work safely. But just knowing *how* to work safely is insufficient! You must also make a *serious* commitment to follow standard safety protocols. In other words, having the knowledge about safety is useless if you do not put that knowledge into practice. What you actually do in the laboratory will determine whether you and your labmates are working in a safe environment.

Chemistry laboratories are potentially dangerous because they commonly house flammable liquids, fragile glassware, toxic chemicals, and equipment that may be under vacuum or at pressures above atmospheric. They may also contain gas cylinders that are under high pressure. The gases themselves may or may not be hazardous—for example, nitrogen is not, whereas hydrogen certainly is—but the fact that their containers are under pressure makes them so. Imagine what might happen if a cylinder of nitrogen fell and ruptured: You could have a veritable rocket on your hands, and, if the tank contained hydrogen, the "rocket" might even come equipped with a fiery tail! This is another way of saying *all* substances are hazardous under certain conditions.

Fortunately the laboratory need be no more dangerous than a kitchen or bathroom, but this depends on you *and* your labmates practicing safety as you work. Should you observe others doing anything that is unsafe, let them know about it in a friendly manner. Everyone will benefit from your action. We'll alert you repeatedly to the possible dangers associated with the chemicals and apparatus that you will use so that you can become well trained in safe laboratory practice. Mastery of the proper procedures is just as important in the course as obtaining high yields of pure products, and carefully reading our suggestions will assist you in achieving this goal. Some safety information will be contained in the text describing a particular experiment or in the experimental procedure itself. It will also appear in highlighted sections titled "**Safety Alert.**" These are designed to draw your special attention to aspects of safety that are of particular importance. We urge you to read these sections carefully and follow the guidelines in them carefully. You will then be fully prepared to have the fun and fulfillment of the laboratory experience.

1.9 SAFETY: GENERAL DISCUSSION

We highlight here, in the form of a Safety Alert, some general aspects regarding safe practices in the laboratory. Such alerts will appear throughout the textbook and should be read carefully.

SAFETY ALERT

Personal Attire

1. ***Do not wear shorts or sandals in the laboratory;*** **the laboratory is *not* a beach! Proper clothing gives protection against chemicals that may be spilled accidentally. It is advisable to wear a laboratory coat, but in any case, the more skin that is protected by clothing the better.**
2. ***Always wear safety glasses or goggles in the laboratory.*** **This applies even when you are writing in your laboratory notebook or washing glassware, since nearby workers may have an accident. It is best *not* to wear contact lenses in the laboratory. Even if you are wearing eye protection, chemicals may get into your eyes, and you may not be able to get the contact lenses out before damage has occurred. Should you have to wear corrective glasses while working in the laboratory, make certain that the lenses are shatterproof. Wearing goggles over such glasses is recommended because the goggles give additional protection from chemicals entering your eyes from the sides of the lenses.**
3. ***Wear suitable protective gloves, which may be made of latex or a plastic such as chloroprene, when working with particularly hazardous chemicals.*** **Some reagents are especially hazardous if they come into contact with your skin. The ones you are most likely to encounter in the organic laboratory are concentrated acids and bases, and bromine and its solutions. Check with your instructor whenever you are uncertain whether you should be wearing gloves when handling reagents.**

General Considerations

1. ***Become familiar with the layout of the laboratory room.*** **Locate the exits from the room and the fire extinguishers, fire blankets, eyewash fountains, safety showers, and first-aid kits in and near your workspace. Consult with your instructor regarding the operation and purpose of each of the safety-related devices.**
2. ***Find the nearest exits from your laboratory room to the outside of the building.*** **Should evacuation of the building be necessary, use stairways rather than elevators to exit. Remain calm during the evacuation, and walk rather than run to the exit.**
3. ***Become knowledgeable about basic first-aid procedures.*** **The damage from accidents will be minimized if first aid is applied promptly. Read the section "First Aid in Case of an Accident" on the inside front cover of this book.**
4. ***Never work alone in the laboratory.*** **In the event of an accident, you may need the immediate help of a coworker. Should you have to work in the laboratory outside of the regularly scheduled periods, do so only with the express permission of your instructor and in the presence of at least one other person.**
5. **Before performing any experiment, you should perform a hazard analysis by reviewing the set-up for the experiment and the chemicals that will be used and identifying any potential hazards. You should consider how these hazards might be eliminated or mitigated and what you will do in case something goes wrong.**

Apparatus and Chemicals

1. ***Always check carefully for imperfections in the glassware that you will be using.*** **This should be done not only when checking into the laboratory for the first time but also when setting up the apparatus needed for each experiment. Look for cracks, chips, or other imperfections in the glass that weaken it. Use care in storing your glassware so that it is not damaged when you open or close the locker or drawer.**

   Pay particular attention to the condition of round-bottom flasks and condensers. The flasks often have "star" cracks (multiple cracks emanating from a central point) as a result of being banged against a hard surface. Heating or cooling a flask having this type of flaw may cause the flask to rupture with loss of its contents. This could result in a serious fire, not just loss of the desired product. To detect such cracks, hold the flask up to the light and look at all its surfaces closely. With respect to condensers, their most vulnerable points are the ring seals—the points where the inner tube and the water jacket of the condenser are joined. Special care must be given to examining these seals for defects, because if cracks are present water might leak into your apparatus and contaminate your product or, worse, cause violent reactions.

   If you detect imperfections in your glassware, consult with your teacher immediately regarding replacement. Cracked or seriously chipped apparatus should always be replaced, but glassware with slight chips may still be safe to use.

2. ***Dispose of glassware properly.*** **The laboratory should be equipped with a properly labeled special container for broken glassware and disposable glass items such as Pasteur pipets and melting-point capillaries. It is not appropriate to throw such items in the regular trash containers, because maintenance personnel may injure themselves while removing the trash. Broken thermometers are a special problem because they usually contain mercury, which is toxic and relatively volatile. There should be a separate, closed container for disposal of thermometers. If mercury has spilled as a result of the breakage, it should be cleaned up immediately. Consult with your instructor about appropriate procedures for doing so.**

3. ***Know the properties of the chemicals used in the experiments.*** **Understanding these properties helps you to take the proper precautions when handling them and to minimize danger in case of an accident.** ***Handle all chemicals with care.***

   Refer to MSDSs (Sec. 1.10) to learn about toxicity and other potential hazards associated with the chemicals you use. Most chemicals are at least slightly toxic, and many are ***very*** **toxic and irritating if inhaled or allowed to come in contact with the skin. It is a good laboratory practice to wear suitable protective gloves when handling chemicals, and there may be times when it is imperative to do so. Your instructor will advise you if you do** ***not*** **need to use gloves.**

   Should chemicals come in contact with your skin, they can usually be removed by a thorough and ***immediate*** **washing of the affected area with soap and water. Do** ***not*** **use organic solvents like ethanol or acetone to rinse chemicals from your skin, as these solvents may actually assist the absorption of the substances into your skin.**

4. ***Avoid the use of flames as much as possible.*** **Most organic substances are flammable, and some are highly volatile as well, which increases their potential for being ignited accidentally. Examples of these are diethyl ether, commonly used as a solvent in the organic laboratory, and acetone. Occasionally,**

open flames may be used for flame-drying an apparatus or distilling a high-boiling liquid. In such cases, a Safety Alert section will give special precautions for their use. Some general guidelines follow.

a. ***Never use an open flame without the permission of your instructor.***

b. ***Never use a flame to heat a flammable liquid in an open container.*** **Use a water or steam bath, hot plate, aluminum block, or similar electrical heat device instead. If a flammable liquid must be heated with an open flame, equip the container holding the liquid with a *tightly* fitting reflux condenser.**

Information about the flammability of many commonly used organic solvents is provided in Table 3.1. Do *not* assume that a solvent is not flammable just because it is not listed in the table, however. In such cases, refer to the MSDSs (Sec. 1.10) or other sources to determine flammability.

c. ***Do not pour flammable liquids when there are open flames within several feet.*** **The act of transferring the liquid from one container to another will release vapors into the laboratory, and these could be ignited by a flame some distance away.**

d. ***Do not pour flammable water-insoluble organic solvents into drains or sinks.*** **First of all, this is an environmentally unsound way to dispose of waste solvents, and second, the solvents may be carried to locations where there are open flames that could ignite them. Water-soluble solvents can be flushed down the drain if local regulations permit; consult with your instructor about this.**

5. ***Avoid inhaling vapors of organic and inorganic compounds.*** **Although most of the pleasant and unpleasant odors you encounter in everyday life are organic in nature, it is prudent not to expose yourself to such vapors in the laboratory. Work at a fume hood when handling particularly noxious chemicals, such as bromine or acetic anhydride, and, if possible, when performing reactions that produce toxic gases.**

6. ***Never taste anything in the laboratory unless specifically instructed to do so.*** **You should also never eat or drink in the laboratory, as your food may become contaminated by the chemicals that are being used.**

7. ***Minimize the amounts of chemicals you use and dispose of chemicals properly.*** **This aspect of laboratory practice is so important that we have devoted a portion of Section 1.10 to it. Read the relevant paragraphs *carefully* and consult with your instructor if there are any questions about the procedures.**

1.10 SAFETY: MATERIAL SAFETY DATA SHEETS (MSDSs)

The variety and potential danger of chemicals used in the organic chemistry laboratory probably exceed that of any laboratory course you have had. It is imperative to understand the nature of the substances with which you are working. Fortunately, the increased emphasis on the proper handling of chemicals has led to a number of publications containing information about the chemical, physical, and toxicological properties of the majority of organic and inorganic compounds used in the experiments in this textbook. A comprehensive source is *The Sigma-Aldrich Library of Chemical Safety Data* (Reference 6), and it or similar compilations should be available in your library or some other central location. Alternatively, you can usually access MSDS information by typing the name of the chemical of interest into the

Name	Ether	**Reviews and standards**	OSHA standard-air: TWA 400 ppm.
Other names	Diethyl ether	**Health hazards**	May be harmful by inhalation, ingestion, or skin absorption. Vapor or mist is irritating to the eyes, mucous membranes, and upper respiratory tract. Causes skin irritation. Exposure can cause coughing, chest pains, difficulty in breathing, and nausea, headache, and vomiting.
CAS Registry No.	60-29-7	**First aid**	In case of contact, immediately flush eyes or skin with copious amounts of water for at least 15 min while removing contaminated clothing and shoes. If inhaled, remove to fresh air. If not breathing, give artificial respiration; if breathing is difficult, give oxygen. If ingested, wash out mouth with water. Call a physician.
Structure	$(CH_3CH_2)_2O$	**Incompatibilities**	Oxidizing agents and heat.
MP	–116 °C	**Extinguishing media**	Carbon dioxide, dry chemical powder, alcohol, or polymer foam.
BP	34.6 °C (760 torr)	**Decomposition products**	Toxic fumes of carbon monoxide, carbon dioxide.
FP	–40 °C	**Handling and storage**	Wear appropriate respirator, chemical-resistant gloves, safety goggles, other protective clothing. Safety shower and eye bath. Do not breathe vapor. Avoid contact with eyes, skin, and clothing. Wash thoroughly after handling. Irritant. Keep tightly closed. Keep away from heat, sparks, and open flame. Forms explosive peroxides on prolonged storage. Refrigerate. Extremely flammable. Vapor may travel considerable distance to source of ignition. Container explosion may occur under fire conditions. *Danger:* Tends to form explosive peroxides, especially when anhydrous. Inhibited with 0.0001% BHT.
Appearance	Colorless liquid	**Spillage**	Shut off all sources of ignition. Cover with activated carbon adsorbent, place in closed containers, and take outdoors.
Irritation data	Human eye 100 ppm	**Disposal**	Store in clearly labeled containers until container is given to approved contractor for disposal in accordance with local regulations.
Toxicity data	Man, oral LDL_0 260 mg/kg		

Figure 1.3
Summary of MSDS for diethyl ether.

query box of your browser and using the associated search function. The data provided by these sources are basically summaries of the information contained in the MSDSs published by the supplier of the chemical of interest. Your instructor may be able to provide these sheets because by federal regulation an MSDS must be delivered to the buyer each time a chemical is purchased.

The information in an MSDS can be overwhelming. For example, the official MSDS for sodium bicarbonate is some six pages long. Even the summaries provided in most compilations are quite extensive, as illustrated in Figure 1.3, which contains specific data for diethyl ether. Entries regarding the structure and physical properties of the compound, including melting point (mp), boiling point (bp), and flash point (fp), are included, along with its CAS (Chemical Abstracts Service) Registry Number, which is unique for each different chemical substance, and RTECS (Registry of Toxic Effects of Chemical Substances) number. Further data are provided concerning its toxicity, the permissible levels set by OSHA for exposure to it in the air you breathe (time-weighted average of 400 ppm), and possible health consequences resulting from contact with the compound. For diethyl ether, the entry for "Toxicity Data" represents the *lowest* recorded *lethal* concentration for ingestion of the chemical. Valuable information is also given regarding first-aid procedures, classes of substances with which diethyl ether reacts and thus is "incompatible" with, products of its decomposition, and materials suitable for extinguishing fires involving ether. Finally, protocols for safe handling and storage are included, along with procedures for disposing and cleaning up spills of diethyl ether.

Accessing MSDS information from commercial sources can be very time-consuming, although it is useful to refer to one or more of them if you need more complete MSDS information than is available online (see the online resources associated with this textbook) or if you are to use or produce a chemical that is not listed on it. We've developed the Web-based MSDSs to provide you with a rapid and convenient way to obtain important information on the chemicals you will be using or producing in the experimental procedures performed when using this textbook. The data we've provided online for this textbook are much more abbreviated than those in other sources, as seen in Figure 1.4. In developing our summaries of MSDS data, we've focused on just those data most relevant to your needs in the introductory organic laboratory.

We noted in the discussion of notebook formats (Sec. 1.6) that you may be required to summarize MSDS data in your laboratory book. This could be a daunting assignment, given the amount of information with which you might be faced, as illustrated in Figure 1.3. To assist you in doing this, we have provided one possible format for a summary in Figure 1.5. A summary for a particular chemical has to be provided only once and can be recorded at the end of your laboratory notebook on pages reserved for that purpose. Whenever the chemical is encountered in later experiments, you would only need to refer to the location of the summary of its MSDS information. *However*, you should reread the MSDS information so that you can continue to handle the chemical properly. This same recommendation applies if you have a file of MSDS-related printouts from the online resources for this textbook.

To summarize, you may think that reading about and recording data like those contained in Figures 1.3–1.5 is not a good investment of time. This is absolutely *wrong!* By knowing more about the chemicals that are used in the laboratory, you will be able to work safely and to deal with accidents, should they occur. The end result will be that you accomplish a greater amount of laboratory work and have a more valuable educational experience.

1.11 SAFETY: DISPOSAL OF CHEMICALS

The proper disposal of inorganic and organic chemicals is one of the biggest responsibilities that you have in the organic laboratory. Your actions, and those of your labmates, can minimize the environmental impact and even financial cost to

Diethyl Ether
$C_4H_{10}O$

CAS No.	PS	Color	Odor	FP	BP	MP	d	VP	VD	Sol
60-29-7	Liquid	Colorless	Sweet	40	35	−116	0.7	442 @ 20	2.6	6.9 @ 20

Types of Hazards/Exposures	Acute Hazards/Symptoms	Prevention	First Aid/Fire
Fire	*Severe* fire hazard, *severe* explosion hazard; may form explosive peroxides; vapors or gases may ignite at distant ignition sources.	*No* flames, *no* sparks, *no* contact with hot surfaces.	Alcohol-resistant foam, carbon dioxide, regular dry chemical powder, water.
Inhalation	Central nervous system depression with drowsiness, dizziness, nausea, headache, and lowering of the pulse and body temperature.	Ventilation, local exhaust.	Remove from exposure immediately and seek medical advice.
Skin	Irritation, defatting, and drying of the skin.	Protective gloves and clothing.	Remove contaminated clothes/jewelry; thoroughly wash skin with soap and water; and seek medical advice.
Eyes	Painful inflammation.	Safety goggles.	Thoroughly flush eyes with water for several min, removing contact lenses if possible, and seek medical advice immediately.
Ingestion	Central nervous system depression with nausea, vomiting, drowsiness, dizziness; stomach may become promptly distended, which may hinder breathing.	Do *not* eat or drink in the laboratory.	Seek medical advice immediately.
Carcinogenicity	Not a known carcinogen.	**Mutagenicity**	Possible mutagen.

For more detailed information, consult the Material Safety Data Sheet for this compound.
Abbreviations: CAS No. = Chemical Abstracts Service Registry Number; PS = physical state; FP = flash point (°C); BP = boiling point (°C) @ 760 torr unless otherwise stated; MP = melting point (°C); d = density or specific gravity (g/mL); VP = vapor pressure (torr) at specified temperature (°C); VD = vapor density relative to air (1.0); Sol = solubility in water (g/100 mL) at specified temperature; N/A = not available or not applicable.

Figure 1.4
Example of MSDS data provided online for this textbook.

your school for handling the waste chemicals that are necessarily produced in the experiments you do.

The experimental procedures in this textbook have been designed at a scale that should allow you to isolate an amount of product sufficient to see and manipulate, but they also involve the use of minimal quantities of reactants, solvents, and

Compound	Health Hazards, First Aid, Incompatibilities, Extinguishing Media, and Handling
Diethyl Ether	May be harmful by inhalation, ingestion, or skin absorption. Avoid contact with eyes, skin, and clothing. In case of contact, immediately flush eyes or skin with copious amounts of water. Keep away from hot surfaces, sparks, and open flames. Extremely flammable. Vapor may travel considerable distance to source of ignition. If spilled, shut off all sources of ignition. Extinguish fire with carbon dioxide, dry chemical extinguisher, foam, or water.

Figure 1.5
Abstract of MSDS for diethyl ether.

drying agents. Bear in mind, however, that minimizing the amounts of chemicals that are used is only the *first* part of an experimental design that results in the production of the least possible quantity of waste. The *second* part is to reduce the amounts of materials that you, the experimentalist, *define* as waste, thereby making the material subject to regulations for its disposal. From a legal standpoint, the laboratory worker is empowered to declare material as waste; that is, unneeded materials are not waste until you say they are! Consequently, a part of most of the experimental procedures in this textbook is reduction of the quantity of residual material that eventually must be consigned to waste. This means some additional time will be required for completion of the experiment, but the benefits—educational, environmental, and economic in nature—fully justify your efforts. The recommended procedures that should be followed are described under the heading **Wrapping It Up.**

How do you properly dispose of spent chemicals at the end of an experiment? In some cases this involves simply flushing chemicals down the drain with the aid of large volumes of water. As an example, solutions of sulfuric acid can be neutralized with a base such as sodium hydroxide, and the aqueous solution of sodium sulfate that results can safely be washed into the sanitary sewer system. However, the environmental regulations that apply in your particular community may require use of alternative procedures. *Be certain to check with your instructor before flushing any chemicals down the drain!*

For water-insoluble substances, and even for certain water-soluble ones, this option is not permissible under *any* circumstances, and other procedures must be followed. The laboratory should be equipped with various containers for disposal of liquid and solid chemicals; the latter should not be thrown in a trash can, because this exposes maintenance and cleaning personnel to potential danger, and it is environmentally unsound. The containers must be properly labeled as to what can be put in them, because it is very important for safety and environmental reasons that different categories of spent chemicals be segregated from one another. Thus, you are likely to find the following types of containers in the organic laboratory: hazardous solids, nonhazardous solids, halogenated organic liquids, hydrocarbons, and oxygenated organic liquids. Each student must assume the responsibility for seeing that her or his spent chemicals go into the appropriate container; otherwise dangerous combinations of chemicals might result and/or a much more expensive method of disposal be required.

REFERENCES

1. Lunn, G.; Sansone, E. B. *Destruction of Hazardous Chemicals in the Laboratory*, 3rd ed., John Wiley & Sons, New York, 2012. A handbook providing procedures for decomposition of materials or classes of materials commonly used in the laboratory.
2. Committee on Hazardous Substances in the Laboratory. *Prudent Practices for Disposal of Chemicals from Laboratories*, National Academy Press, Washington, D.C., 1995. An excellent reference containing information for the minimization of waste generated in the laboratory and for the proper handling and disposal of waste chemicals, both organic and inorganic. Available at no cost online at www.nap.edu/catalog.php?record_id=4911#toc.
3. Young, J. A., ed. *Improving Safety in the Chemical Laboratory: A Practical Guide*, 2nd ed., John Wiley & Sons, New York, 1991. A book containing thorough discussions of the full range of safe practices in the laboratory.
4. Lide, D. A., ed. *CRC Handbook of Chemistry and Physics*, annual editions, CRC Press, Boca Raton, FL. Available online to subscribers at www.hbcpnetbase.com.
5. Speight, J. G., ed. *Lange's Handbook of Chemistry*, 16th ed., McGraw-Hill, New York, 2005. Available online to subscribers on McGraw-Hill's site Access Engineering.
6. Lenga, R. E.; Votoupal, K. L., eds. *The Sigma-Aldrich Library of Chemical Safety Data*, 2nd ed., Sigma-Aldrich, Milwaukee, WI, 1988.
7. O'Neil, M. J., ed. *The Merck Index of Chemicals and Drugs*, 15th ed., Merck and Co., Rahway, NJ, 2013. Available free online at www.rsc.org/merck-index.
8. Armour, M. A. *Hazardous Laboratory Chemical Disposal Guide*, 3rd ed., CRC Press, Boca Raton, FL, 2003. Available online at bib.tiera.ru/b/126474.

EXPERIMENTAL PROCEDURES

Simple Distillation

Purpose To demonstrate the technique for purification of a volatile organic liquid containing a nonvolatile impurity.

SAFETY ALERT

1. **Wear safety glasses or goggles and suitable protective gloves while performing the experiments.**
2. **Cyclohexane is highly flammable, so be sure that burners are not being used in the laboratory. Use *flameless* heating (Sec. 2.9).**
3. **Examine your glassware for cracks and other weaknesses before assembling the distillation apparatus. Look for "star" cracks in round-bottom flasks, because these can cause a flask to break upon heating.**
4. **Proper assembly of glassware is important to avoid possible breakage and spillage or the release of distillate vapors into the room. Be certain that all connections in the apparatus are tight before beginning the distillation. Have your instructor examine your setup after it is assembled.**
5. **The apparatus used in these experiments *must* be open to the atmosphere at the receiving end of the condenser. *Never heat a closed system,* because the pressure buildup may cause the apparatus to explode!**
6. **Be certain that the water hoses are *securely* fastened to your condensers so that they will not pop off and cause a flood. If heating mantles or oil baths are used for heating in this experiment, water hoses that come loose may cause water to spray onto electrical connections or into the heating sources, either of which is potentially dangerous.**
7. **Avoid excessive inhalation of organic vapors at all times.**

MINISCALE PROCEDURE

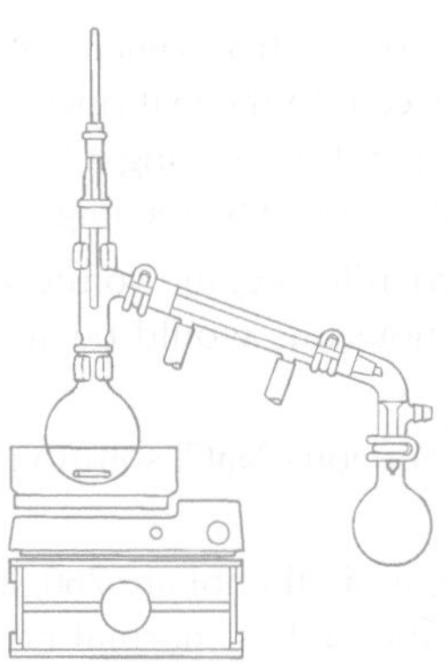

Preparation Refer to the online resources to access videos, Pre-Lab Exercises, and read the MSDSs for the chemicals used or produced in this procedure. Read or review Sections 2.2, 2.4, 2.9, 2.11, and 2.13.

Apparatus A 25-mL round-bottom flask, ice-water bath, apparatus for simple distillation, magnetic stirring, and *flameless* heating.

Setting Up Place 10 mL of cyclohexane containing a nonvolatile dye in the round-bottom flask. Add a stirbar to the flask to ensure smooth boiling, and assemble the simple distillation apparatus shown in Figure 2.37a. Be sure to position the thermometer in the stillhead so the *top* of the mercury thermometer bulb is level with the *bottom* of the sidearm of the distillation head. Have your instructor check your apparatus *before* you start heating the stillpot.

Distillation Start the magnetic stirrer and begin heating the stillpot. As soon as the liquid begins to boil *and the condensing vapors have reached the thermometer bulb,* regulate the heat supply so that distillation continues steadily at a rate of 2–4 *drops per second;* if a drop of liquid cannot be seen suspended from the end of the thermometer, the rate of distillation is too *fast.* As soon as the distillation rate is adjusted and the head temperature is constant, note and record the temperature. Continue the distillation and periodically record the head temperature. Discontinue heating when only 2–3 mL of impure cyclohexane remains in the distillation flask. Record the volume of distilled cyclohexane that you obtain.

Optional Procedure

You may be required to perform this distillation using the shortpath apparatus discussed in Section 2.13 and illustrated in Figure 2.37b. After assembling the equipment, make certain that the *top* of the mercury in the thermometer bulb is level with the *bottom* of the sidearm of the distillation head. The preferred way to collect the distillate in this distillation is to attach a dry round-bottom flask to the vacuum adapter and put a drying tube containing calcium chloride on the sidearm of the adapter to protect the distillate from moisture. The receiver should be cooled in an ice-water bath to prevent loss of product by evaporation and to ensure complete condensing of the distillate.

WRAPPING IT UP

Unless directed otherwise, return the *distilled* and *undistilled cyclohexane* to a bottle marked "Recovered Cyclohexane."

EXERCISES

1. Define the following terms:
   a. simple distillation
   b. head temperature
   c. pot temperature
   d. Raoult's law
   e. ideal solution
   f. Dalton's law
2. Sketch and completely label the apparatus required for a simple distillation.
3. Why should you never heat a closed system, and how does this rule apply to a distillation?
4. Explain the role of the stirbar that is normally added to a liquid that is to be heated to boiling.
5. In a miniscale distillation, the top of the mercury bulb of the thermometer placed at the head of a distillation apparatus should be adjacent to the exit opening to the condenser. Explain the effect on the observed temperature reading if the bulb is placed (a) below the opening to the condenser or (b) above the opening.
6. Distillation is frequently used to isolate the nonvolatile organic solute from a solution containing an organic solvent. Explain how this would be accomplished using a simple distillation.
7. Using Raoult's and Dalton's laws, explain why an aqueous NaCl solution will have a higher boiling point than pure water.
8. At 100 °C, the vapor pressures for water, methanol, and ethanol are 760, 2625, and 1694 torr, respectively. Which compound has the highest normal boiling point and which the lowest?

4.4 FRACTIONAL DISTILLATION

It is easy to separate a volatile compound from a nonvolatile one by simple distillation (Sec. 4.3). The same technique may also be used to separate volatile compounds from one another if their boiling points differ by at least 40–50 °C. If this is not the case, the technique of fractional distillation is normally used to obtain each volatile component of a mixture in pure form. The theoretical basis of this technique is the subject of the following discussion, and a potential practical application of fractional distillation that could lessen the air pollution produced by internal combustion engines is described in the Historical Highlight *Reducing Automobile Emissions*, which is available online.

Theory

For simplicity, we'll only consider the theory for separating *ideal solutions* (Sec. 4.3) consisting of two volatile components, designated X and Y. Solutions containing more than two such components are often encountered, and their behavior on distillation may be understood by extension of the principles developed here for a binary system.

The vapor pressure of a compound is a measure of the ease with which its molecules escape the surface of a liquid. When the liquid is composed of two volatile components, in this case X and Y, the number of molecules of X and of Y in a given volume of the vapor above the mixture will be proportional to their respective partial vapor pressures. This relationship is expressed mathematically by Equation 4.5, where N'_X/N'_Y is the ratio of the mole fractions of X and Y in the *vapor* phase. The mole fraction of each component may be calculated from the equations $N'_X = P_X/(P_X + P_Y)$ and $N'_Y = P_Y/(P_X + P_Y)$. The partial vapor pressures, P_X and P_Y, are determined by the composition of the liquid solution according to Raoult's law (Eq. 4.2). Since the solution boils when the sum of the partial vapor pressures of X and Y is equal to the external pressure, as expressed by Dalton's law (Eq. 4.4), the boiling temperature of the solution is determined by its composition.

$$\frac{N'_X}{N'_Y} = \frac{P'_X}{P'_X} = \frac{P^\circ_X N_x}{P^\circ_Y N_Y} \tag{4.5}$$

The relationship between temperature and the composition of the liquid and vapor phases of ideal binary solutions is illustrated in Figure 4.3 for mixtures of benzene, bp 80 °C (760 torr), and toluene, bp 111 °C (760 torr). The lower curve, the **liquid line,** gives the boiling points of all mixtures of these two compounds. The upper curve, the **vapor line,** is calculated using Raoult's law and defines the composition of the vapor phase in equilibrium with the boiling liquid phase at the same temperature. For example, a mixture whose composition is 58 mol % benzene and 42 mol % toluene will boil at 90 °C (760 torr), as shown by point A in Figure 4.3. The composition of the vapor in equilibrium with the solution when it *first* starts to boil can be determined by drawing a horizontal line from the *liquid line* to the *vapor line;* in this case, the vapor has the composition 78 mol % benzene and 22 mol % toluene, as shown by point B in Figure 4.3. This is a key point, for it means that at any given temperature the *vapor phase is richer in the more volatile component than is the boiling liquid with which the vapor is in equilibrium.* This phenomenon provides the basis of **fractional distillation.**

When the liquid mixture containing 58 mol % benzene and 42 mol % toluene is heated to 90 °C (760 torr), its boiling point, the vapor formed initially contains 78 mol % benzene and 22 mol % toluene. If this first vapor is condensed, the condensate would also have this composition and thus would be much richer in benzene than the original liquid mixture from which it was distilled. After this vapor is removed from the original mixture, the liquid remaining in the stillpot will contain a smaller mol % of benzene and a greater mol % of toluene because more benzene

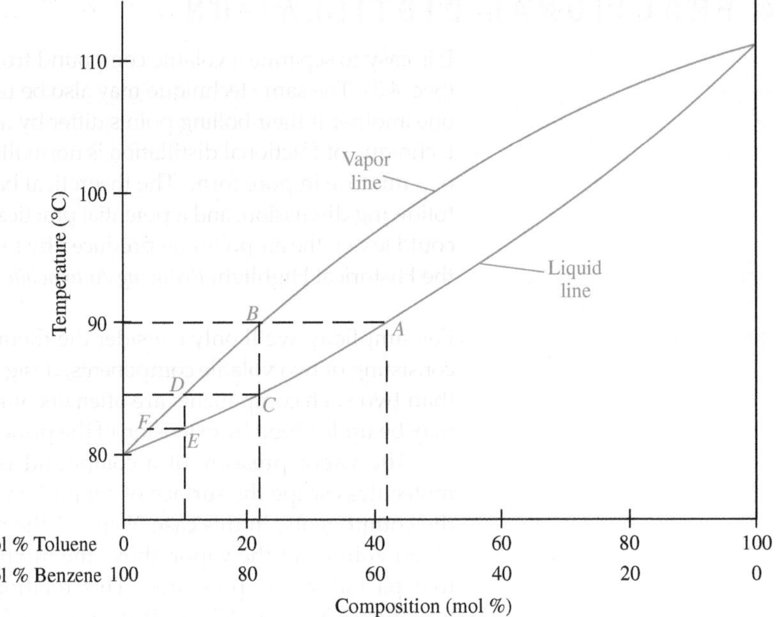

Figure 4.3
Temperature–composition diagram for binary mixture of benzene and toluene.

than toluene was removed by vaporization. The boiling point of the liquid remaining in the distilling flask will rise as a result. As the distillation continues, the boiling point of the mixture will steadily increase until it approaches or reaches the boiling point of pure toluene. The composition of the distillate will change as well and will ultimately consist of "pure" toluene.

Now let's return to the first few drops of distillate that are obtained by condensing the vapor initially formed from the original mixture. This condensate, as noted earlier, has a composition identical to that of the vapor from which it is produced. Were this liquid to be collected and then redistilled, its boiling point would be the temperature at point *C*, namely 85 °C; this boiling temperature is easily determined by drawing a vertical line from the vapor line at point *B* to the liquid line at point *C*, which corresponds to the composition of the distillate initially produced. The first distillate obtained at this temperature would have the composition *D*, 90 mol % benzene and 10 mol % toluene; this composition is determined from the intersection with the vapor line of the horizontal line from point *C* on the liquid line.

In theory, this process could be repeated again and again to give a very small amount of pure benzene. Similarly, collecting the *last* small fraction of each distillation and redistilling it in the same stepwise manner would yield a very small amount of pure toluene. If larger amounts of the initial and final distillates were collected, reasonable quantities of materials could be obtained, but a large number of individual simple distillations would be required. This process would be extremely tedious and time-consuming. Fortunately, the repeated distillation can be accomplished almost automatically in a single operation by using a **fractional distillation column,** the theory and use of which are described later in this section.

Most homogeneous solutions of volatile organic compounds behave as ideal solutions, but some of them exhibit *nonideal* behavior. This occurs because unlike molecules are affected by the presence of one another, thereby causing deviations from Raoult's law for *ideal* solutions (Eq. 4.2). When nonideal solutions have vapor pressures *higher* than those predicted by Raoult's law, the solutions are said to exhibit *positive* deviations from it; solutions having vapor pressures lower than predicted are thus considered to represent *negative* deviations from the law. In the present discussion, we'll consider only positive deviations associated with binary solutions, as such deviations are generally most important to organic chemists.

To produce positive deviations in a solution containing two volatile liquids, the forces of attraction between the molecules of the two components are *weaker* than those between the molecules of each individual component. The combined vapor pressure of the solution is thus *greater* than the vapor pressure of the pure, more volatile component for a particular range of compositions of the two liquids. This situation is illustrated in Figure 4.4, in which it may be seen that mixtures in the composition range between *X* and *Y* have boiling temperatures *lower* than the boiling temperature of either pure component. The *minimum-boiling* mixture, composition *Z* in Figure 4.4, may be considered as though it is a third component of the binary mixture. It has a *constant* boiling point because the vapor in equilibrium with the liquid has a composition *identical* to that of the liquid itself. The mixture is called a **minimum-boiling azeotrope.** Fractional distillation of such mixtures will *not* yield both of the components in pure form; rather, only the azeotropic mixture *and* the component present in *excess* of the azeotropic composition will be produced from the fractionation. For example, pure ethanol cannot be obtained by fractional distillation of aqueous solutions containing less than 95.57% ethanol, the azeotropic composition, even though the boiling point of this azeotrope is only 0.15 °C below that of pure ethanol. Since optimal fractional distillations of aqueous solutions containing less than 95.57% ethanol yield this azeotropic mixture, "95% ethyl alcohol" is readily available. Pure or "absolute" ethanol is more difficult to obtain from aqueous solutions. However, it can be prepared by removing the water chemically, through the use of a drying agent such as molecular sieves (Sec. 2.24), or by distillation of a ternary mixture of ethanol-water-benzene.

Azeotropic distillation is a useful technique for removing water from organic solutions. For example, toluene and water form an azeotrope having a composition of 86.5 wt % toluene and 13.5 wt % water, and so distillation of a mixture of these two effectively removes water from a mixture. This technique is used in the Experimental Procedure of Section 18.4 for driving an equilibrium in which water is being formed to completion. Azeotropic distillation may also be used to dry an organic liquid that is to be used with reagents that are sensitive to the presence of water. This application is found in the Experimental Procedure of Section 15.2, in which *anhydrous* *p*-xylene is required for a Friedel-Crafts alkylation reaction.

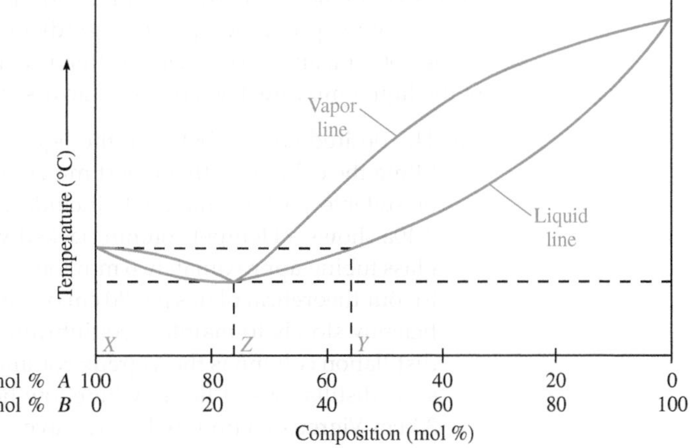

Figure 4.4
Temperature–composition diagram for minimum-boiling azeotrope.

Fractional Distillation Columns and Their Operation

There are many types of fractional distillation columns, but all can be discussed in terms of a few fundamental characteristics. The column provides a vertical path through which the vapor must pass from the stillpot to the condenser before being collected in the receiver (Fig. 2.39). This path is significantly longer than in a simple distillation apparatus. As the vapor from the stillpot rises up the column, some of it condenses *in the column* and returns to the stillpot. *If the lower part of the distilling column is maintained at a higher temperature than the upper part of the column,* the condensate will be partially revaporized as it flows down the column. The uncondensed vapor, together with that produced by revaporization of the condensate in the column, rises higher and higher in the column and undergoes a repeated series of condensations and revaporizations. This repetitive process is equivalent to performing a number of simple distillations *within* the column, with the vapor phase produced in each step becoming increasingly richer in the *more* volatile component; the condensate that flows down the column correspondingly becomes richer in the less volatile component.

Each step along the path *A-B-C-D-E-F* of Figure 4.3 represents a *single* ideal distillation. One type of fractional distillation column, the bubble-plate column, was designed to effect one such step for each **plate** it contained. This led to the description of the efficiency of any fractional distillation column in terms of its equivalency to such a column in **theoretical plates.** Another index of the separating efficiency of a fractional distillation column is the **HETP,** which stands for ***h**eight **e**quivalent* to a ***t**heoretical **p**late* and is the vertical length of a column that is necessary to obtain a separation efficiency of one theoretical plate. For example, a column 60 cm long with an efficiency of 30 plates has an HETP value of 2 cm. Such a column would usually be better for research purposes than a 60-plate column that is 300 cm long (HETP = 5 cm) because of the small liquid capacity and **hold-up** of the shorter column. "Hold-up" refers to the condensate that remains in a column during and after distillation. When small amounts of material are to be distilled, a column must be chosen that has an efficiency, HETP, adequate for the desired separation and also a low to moderate hold-up.

As stated earlier, equilibrium between liquid and vapor phases must be established in a fractional distillation column so that the more volatile component is selectively carried to the top of the column and into the condenser, where the vapor condenses into the distillate. After all of the more volatile component is distilled, the less volatile one remains in the column and the stillpot; the heat supplied to the stillpot is then further increased to distill the second component. The most important requirements for performing a successful fractional distillation are (a) intimate and extensive contact between the liquid and the vapor phases in the column, (b) maintenance of the proper temperature gradient along the column, (c) sufficient length of the column, and (d) sufficient difference in the boiling points of the components of the liquid mixture. Each of these factors is considered here.

a. The desired contact between the liquid and vapor phases can be achieved by filling the column with an inert material having a large surface area. Examples of suitable packing materials include glass, ceramic, or metal pieces. Figure 2.40a shows a Hempel column packed with Raschig rings, which are pieces of glass tubing approximately 6 mm long. This type of column will have from two to four theoretical plates per 30 cm of length, if the distillation is carried out sufficiently slowly to maintain equilibrium conditions. Another type of fractional distillation column is the Vigreux column (Fig. 2.40b), which is useful for small-scale distillations of liquid where low hold-up is of paramount importance. A 30-cm Vigreux column will only have 1–2 theoretical plates and consequently will be less efficient than the corresponding Hempel column. The Vigreux column has the advantage of a hold-up of less than 1 mL as compared with 2–3mL for a Hempel column filled with Raschig rings.

b. Temperature gradient refers to the difference in temperature between the top and bottom of the column. The maintenance of the proper temperature gradient within the column is particularly important for an effective fractional distillation. Ideally, the temperature at the bottom of the column should be approximately equal to the boiling temperature of the solution in the stillpot, and it should decrease continually in the column until it reaches the boiling point of the more volatile component at the head of the column. The significance of the temperature gradient is seen in Figure 4.3, where the boiling temperature of the distillate decreases with each succeeding step, for example, *A* (90 °C) to *C* (85 °C) to *E* (82 °C).

The necessary temperature gradient from stillpot to stillhead in most distillations will be established *automatically* by the condensing vapors *if* the rate of distillation is properly adjusted. Frequently, this gradient can be maintained only by insulating the column with a material such as glasswool around the outside of the column. Insulation helps reduce heat losses from the column to the atmosphere. Even when the column is insulated, an insufficient amount of vapor may be produced to heat the column if the stillpot is heated too slowly, so that little or no condensate reaches the head. This rate must then be increased, but it must be kept below the point where the column is flooded. A **flooded column** is characterized by a column or "plug" of liquid that may be observed within the distillation column, often at the joint between it and the stillpot.

Factors directly affecting the temperature gradient in the column are the rate of heating of the stillpot and the rate at which vapor is removed at the stillhead. If the heating is too vigorous or the vapor is removed too rapidly, the entire column will heat up almost uniformly, and there will be no fractionation and thus no separation of the volatile components. On the other hand, if the stillpot is not heated strongly enough and if the vapor is removed too slowly at the top, the column will flood with returning condensate. Proper operation of a fractional distillation column thus requires *careful* control of the heat supplied to the stillpot and of the rate at which the distillate is removed at the stillhead. This rate should be *no more than one drop* every 2–3 sec.

The ratio of the amount of condensate returning to the stillpot and the amount of vapor removed as distillate per unit time is defined as the **reflux ratio.** A ratio of 10:1, for example, means that 10 drops of condensate return to the stillpot for each drop of distillate that is obtained. In general, the higher the reflux ratio, the more efficient the fractional distillation.

c. Correct column length is difficult to determine in advance of performing a fractional distillation. The trial-and-error technique must normally be used, and if a particular column does not efficiently separate a certain mixture, a longer column or a different type of column or column packing must be selected.

d. The difference in boiling points between the two pure components of a mixture should be no less than 20–30 °C in order for a fractional distillation to be successful when a Hempel column packed with Raschig rings or a similar type of packing is used. As mentioned previously, modifications in column length and type may result in the successful separation of mixtures having smaller boiling point differences.

In summary, the most important variables that can be controlled experimentally in a fractional distillation are proper selection of the column and column packing, adequate insulation of the column, and careful control of the rate of heating so as to provide the proper reflux ratio and a favorable temperature gradient within the column. Under such conditions, two different temperature **plateaus** will be observed in the fractional distillation of a typical binary mixture (Fig. 4.5). The head temperature should first rise to the normal boiling point of the more volatile component and remain there until that component is mostly removed (Fig. 4.5, Fraction 1). The head temperature may then drop somewhat, indicating that the more volatile component has largely been removed. As additional heat is provided to the stillpot, the less volatile component will begin to distill, and the head temperature will rise to the boiling point of the second component (Fig. 4.5, Fraction 2). If the separation is efficient, the volume of this fraction, which contains a mixture of the two components, will be small. The head temperature should then remain constant at the normal boiling point of the less volatile component until most of it has distilled (Fig. 4.5, Fraction 3).

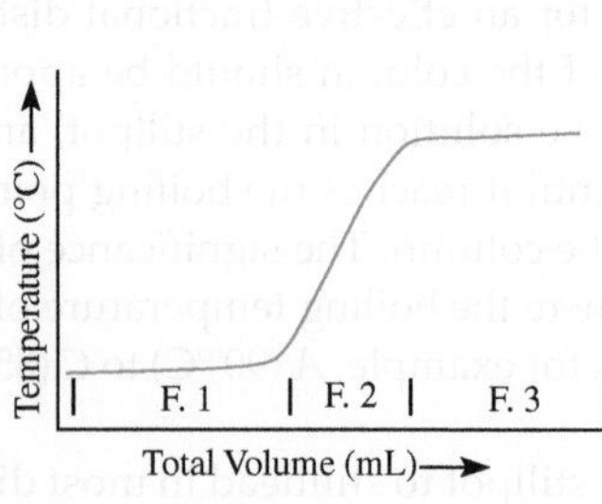

Figure 4.5
Progress curve for typical fractional distillation.

EXPERIMENTAL PROCEDURES

Base and Acid Extractions

Purpose To separate multicomponent mixtures as a function of pH of solution.

SAFETY ALERT

1. **Wear safety glasses or goggles and suitable protective gloves while performing the experiments.**
2. **Do not allow any of the chemicals used in this experiment to come in contact with your skin. If they do, *immediately* wash the affected areas with soap and water.**
3. **Diethyl ether is *extremely* volatile and flammable. Be certain there are *no flames* in your vicinity when using it for extraction and when removing it from the "Neutral Compound."**
4. **Use caution in handling wet glassware, because it can easily slip out of your grasp.**
5. **When extracting a solution, vent the separatory funnel or vial *often* to avoid a buildup of pressure.**

MINISCALE PROCEDURE

Preparation Refer to the online resources to answer Pre-Lab Exercises, access videos, and read the MSDSs for the chemicals used or produced in this procedure. Read or review Sections 2.7, 2.10, 2.11, 2.13, 2.17, 2.21, 2.24, 2.25, 2.29, 3.2, and 3.3.

A. One-Base Extraction

Apparatus Separatory funnel, ice-water bath, apparatus for vacuum filtration, simple distillation, and *flameless* heating.

Dissolution Obtain 2 g of a mixture of benzoic acid and naphthalene. Dissolve the mixture by swirling it with 30 mL of diethyl ether in an Erlenmeyer flask. If any solids remain, add more diethyl ether to effect complete dissolution. Transfer the solution to the separatory funnel.

Extraction Extract the solution with a 15-mL portion of 2.5 *M* (10%) aqueous sodium hydroxide. *Be sure to hold both the stopcock and the stopper of the funnel tightly and frequently vent the funnel by opening its stopcock* (Fig. 2.61). Identify the aqueous layer by the method described in Section 2.21, transfer it to an Erlenmeyer flask labeled "Hydroxide Extract," and transfer the organic solution into a clean Erlenmeyer flask containing two spatula-tips full of *anhydrous* sodium sulfate and labeled "Neutral Compound." Let this solution stand for about 15 min, occasionally swirling it to hasten the drying process. If the solution remains cloudy, add additional portions of sodium sulfate to complete the drying process.★

Precipitating and Drying Cool the "Hydroxide Extract" in an ice-water bath. Carefully acidify this solution with 3 *M* hydrochloric acid, so that the solution is distinctly acidic to pHydrion paper.★ Upon acidification, a precipitate should form; cool the mixture for 10–15 min to complete the crystallization.

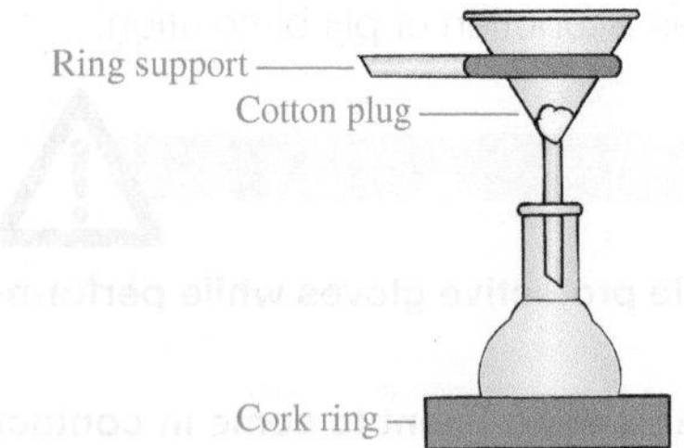

Figure 5.5
Miniscale gravity filtration through a cotton plug.

Collect the precipitate by vacuum filtration (Fig. 2.54) using a Büchner or Hirsch funnel. Wash the solid on the filter paper with a small portion of *cold* water. Transfer the solid to a labeled watchglass, cover it with a piece of filter or weighing paper, and allow the product to air-dry until the next laboratory period. Alternatively, dry the solid in an oven having a temperature of 90–100 °C for about 1 h. After drying, transfer the benzoic acid to a dry, *tared* vial.

Separate the "Neutral Compound" from the drying agent by decantation (Fig. 2.56) or gravity filtration through a cotton plug (Fig. 5.5) into a 100-mL round-bottom flask. Remove the solvent by simple distillation (Fig. 2.37). Alternatively, use rotary evaporation or one of the other techniques described in Section 2.29. Allow the residue to cool to room temperature to solidify, scrape the contents of the flask onto a piece of weighing paper to air-dry, and then transfer it to a dry, *tared* vial.

Analysis and Recrystallization Determine the weight and melting point of each crude product. If you know the relative amounts of benzoic acid (**5**) and naphthalene (**7**) in the original mixture, calculate the percent recovery of each compound. Recrystallize them according to the general procedures provided in Section 3.2 and determine the melting points of the purified materials.

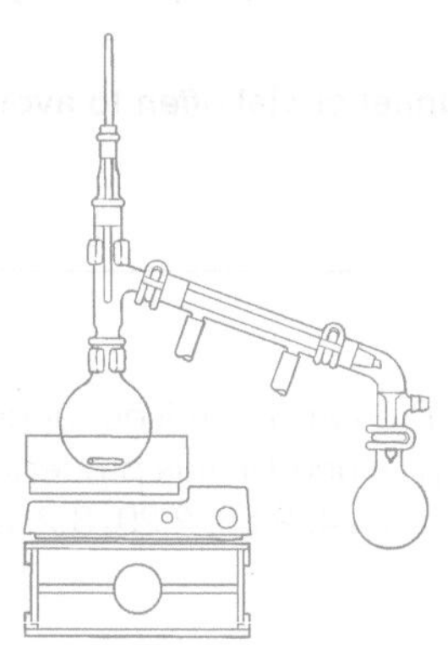

B. Two-Base Extraction

Apparatus Separatory funnel, ice-water bath, apparatus for vacuum filtration, simple distillation, and *flameless* heating.

Dissolution Obtain 2 g of a mixture of benzoic acid, 2-naphthol, and naphthalene. Dissolve the mixture by swirling it with 30 mL of diethyl ether in a 125-mL Erlenmeyer flask. If any solids remain, add more diethyl ether to effect complete dissolution.

Extraction Extract the solution with a 20-mL portion of 1.25 *M* (10%) aqueous sodium bicarbonate (Fig. 2.61). *Caution:* Gaseous carbon dioxide is generated! To prevent accidental loss of material, do the following: After adding the aqueous bicarbonate to the funnel, swirl the *unstoppered* funnel until all foaming has subsided. Then stopper the funnel and, *holding both the stopcock and the stopper of the separatory funnel tightly,* invert the funnel and *immediately* vent it by opening the *stopcock.* Finally, shake the funnel with *frequent* venting until gas is no longer evolved. Separate the layers, transferring the aqueous layer to a 125-mL Erlenmeyer flask labeled "Bicarbonate Extract."★ To ensure properly identifying the aqueous layer, consult Section 2.21. Return the organic solution to the separatory funnel.

Now extract the organic solution with a 20-mL portion of *cold* 2.5 *M* (10%) aqueous sodium hydroxide, venting the funnel frequently during the process. Transfer the aqueous layer to a 125-mL Erlenmeyer flask labeled "Hydroxide Extract." Transfer the organic solution to a 50-mL Erlenmeyer flask labeled "Neutral Compound" and containing two spatula-tips full of *anhydrous* sodium sulfate. Loosely cork the flask containing the organic solution, and let it stand for at least 15 min with occasional swirling to promote drying. If the solution remains cloudy, add additional portions of sodium sulfate to complete the drying process.★

Precipitating and Drying For the "Bicarbonate" and "Hydroxide Extracts," follow the directions given in Part A for the "Hydroxide Extract." Also apply the protocol provided in Part A for the "Neutral Compound" to the corresponding solution obtained in this procedure.

Analysis and Recrystallization Determine the weight and melting point of each crude product. If you know the relative amounts of benzoic acid (**5**), naphthalene (**7**), and 2-naphthol (**11**) in the original mixture, calculate the percent recovery of each compound. Recrystallize them according to the general procedures provided in Section 3.2 and determine the melting points of the purified materials.

C. Acid-Base Extraction

Apparatus Separatory funnel, ice-water bath, apparatus for vacuum filtration, simple distillation, and *flameless* heating.

Dissolution Obtain 1.5 g of a mixture of benzoic acid, 4-nitroaniline, and naphthalene. Dissolve the mixture by swirling it with about 40 mL of dichloromethane in an Erlenmeyer flask. Transfer the solution to the separatory funnel.

Extraction Extract the organic solution three times using 15-mL portions of 3 *M* hydrochloric acid. *Be sure to hold both the stopcock and the stopper of the funnel tightly and frequently vent the funnel by opening its stopcock* (Fig. 2.61). Identify the aqueous layer by the method described in Section 2.21. Combine the three acidic aqueous layers from the extractions in an Erlenmeyer flask labeled "HCl Extract." Return the organic layer to the separatory funnel and extract it two times using 15-mL portions of 3 *M* sodium hydroxide solution. Combine these two aqueous layers in a second flask labeled "Hydroxide Extract." Transfer the organic solution into a clean Erlenmeyer flask containing two spatula-tips full of *anhydrous* sodium sulfate and labeled "Neutral Compound." Let this solution stand for about 15 min, occasionally swirling it to hasten the drying process. If the solution remains cloudy, add additional portions of sodium sulfate to complete the drying process.★

Precipitating and Drying Cool the "HCl Extract" and the "Hydroxide Extract" in an ice-water bath. Neutralize the "HCl Extract" with 6 *M* sodium hydroxide and add a little excess base to make the solution distinctly basic to pHydrion paper. Neutralize the "Hydroxide Extract" with 6 *M* hydrochloric acid and add a little excess acid

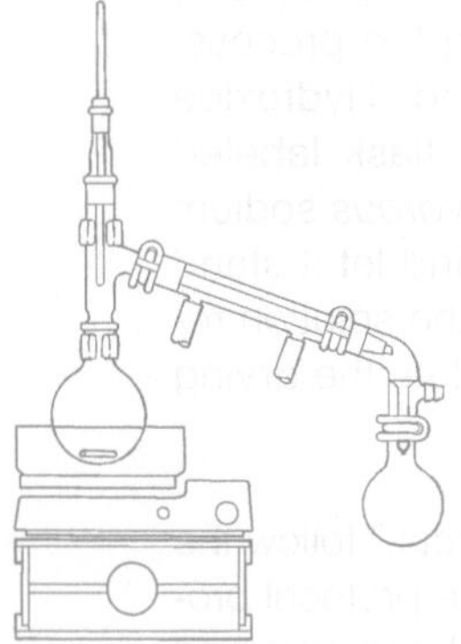

to make the solution distinctly acidic to pHydrion paper.★ Upon neutralization, a precipitate should form in each flask.

Collect the precipitate in the flasks labeled "HCl Extract" and "Hydroxide Extract" by vacuum filtration (Fig. 2.54) using a Büchner or Hirsch funnel. Wash each solid on the filter paper with a small portion of *cold* water. Transfer each solid to a labeled watchglass, cover it with a piece of filter or weighing paper, and allow the product to air-dry until the next laboratory period. Alternatively, dry the solid in an oven having a temperature of 90–100 °C for about 1 h. After drying, transfer the 4-nitroaniline and the benzoic acid each to a different dry, *tared* vial.

Separate the "Neutral Compound" from the drying agent by decantation (Fig. 2.56) or gravity filtration through a cotton plug (Fig. 5.5) into a 100-mL round-bottom flask. Remove the solvent by simple distillation (Fig. 2.37). Alternatively, use rotary evaporation or one of the other techniques described in Section 2.29. Allow the residue to cool to room temperature to solidify, scrape the contents of the flask onto a piece of weighing paper to air-dry, and then transfer it to a dry, *tared* vial.

Analysis and Recrystallization Determine the weight and melting point of each crude product. If you know the relative amounts of benzoic acid (**5**), naphthalene (**7**), and 4-nitroaniline (**13**) in the original mixture, calculate the percent recovery of each compound. Recrystallize them according to the general procedures provided in Section 3.2 and determine the melting points of the purified materials.

WRAPPING IT UP

Place the used *filter papers* in a container for nontoxic solid waste. Flush the *acidic* and *basic* filtrates down the drain. Pour any *diethyl ether* that has been isolated into a container for nonhalogenated organic liquids. Pour any *dichloromethane* that has been isolated into a container for halogenated organic liquids.

EXERCISES

General Questions

1. Using Equation 5.9, show that three extractions with 5-mL portions of a solvent give better recovery than a single extraction with 15 mL of solvent when $K = 0.5$.
2. Show mathematically how Equation 5.17 can be converted to Equation 5.19.
3. Define the following terms:
   a. immiscible liquid phases
   b. distribution or partition coefficient
   c. adsorption
   d. absorption
   e. conjugate base of an acid, HA
   f. conjugate acid of a base, B^-
   g. liquid-liquid extraction
   h. hydrophilic
4. Explain why swirling or shaking a solution and its drying agent hastens the drying process.
5. Assume that the partition coefficient, *K*, for partitioning of compound *A* between diethyl ether and water is 3; that is, *A* preferentially partitions into ether.

a. Given 400 mL of an aqueous solution containing 12 g of compound *A*, how many grams of *A* could be removed from the solution by a *single* extraction with 200 mL of diethyl ether?

b. How many total grams of *A* can be *removed* from the aqueous solution with three successive extractions of 67 mL each?

6. Based on the principle of "like dissolves like," indicate by placing an "x" in the space those compounds listed below that are likely to be soluble in an organic solvent like diethyl ether or dichloromethane and those that are soluble in water.

Compound	*Organic Solvent*	*Water*
a. $C_6H_5CO_2Na$	______	______
b. Naphthalene (7)	______	______
c. Anthracene (15)	______	______
d. Phenol (16)	______	______
e. C_6H_5ONa	______	______
f. Aniline (17)	______	______
g. NaCl	______	______
h. CH_3CO_2H	______	______

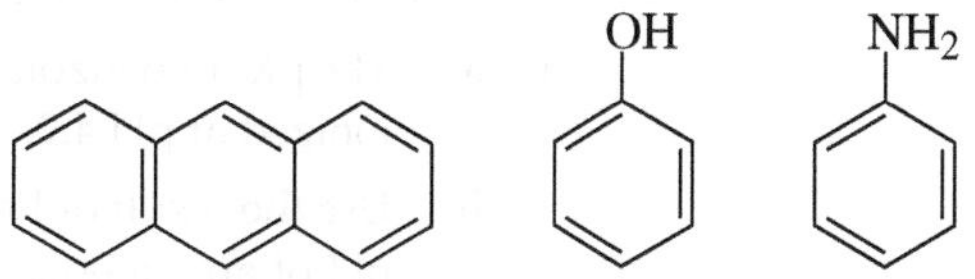

OH NH$_2$

15 Anthracene **16** Phenol **17** Aniline

7. Benzoic acid (**5**) is soluble in diethyl ether but not water; however, benzoic acid is extracted from diethyl ether with aqueous sodium hydroxide.

a. Complete the acid-base reaction below by writing the products of the reaction.

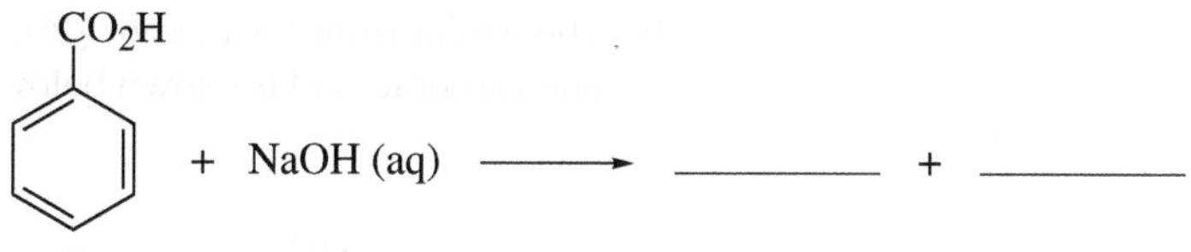

CO_2H + NaOH (aq) ⟶ ________ + ________

5

b. In the reaction of Part **a,** label the acid, the base, conjugate acid, and conjugate base.

c. Indicate the solubility of benzoic acid and its conjugate base in diethyl ether and in water.

8. Aniline (**17**), an amine, is soluble in diethyl ether but not water; however, aniline is extracted from diethyl ether with aqueous hydrochloric acid.

a. Complete the acid-base reaction below by writing the products of the reaction.

$$\text{(17, } C_6H_5NH_2\text{)} + HCl\,(aq) \longrightarrow \_\_\_\_\_\_\_\_ + \_\_\_\_\_\_\_\_$$

NH$_2$

17

b. In the reaction of Part **a,** label the acid, the base, conjugate acid, and conjugate base.

c. Indicate the solubility of aniline and its conjugate acid in diethyl ether and in water.

9. Naphthalene (**7**) is soluble in diethyl ether, but it is insoluble in water regardless of the solution pH. Explain why this compound cannot be readily ionized in aqueous solution.

10. There are three common functional groups in organic chemistry that are readily ionized by adjusting the pH of the aqueous solution during an extraction. Name and write the chemical structure of these three functional groups, and show each of them in both their neutral and ionized forms.

11. a. The pK_a of benzoic acid (**5**) is 4.2. Show mathematically that this acid is 50% ionized at pH 4.2.

b. Use the result of Part **a** to explain why precipitation of **5** is incomplete if the pH of an aqueous solution of benzoate ion (**6**) is lowered only to pH 7 by adding acid.

12. Consider the base monosodium phosphate, Na^+ $(HO)_2P(=O)O^-$. (a) Write the structure of the conjugate acid of this base. (b) Given that the pK_a of this conjugate acid is 2.1, explain why an aqueous solution of monosodium phosphate would be ineffective for extracting benzoic acid (**5**) from a diethyl ether solution.

13. Provide a flowchart analogous to those in Figures 5.1–5.4 for separating a diethyl ether solution containing anthracene (**15**), benzoic acid (**5**), 2-naphthol (**11**), and 4-nitroaniline (**13**). All compounds are solids when pure.

14. The equilibrium for phenol (**16**), sodium phenoxide (**18**), sodium bicarbonate, and carbonic acid is shown below:

$$C_6H_5OH + NaHCO_3 \rightleftharpoons C_6H_5O^-Na^+ + H_2CO_3$$

OH — **16** Phenol; Sodium bicarbonate; O$^-$Na$^+$ — **18** Sodium phenoxide; Carbonic acid

a. The pK_as for phenol and carbonic acid are 10.0 and 6.4, respectively. Determine the K_{eq} for this reaction.

b. Based upon your answer to Part **a,** would sodium bicarbonate be a suitable base for separating phenol from a neutral organic compound via an aqueous extraction?

One-Base Extraction

15. What practical consideration makes aqueous hydroxide rather than aqueous bicarbonate (**9**) the preferred base for extracting benzoic acid (**5**) from diethyl ether?

16. Naphthalene (**7**) has a relatively high vapor pressure for a solid (because of its volatility, naphthalene is the active ingredient in some brands of mothballs). In view of this, what might happen if you placed naphthalene under vacuum or in an oven for several hours to dry it?

17. When benzoic acid (**5**) is partitioned between diethyl ether and aqueous sodium hydroxide solution and the aqueous layer is separated, acidification of the aqueous solution yields a precipitate.

a. Using arrows to symbolize the flow of electrons, show the reaction of benzoic acid (**5**) with hydroxide and draw the structure of the product of this reaction.

b. Using arrows to symbolize the flow of electrons, show the reaction of the product of the reaction in Part **a** with aqueous acid and draw the structure of the product of this reaction.

c. Why does the organic product of the reaction in Part **b** precipitate from aqueous solution?

Two-Base Extraction

18. Why does the sequence for extracting the diethyl ether solution of benzoic acid (**5**), naphthalene (**7**), and 2-naphthol (**11**) start with aqueous bicarbonate and follow with aqueous hydroxide rather than the reverse order?

19. What would be the consequence of acidifying the basic extract containing **12** only to pH 10?

20. Why is caution advised when acidifying the bicarbonate solution of sodium benzoate (**6**)?

Acid-Base Extraction

21. Why is *anhydrous* sodium sulfate added to the organic solution remaining after the extractions with 6 *M* HCl and 6 *M* NaOH?

22. The pK_as of benzoic acid (**5**) and 4-nitroanilinium hydrochloride (**14**) are 4.2 and 1.0, respectively.

a. Determine the K_{eq} for the reaction of benzoic acid (**5**) with 4-nitroaniline (**13**).

b. Based upon your answer to Part **a,** do you think a significant amount of salt would form from mixing equimolar amounts of benzoic acid (**5**) and 4-nitroaniline (**13**)? Explain your reasoning.

EXPERIMENTAL PROCEDURES

Recrystallization

Purpose To explore the techniques for recrystallizing solids.

SAFETY ALERT

1. **Wear safety glasses or goggles while performing the experiments.**
2. **Organic compounds are much more rapidly absorbed through the skin when they are in solution, particularly in water-soluble solvents such as acetone and ethanol. For this reason, do not rinse organic materials off your skin with solvents such as acetone; wash your hands thoroughly with soap and warm water instead.**
3. **Do not use a burner in these procedures unless instructed to do so. Most solvents used for recrystallization are flammable (Table 3.1).**
4. **When using a hot plate, do not set it at its highest value. A moderate setting will prevent overheating and the resultant bumping and splashing of materials from the flask. Do not employ hot plates for heating volatile or flammable solvents; rather, use a steam bath.**
5. **Do not inhale solvent vapors. If a hood is not available to you, clamp an inverted funnel just above the Erlenmeyer flask in which you will be heating solvents. Attach this funnel to a source of vacuum by means of rubber tubing (Fig. 2.71b).**
6. ***Never* add decolorizing carbon to a boiling solution; doing so may cause the solution to boil out of the flask. Add the carbon only when the temperature of the solvent is below the boiling temperature. This same precaution applies when using a filter-aid to assist in the removal of the carbon during the hot filtration step.**

A ▪ *Solvent Selection*

Procedure

Preparation Refer to the online resources to answer Pre-Lab Exercises, access videos, and read the MSDSs for the chemicals used or produced in this procedure. Read or review Sections 2.5, 2.9, and 3.2, and review the solvent properties listed in Table 3.1. Although different criteria are used for defining solubility, plan to use the following definitions in this experiment: (a) soluble—20 mg of solute will dissolve in 0.5 mL of solvent; (b) slightly soluble—some but not all of the 20 mg of solute will dissolve in 0.5 mL of solvent; (c) insoluble—none of the solute appears to dissolve in 0.5 mL of solvent. *Be certain to record all your observations regarding solubilities in your notebook!*

Apparatus Test tubes (10-mm × 75-mm), hot-water (80–100 °C) or steam bath.

Protocol For *known* compounds, place about 20 mg (a microspatula-tip full) of the finely crushed solid in a test tube and add about 0.5 mL of water using a calibrated Pasteur pipet. Stir the mixture with a glass rod or microspatula to determine whether the solid is soluble in water at room temperature. If the solid is not completely soluble at room temperature, warm the test tube in the hot-water or steam bath, and stir or swirl its contents to determine whether the solid is soluble in hot water.

If any of your solutes are soluble in the hot solvent but only slightly soluble or insoluble at room temperature, allow the hot solution to cool slowly to room temperature and compare the quantity, size, color, and form of the resulting crystals with the original solid material.

Repeat the solubility test for the solutes using 95% ethanol and then petroleum ether (bp 60–80 °C, 760 torr). After completing these additional tests, record which of the three solvents you consider best suited for recrystallization of each of the solutes.

Compounds **1–4** contain a variety of functional groups that impart differing solubility properties to the molecules and are possible substrates on which to practice the technique of determining solubilities. Other known compounds may be assigned by your instructor.

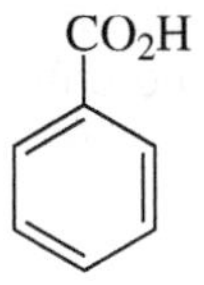

CO_2H — **1** Benzoic acid

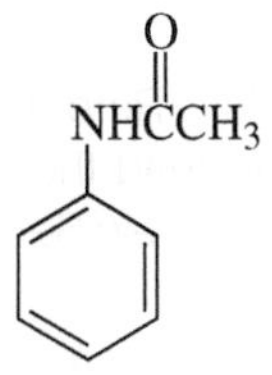

$NHCCH_3$ (with C=O) — **2** Acetanilide

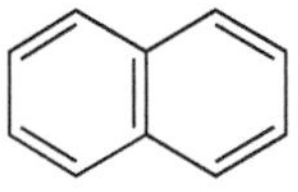

3 Naphthalene

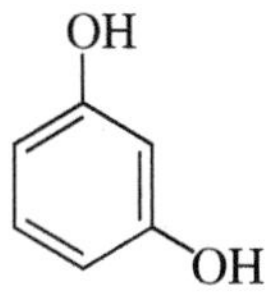

OH, OH — **4** Resorcinol

For *unknown* compounds, a *systematic* approach is important for determining their solubility. First, select the solvents from Table 3.1 to be used in the tests. It should not be necessary to test all the solvents, but you should consider trying those that are denoted with the symbol ‡ in the table. Your instructor may also suggest solvents to evaluate.

After selecting the solvents, obtain enough clean, dry test tubes so that there is one for each solvent to be tested. Place about 20 mg (a microspatula-tip full) of the finely crushed unknown in each test tube and add about 0.5 mL of a solvent to a tube containing the solid. Stir each mixture and determine the solubility of the unknown in each solvent at room temperature. Use the definitions of *soluble, slightly soluble, or insoluble* given earlier.

If the unknown is insoluble in a particular solvent, warm the test tube in the hot-water or steam bath. Stir or swirl the contents of the tube and note whether the unknown is soluble in hot solvent. If the solid is soluble in the hot solvent but only slightly soluble or insoluble at room temperature, allow the hot solution to cool to room temperature slowly. If crystals form in the cool solution, compare their quantity, size, color, and form with the original solid material and with those obtained from other solvents.

It is a good idea to test the solubility of a solute in a variety of solvents. Even though nice crystals may form in the first solvent you try, another one might prove better if it provides either better recovery or higher-quality crystals. To assist in determining the best solvent to use in recrystallizing an unknown, you should construct a table containing the solubility data you gather by the systematic approach described above.

If these solubility tests produce no clear choice for the solvent, mixed solvents might be considered. Review the discussion presented earlier in this section for the procedure for using a mixture of two solvents. Before trying any combinations of solvent pairs, take about 0.2 mL of each *pure* solvent being considered and mix them to ensure that they are miscible in one another. If they are not, that particular combination *cannot* be used.

B ■ *Recrystallizing Impure Solids*

MINISCALE PROCEDURES

Preparation Refer to the online resources to answer Pre-Lab Exercises, access videos, and read the MSDSs for the chemicals used or produced in this procedure. Read or review Sections 2.6, 2.7, 2.9, 2.11, 2.17, and 2.18.

1. Benzoic Acid

Apparatus Two 50-mL Erlenmeyer flasks, graduated cylinder, ice-water bath, apparatus for magnetic stirring, vacuum filtration, and *flameless* heating.

Dissolution Place 1.0 g of impure benzoic acid in an Erlenmeyer flask equipped for magnetic stirring or with boiling stones. Measure 25 mL of water into the graduated cylinder and add a 10-mL portion of it to the flask. Heat the mixture to a gentle boil and continue adding water in 0.5-mL portions until no more solid appears to dissolve in the boiling solution. Record the total volume of water used; no more than 10 mL should be required. *Caution:* Because the sample may be contaminated with insoluble material, pay close attention to whether additional solid is dissolving as you add more solvent; if it is not, *stop adding solvent.*

Decoloration Pure benzoic acid is colorless, so a colored solution indicates that treatment with decolorizing carbon (Sec. 2.18) is necessary. *Caution:* Do *not* add decolorizing carbon to a *boiling* solution! Allow the solution to cool slightly, add a microspatula-tip full of carbon, and reheat to boiling for a few minutes. To aid in removing the finely divided carbon by filtration, allow the solution to cool slightly, add about 0.2 g of a filter-aid (Sec. 2.17), and reheat.

Hot Filtration and Crystallization If there are insoluble impurities or decolorizing carbon in the solution, perform a hot filtration (Sec. 2.17) using a 50-mL Erlenmeyer flask to receive the filtrate (Fig. 2.52). Rinse the empty flask with about 1 mL of *hot* water and filter this rinse into the original filtrate. If the filtrate remains colored, repeat the treatment with decolorizing carbon. Cover the opening of the flask with a piece of filter paper, an inverted beaker, or loose-fitting cork to exclude airborne impurities from the solution, and allow the filtrate to stand undisturbed until it has cooled to room temperature and no more crystals form.★ To complete the crystallization, place the flask in an ice-water bath for at least 15 min.

Isolation and Drying Collect the crystals on a Büchner or Hirsch funnel by vacuum filtration (Fig. 2.54) and wash the filter cake with two small portions of *cold* water. Press the crystals as dry as possible on the funnel with a clean cork or spatula. Spread the benzoic acid on a watchglass, protecting it from airborne contaminants with a piece of filter paper, and air-dry it at room temperature or in an oven. Be certain that the temperature of the oven is 20–30 °C below the melting point of the product!

Analysis Determine the melting points of the crude and recrystallized benzoic acid, the weight of the latter material, and calculate your percent recovery using Equation 3.1.

$$\text{Percent recovery} = \frac{\text{Weight of pure crystals recovered}}{\text{Weight of original sample}} \times 100 \qquad (3.1)$$

2. *Acetanilide*

Apparatus Two 50-mL Erlenmeyer flasks, graduated cylinder, ice-water bath, apparatus for magnetic stirring, vacuum filtration, and *flameless* heating.

Dissolution Place 1.0 g of impure acetanilide in an Erlenmeyer flask equipped for magnetic stirring or with boiling stones. Measure 20 mL of water into the graduated cylinder and add a 10-mL portion of it to the flask. Heat the mixture to a gentle boil.

A layer of oil should form when the stated amount of water is added. (If you have not done so already, review the discussion of *Crystallization* in this section, focusing on how to crystallize compounds that form oils.) This layer consists of a solution of water in acetanilide. More water must be added to effect complete solution of the acetanilide in water. However, even if a homogeneous solution is produced at the boiling point of the mixture, an oil may separate from it as cooling begins. The formation of this second liquid phase is known to occur only under specific conditions: The acetanilide-water mixture must have a composition that is between 5.2% and 87% in acetanilide and be at a temperature above 80 °C. Because the solubility of acetanilide in water at temperatures near 100 °C exceeds 5.2%, a homogeneous solution formed by using the minimum quantity of water meets these criteria. Such a solution will yield an oil on cooling to about 83 °C; solid begins to form below this temperature.

Continue adding 3–5 mL of water in 0.5-mL portions to the boiling solution until the oil has completely dissolved. *Caution:* Because the sample may be contaminated with insoluble material, pay close attention to whether additional solid is dissolving as you add more solvent; if it is not, *stop adding solvent.* Once the acetanilide has just dissolved, add an additional 1 mL of water to prevent formation of oil during the crystallization step. If oil forms at this time, reheat the solution and add a little more water. Record the total volume of water used.

Continue the procedure by following the directions for *Decoloration, Hot Filtration and Crystallization, and Isolation and Drying* given for benzoic acid in Part 1.

Analysis Determine the melting points of the crude and recrystallized acetanilide, the weight of the latter material, and calculate your percent recovery using Equation 3.1.

3. Naphthalene

Apparatus Two 50-mL Erlenmeyer flasks, graduated cylinder, ice-water bath, apparatus for magnetic stirring, vacuum filtration, and *flameless* heating.

Dissolution Naphthalene may be conveniently recrystallized from methanol, 95% ethanol, or 2-propanol. Because these solvents are somewhat toxic and/or flammable, proper precautions should be taken. The sequence of steps up through the hot filtration should be performed in a hood if possible. Alternatively, if instructed to do so, position an inverted funnel connected to a vacuum source above the mouth of the flask being used for recrystallization (Fig. 2.71b).

Place 1.0 g of impure naphthalene in an Erlenmeyer flask equipped for magnetic stirring or with boiling stones and dissolve it in the minimum amount of boiling alcohol. *Caution:* Because the sample may be contaminated with insoluble material, pay close attention to whether additional solid is dissolving as you add more solvent; if it is not, *stop adding solvent.* Then add 0.5 mL of additional solvent to ensure that premature crystallization will not occur during subsequent transfers. Record the total volume of solvent used.

Continue the procedure by following the directions for *Decoloration, Hot Filtration and Crystallization, and Isolation and Drying* given for benzoic acid in Part 1; however, use the solvent in which you dissolved the naphthalene rather than water.

Analysis Determine the melting points of the crude and recrystallized naphthalene, the weight of the latter material, and calculate your percent recovery using Equation 3.1.

4. Unknown Compound

Apparatus Two 50-mL Erlenmeyer flasks, graduated cylinder, ice-water bath, apparatus for magnetic stirring, vacuum filtration, and *flameless* heating.

Dissolution *Accurately* weigh about 1 g of the unknown compound and transfer it to an Erlenmeyer flask equipped for magnetic stirring or with boiling stones. Measure about 15 mL of the solvent you have selected on the basis of solubility tests into a graduated cylinder and add 10 mL of it to the flask. Bring the mixture to a gentle boil using *flameless* heating unless water is the solvent, add a 1-mL portion of the solvent, and again boil the solution. Continue adding 3-mL portions of solvent, one portion at a time, until the solid has completely dissolved. Bring the solution to boiling after adding each portion of solvent. *Caution:* Because the sample may be contaminated with insoluble material, pay close attention to whether additional solid is dissolving as you add more solvent; if it is not, *stop adding solvent.* Record the total volume of solvent that is added.

Continue the procedure by following the directions for *Decoloration, Hot Filtration and Crystallization, and Isolation and Drying* given for benzoic acid in Part 1.

Analysis Determine the melting points of the crude and recrystallized unknown, the weight of the latter material, and calculate your percent recovery using Equation 3.1.

5. Mixed-Solvent Crystallization

Apparatus Two 25-mL Erlenmeyer flasks, graduated cylinder or calibrated Pasteur pipet, ice-water bath, apparatus for magnetic stirring, vacuum filtration, and *flameless* heating.

Dissolution Place 1.0 g of impure benzoic acid or acetanilide in an Erlenmeyer flask equipped for magnetic stirring or with boiling stones. Add 2 mL of 95% ethanol and heat the mixture to a gentle boil. If necessary, continue adding the solvent in 0.5-mL portions until no more solid appears to dissolve in the boiling solution. *Caution:* Because the sample may be contaminated with insoluble material, pay close attention to whether additional solid is dissolving as you add more solvent; if it is not, *stop adding solvent.* Record the total volume of 95% ethanol used.

Decoloration If the solution is colored, treat it with decolorizing carbon (Sec. 2.18) and a filter-aid according to the procedure given for benzoic acid in Part 1.

Hot Filtration and Crystallization If there are insoluble impurities or decolorizing carbon in the solution, perform a hot filtration (Sec. 2.17) using a 25-mL Erlenmeyer flask to receive the filtrate (Fig. 2.52). Rinse the empty flask with about 0.5 mL of *hot* 95% ethanol and filter this rinse into the original filtrate. If the filtrate remains colored, repeat the treatment with decolorizing carbon.

Reheat the decolorized solution to boiling and add water dropwise from a Pasteur pipet until the boiling solution remains cloudy or precipitate appears; this may require adding several milliliters of water. Then add a few drops of 95% ethanol to produce a clear solution at the boiling point. Remove the flask from the heating source, and follow the same directions as given for benzoic acid in Part 1 to complete both this stage of the procedure and *Isolation and Drying.*

Analysis Determine the melting points of the crude and recrystallized product, the weight of the latter material, and calculate your percent recovery using Equation 3.1.

WRAPPING IT UP

Flush any *aqueous filtrates* or *solutions* down the drain. With the advice of your instructor, do the same with the *filtrates* derived from use of *alcohols, acetone,* or other *water-soluble solvents.* Use the appropriate containers for the *filtrates* containing *halogenated solvents* or *hydrocarbon solvents.* Put *filter papers* in the container for nontoxic waste, unless instructed to do otherwise.

EXERCISES

1. Define or describe each of the following terms as applied to recrystallization:
   - **a.** solution recrystallization
   - **b.** temperature coefficient of a solvent
   - **c.** the relationship between dielectric constant and polarity of a solvent
   - **d.** petroleum ether
   - **e.** mixed solvents
   - **f.** solvent selection
   - **g.** filter-aid
   - **h.** hot filtration
   - **i.** seeding
   - **j.** vacuum filtration
   - **k.** mother liquor
   - **l.** filtrate
   - **m.** solute
   - **n.** solvent
   - **o.** occlusion
2. Provide the IUPAC name for ethyl acetate and acetone.
3. For which of the following situations is it appropriate to perform a recrystallization? More than one answer may be circled.
   - **a.** To purify an impure liquid.
   - **b.** To purify an impure solid.
   - **c.** The melting point of a compound is depressed and melts over a wide range.
   - **d.** The melting point of a compound is sharp and agrees with the literature value.
   - **e.** An impure solid is soluble in all possible recrystallization solvents that are available.
4. List the steps in the systematic procedure for miniscale recrystallization, briefly explaining the purpose of each step.
5. In performing a hot filtration at the miniscale level, what might happen if the filter funnel is not preheated before the solution is poured through it?
6. Describe the use of the following pieces of equipment during recrystallizations at the miniscale level.
   - **a.** filter flask
   - **b.** filter trap
   - **c.** Büchner funnel
7. Why should the filter flask not be connected directly to a water aspirator pump when performing a vacuum filtration?

8. List the steps in the systematic procedure for microscale recrystallization, briefly explaining the purpose of each step.
9. Why is a Pasteur filter-tip pipet preferred to a regular Pasteur pipet for transferring hot volatile solutions?
10. In performing a hot filtration at the microscale level, what might happen if the Pasteur filtering and filter-tip pipets are not preheated before filtration?
11. Why is a Craig tube filtration ineffective for removing finely divided particles from a solution?
12. Briefly explain how a colored solution may be decolorized.
13. Briefly explain how insoluble particles can be removed from a hot solution.
14. When might Celite, a filter-aid, be used in recrystallization, and why is it used?
15. List five criteria that should be used in selecting a solvent for a recrystallization.
16. How does the principle of *like dissolves like* explain the differing solubilities of solutes in various solvents?
17. The following solvent selection data were collected for two different impure solids:

Solid A

Solvent	*Solubility at Room Temperature*	*Solubility When Heated*	*Crystals Formed When Cooled*
Methanol	Insoluble	Insoluble	—
Ethyl acetate	Insoluble	Soluble	Very few
Cyclohexane	Insoluble	Soluble	Many
Toluene	Insoluble	Soluble	Very few

Solid B

Solvent	*Solubility at Room Temperature*	*Solubility When Heated*	*Crystals Formed When Cooled*
Water	Soluble	—	—
Ethanol	Soluble	—	—
Dichloromethane	Insoluble	Insoluble	—
Petroleum ether	Insoluble	Insoluble	—
Toluene	Insoluble	Insoluble	—

Based on these results, what solvents or mixture of solvents might you consider using to recrystallize solids A and B? Explain.

18. Briefly describe how a mixture of sand and benzoic acid, which is soluble in hot water, might be separated to provide pure benzoic acid.
19. Look up the solubility of benzoic acid in hot water. According to the published solubility, what is the minimum amount of water in which 1 g of benzoic acid can be dissolved?

20. The solubility of benzoic acid at 0 °C is 0.02 g per 100 mL of water, and that of acetanilide is 0.53 g per 100 mL of water. If you performed either of these recrystallizations, calculate, with reference to the total volume of water you used in preparing the hot solution, the amount of material in your experiment that was unrecoverable by virtue of its solubility at 0 °C.

21. Assuming that either solvent is otherwise acceptable in a given instance, what advantages does ethanol have over 1-octanol as a crystallization solvent? hexane over pentane? water over methanol?

22. In the course of a synthesis of an important antibiotic, an impure solid was obtained as one of the intermediates. The solubility of this material in various solvents is shown below.

	Water	*Ethanol*	*Toluene*	*Petroleum Ether*	*2-Butanone*	*Acetic Acid*
Cold	Insoluble	Soluble	Insoluble	Insoluble	Soluble	Slightly soluble
Hot	Slightly soluble	Soluble	Soluble	Insoluble	Soluble	Soluble

a. Which of the solvents above would be the most suitable for recrystallization of the impure solid? Explain your reasoning.

b. Provide a reason why each of the following solvents would *not* be a suitable solvent for recrystallization of this material: ethanol, petroleum ether.

c. Write the chemical structure for each of the solvents in the table above.

d. Which solvent is the most polar? least polar?

23. The goal of the recrystallization procedure is to obtain purified material with a maximized recovery. For each of the items listed, explain why this goal would be adversely affected.

a. In the solution step, an unnecessarily large volume of solvent is used.

b. The crystals obtained after filtration are not washed with fresh cold solvent before drying.

c. The crystals referred to in (**b**) are washed with fresh hot solvent.

d. A large quantity of decolorizing carbon is used.

e. Crystals are obtained by breaking up the solidified mass of an oil that originally separated from the hot solution.

f. Crystallization is accelerated by immediately placing the flask of hot solution in an ice-water bath.

24. A second crop of crystals may be obtained by concentrating the vacuum filtrate and cooling. Why is this crop of crystals probably less pure than the first crop?

25. Explain why the rate of dissolution of a crystalline substance may depend on the size of its crystals.

26. In the technique of recrystallization, one step involves heating the solvent containing the solute to its boiling point and, after the solution is cooled to room temperature, cooling it further in an ice-water bath. Why is it important to operate at these temperature extremes during a recrystallization?

27. In the process of a recrystallization, if crystals do not form upon cooling the solution, it is often recommended that the inside of the flask be scratched at the air-liquid interface with a glass stirring rod. What purpose does this serve, and how does it work? What else might be done to induce crystallization?
28. Should some loss of sample mass be expected even after the most carefully executed recrystallization? Explain.
29. In general, what solvent should be used to rinse the filter cake during the vacuum filtration step of a recrystallization? Should this solvent be cooled prior to use?
30. Why do you seldom see high-boiling solvents used as recrystallization solvents?
31. At the end of a recrystallization, where should the *impurities* be located?
32. A student has been asked to recrystallize 1.0 g of impure stilbene from ethanol. Provide a set of standard step-by-step instructions for recrystallization of this sample so as to maximize the purity and yield obtained.
33. An important product from a multistep synthesis must be recrystallized to remove a small amount of an impurity. However, all the available solvents each individually fail to be suitable recrystallization solvents. Offer a solution to this problem using only the available solvents. (*Hint:* Consider binary solvents.)
34. A suspension of decolorizing carbon (charcoal) is often administered to poison victims.
    a. Speculate on the purpose decolorizing carbon serves in this particular application. (*Hint:* It is similar to the way in which decolorizing carbon is used in a recrystallization.)
    b. How is the charcoal ultimately removed from the victim?

EXPERIMENTAL PROCEDURE

Separation of Syn- *and* Anti-*Azobenzenes by* TLC

Purpose To identify solvent mixtures that will separate *syn*- and *anti*-azobenzenes using thin-layer chromatography.

SAFETY ALERT

1. **Wear safety glasses or goggles and suitable protective gloves while performing the experiment.**
2. **Petroleum ether, ethanol, and acetone are highly volatile and flammable solvents. Be certain there are *no flames* in the vicinity during this experiment.**
3. **Since azobenzene is a suspected carcinogen, avoid contacting it with your skin or ingesting it.**

Procedure

Preparation Refer to the online resources to answer Pre-Lab Exercises, access videos, and read the MSDSs for the chemicals used or produced in this procedure.

Apparatus A wide-mouth bottle with a screw-top cap, 3-cm × 10-cm silica gel TLC plates, capillary pipet.

Setting Up Prepare a developing chamber by placing a folded filter paper lengthwise in a wide-mouth bottle (Fig. 6.3). As directed by your instructor, prepare three or four mixtures of eluants that contain different ratios of varying pairs of the following solvents: petroleum ether, bp 60–80 °C (760 torr), chloroform, acetone, and ethanol. For example, prepare 10 mL of a 90:10 mixture of petroleum ether and chloroform to use as one eluant. Add an amount of the eluant to the developing chamber so that it forms a 1-cm layer on the bottom of the container. Screw the cap onto the bottle *tightly*, and *shake* the container *well* to saturate the atmosphere of the chamber with vapors of the solvent.

Preparing and Developing a Plate Obtain three or four 3-cm × 10-cm strips of silica gel chromatogram sheets *without* a fluorescent indicator. Handle the strip *only* by the sides to avoid contaminating the plate with oils from your hands. Place one pencil dot about 1 cm from the left side and about 1 cm from one end of one sheet and another about 1 cm from the right side the same distance from the bottom as the first. Using a capillary pipet, carefully apply a *small* spot of a 10% solution of commercial azobenzene in toluene, which you should obtain from your instructor, over one of the pencil dots. Do not allow the spot to diffuse to a diameter of more than 1–2 mm during application of the sample. Repeat this process for each strip. Allow the spots to dry and then expose the plates to sunlight for one to two hours (or a sunlamp for about 20 min).

When the irradiation is complete, apply another spot of the *original* solution on the plate over the second pencil dot in the same manner as just described and allow each strip to dry. Place a strip in the developing chamber, being careful not to splash solvent onto the plate. Both spots *must be above* the solvent level. Allow the solvent to move to within approximately 2–3 mm of the top of the strip and then remove the strip. Repeat this process for each additional strip using a different eluting solvent as directed by your instructor. Mark the position of the solvent front with a pencil, and allow the plate to air-dry.

Analysis Note the number of spots arising from each of the two original spots. Pay particular attention to the relative intensities of the two spots nearest the starting point in each of the samples; these are *syn*-azobenzenes. Calculate the R_f-values of each of the spots on your developed plate. In your notebook, include a picture of the developed plate drawn to scale as a permanent record. Identify the solvent mixture that gave the best separation of *syn*- and *anti*-azobenzene.

Discovery Experiment

Analysis of Analgesics by TLC

Design and execute an experimental procedure for testing over-the-counter analgesics such as Excedrin, Tylenol, and Advil for the presence of caffeine (**3**) and/or acetaminophen (**4**). A 50:50 (v:v) mixture of ethanol and dichloromethane can be used to extract the active ingredients.

3
Caffeine

HO–C_6H_4–NHC(O)CH_3

4
Acetaminophen

WRAPPING IT UP

Put the *unused eluants* containing mixtures of only *petroleum ether, acetone,* and *ethanol* in the container for nonhalogenated organic liquids and any unused mixtures containing *chloroform* in the container for halogenated organic liquids. Put the dry chromatographic plates in the hazardous solid waste container, since they contain small amounts of azobenzene.

EXERCISES

1. Explain why TLC is not suitable for use with compounds that have boiling points below about 150 °C (760 torr).
2. What may occur if a mixture containing a component that is very sensitive to acidic conditions is subjected to a TLC analysis in which silica gel serves as the stationary phase?

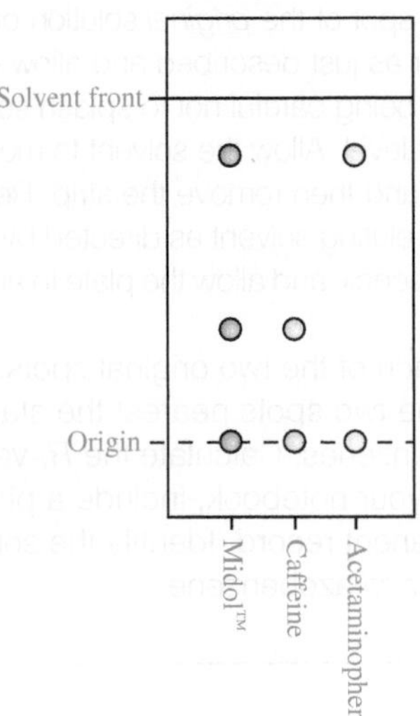

Figure 6.6
TLC analysis of mixture.

3. In a TLC experiment, why should the spot not be immersed in the solvent in the developing chamber?
4. Explain why the solvent must not be allowed to evaporate from the plate during development.
5. Explain why the diameter of the spot should be as small as possible.
6. Which of the two diastereomers of azobenzene would you expect to be more thermodynamically stable? Why?
7. From the results of the TLC experiment with the azobenzenes, describe the role of sunlight.
8. A student obtained the silica gel TLC plate shown in Figure 6.6 by spotting samples of Midol, caffeine, and acetaminophen on the plate and eluting with petroleum ether:chloroform (9:1 v:v).
   a. What are the R_f-values of acetaminophen and of caffeine, respectively?
   b. Based on this TLC analysis, what are the ingredients in a tablet of Midol?
   c. What are the mobile and stationary phases, respectively, in this TLC experiment?
   d. No spots were observed visually when the TLC plate was removed from the developing chamber. How might the student effect visualization of the spots?
   e. Another student accidentally used Midol PM in her experiment and observed only one spot. Speculate as to which spot was absent and offer a possible explanation for the difference in this student's result.
9. Carboxylic acids often produce a streak rather than a spot when analyzed on silica gel TLC plates. Adding a drop or two of acetic acid to the eluant reduces streaking.
   a. Explain why carboxylic acids may streak on silica gel TLC plates and why adding acetic acid to the eluent reduces streaking.
   b. Amines also often streak on silica gel TLC. What might you add to the eluant to reduce such streaking?

EXPERIMENTAL PROCEDURE

Relative Rates of Free-Radical Chain Bromination

Discovery Experiment

Purpose To determine the relative reactivities of different types of hydrogen atoms toward bromine atoms.

SAFETY ALERT

1. **Wear safety glasses or goggles and suitable protective gloves while performing the experiments.**
2. ***Bromine is a hazardous chemical that may cause serious chemical burns.* Do *not* breathe its vapors or allow it to come into contact with skin. Perform all operations involving the transfer of the pure liquid or its solutions at a hood. If you get bromine on your skin, wash the area immediately with soap and warm water and soak the affected area in 0.6 *M* sodium thiosulfate solution for up to 3 h if the burn is particularly serious.**
3. **Keep the 1 *M* bromine in dichloromethane solution in the hood. Dispense 0.5-mL portions of it, using a pipet pump, calibrated Pasteur filter-tip pipet, or a buret fitted with a Teflon stopcock.**
4. **Bromine reacts with acetone to produce the powerful lachrymator α-bromoacetone, $BrCH_2COCH_3$. Do *not* rinse glassware containing residual bromine with acetone!**
5. **Avoid inhalation of the vapors of any of the materials being used in this experiment.**

Procedure

Preparation Refer to the online resources to answer Pre-Lab Exercises, access videos, and read the MSDSs for the chemicals used or produced in this procedure. Review Sections 2.5 and 2.10.

Construct a table in your notebook with the following four main headings: (a) "Hydrocarbon"; (b) "Types of Hydrogen Atoms," entries under which will include the terms 1° aliphatic, 2° benzylic, and so on; (c) "Conditions," with the subheadings RT, RT/hν; and (d) "Elapsed Time," entries under which will be the time required for reaction as measured by decoloration.

Carefully plan your execution of this experiment, because proper labeling of test tubes and managing of time once the reactions have been started are critical. You will perform two separate experimental trials, with one trial starting 5–10 min after the other.

Apparatus Fourteen 13-mm × 100-mm test tubes and corks, six 10-mm × 75-mm test tubes, six Pasteur pipets, filter-tip pipet, ice-water bath, light source.

Setting Up Organize *twelve* 13-mm × 100-mm test tubes into pairs and label each tube in the pair with the name or number of the hydrocarbon **8–13** that you will add to it. Measure 2.5 mL of dichloromethane into each of these tubes and then add 0.5 mL (10 drops) of the hydrocarbon for which it is labeled. Label the *two* remaining 13-mm × 100-mm test tubes "Control" and add 3 mL of dichloromethane to them. Place the *seven* pairs of labeled tubes in a beaker. Working at the hood, dispense 0.5 mL of a 1 *M* solution of bromine in dichloromethane into each of the *six* small test tubes and into one of the larger tubes labeled "Control."

Bromination In rapid succession, add the solution of bromine to each of the hydrocarbon-containing tubes. Do this with agitation to ensure good mixing and record the time of the additions. After all the additions are made, loosely cork each tube to prevent loss of solvent and bromine. Monitor all the tubes, including that labeled "Control," and record the elapsed time required for the discharge, if any, of the color of each solution.

After about 5 min, again dispense 0.5 mL of 1 *M* bromine solution into the six small test tubes used originally for this reagent *and* also into the remaining tube labeled "Control." Working as before, add the solution of bromine to each of the hydrocarbon-containing tubes. Place the six tubes containing the resulting solutions and the tube labeled "Control" in a beaker located 14–16 cm above an unfrosted 100- or 150-watt light bulb so that all the solutions are exposed to the same amount of light. Monitor these seven tubes and record the elapsed time required for the discharge, if any, of the color of each solution.

Terminate your observations of both sets of samples after about 1 h.

Analysis Evaluate the intensity of color remaining in any of the tubes relative to that of the "Control" samples and record the results in your notebook. Obtain IR and ^{1}H NMR spectra of your starting materials and compare them with those of authentic samples (Figs. 9.6–9.17).

WRAPPING IT UP

Decolorize any *solutions* in which the color of bromine is visible by the dropwise addition of cyclohexene; then discard the resulting solutions together with *all other solutions* in a container for halogenated organic liquids.

EXERCISES

1. Draw the structure of the major monobrominated product expected from each of the hydrocarbons used in this experiment.
2. Comment on the need for light in order for bromination to occur with some of the hydrocarbons.
3. Why is a "Control" sample needed in this experiment?
4. Perform the calculations necessary to demonstrate that bromine is indeed the limiting reagent (Sec. 1.6). The densities and molar mass needed to complete the calculations can be found in the abbreviated MSDSs on the website or various handbooks of chemistry.
5. How is polyhalogenation minimized in this experiment?

6. Using curved arrows to symbolize the flow of electrons, show the mechanism for the propagation steps that convert **10** into the corresponding monobromide, and provide two possible termination steps for the process.
7. Answer the questions below for substrates **8–13**.
   a. Which is statistically the most likely to form a monobromide? Briefly explain your answer.
   b. Which is the most likely to form a single isomer of a monobromide? Briefly explain your answer.
   c. Which is expected to produce the *most* stable radical? Briefly explain your answer.
   d. Which is expected to produce the *least* stable radical? Briefly explain your answer.
8. Arrange the six hydrocarbons **8–13** in *increasing* order of reactivity in free-radical chain bromination.
9. a. On the basis of the observed order of reactivity of the hydrocarbons, deduce the order of reactivity of the seven different types of hydrogens found in these compounds, that is, (1) primary aliphatic, (2) secondary aliphatic, (3) tertiary aliphatic, (4) primary benzylic, (5) secondary benzylic, (6) tertiary benzylic, and (7) aromatic.
   b. Outline the logic you used to arrive at your sequence in Part **a.**
10. Consider the free-radical halogenation of an alkane. You may wish to refer to your lecture textbook and to tables of bond dissociation energies when answering these questions.
    a. Why is the bromination much more regioselective than chlorination?
    b. Why are fluorinations extremely dangerous? (*Hint:* Consider heats of reaction of the propagation steps.)
    c. Why is it difficult to generate an alkyl iodide by free-radical chain halogenation?
11. How does the Hammond postulate explain
    a. the greater selectivity for bromination versus chlorination of an alkane?
    b. the fact that the relative reactivity of C–H bonds of an alkane for free-radical chain halogenation is $3° > 2° > 1°$?
12. Why is a 1° benzylic radical more stable than a 1° aliphatic radical?

Refer to the online resources and use the spectra viewer and Tables 8.1–8.8 as needed to answer the blue-numbered questions on spectroscopy.

13. Consider the IR spectra of compounds **8–11** (Figs. 9.6, 9.8, 9.10, and 9.12), all of which contain a phenyl ring. What absorption(s) in the spectra denote the presence of this ring?
14. Consider the NMR data for compounds **8–13** (Figs. 9.7, 9.9, 9.11, 9.13, 9.15, and 9.17).
    a. In the ^{1}H NMR spectra, assign the various resonances to the hydrogen nuclei responsible for them.
    b. In the ^{13}C NMR spectra of these compounds, assign the various resonances to the carbon nuclei responsible for them.

SPECTRA

Starting Materials

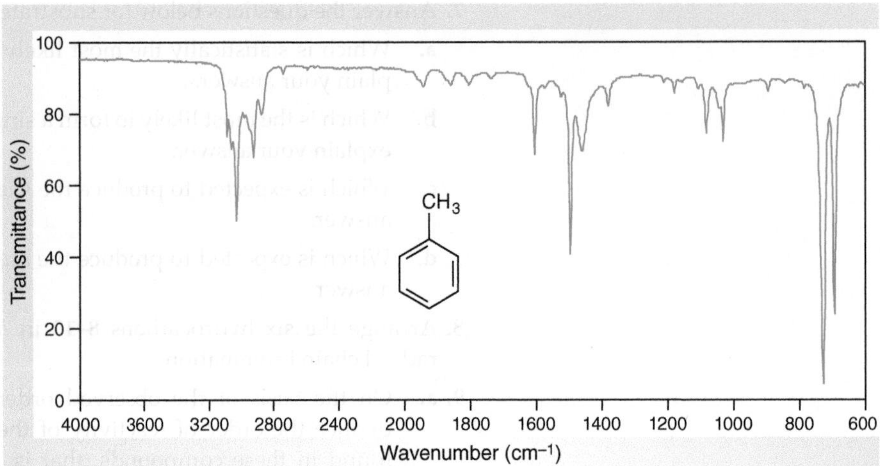

Figure 9.6
IR spectrum of toluene (neat).

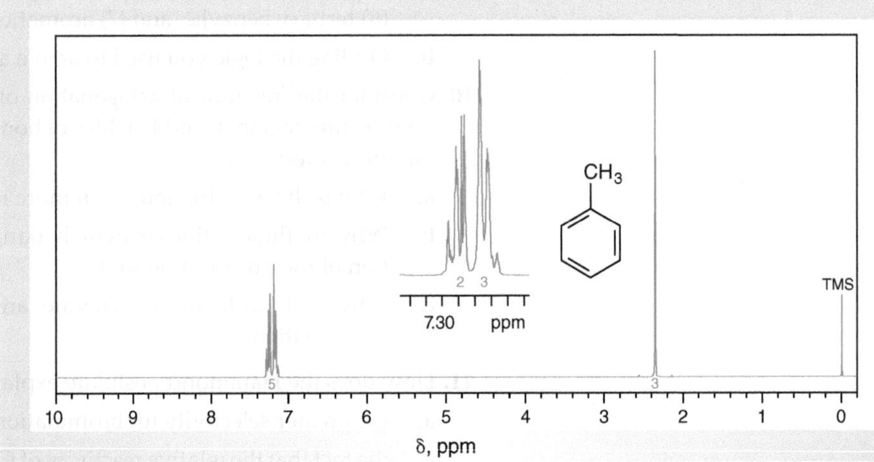

Figure 9.7
NMR data for toluene ($CDCl_3$).

(a) ^{1}H NMR spectrum (300 MHz).
(b) ^{13}C NMR data: δ 21.4, 125.3, 128.2, 129.0, 137.8.

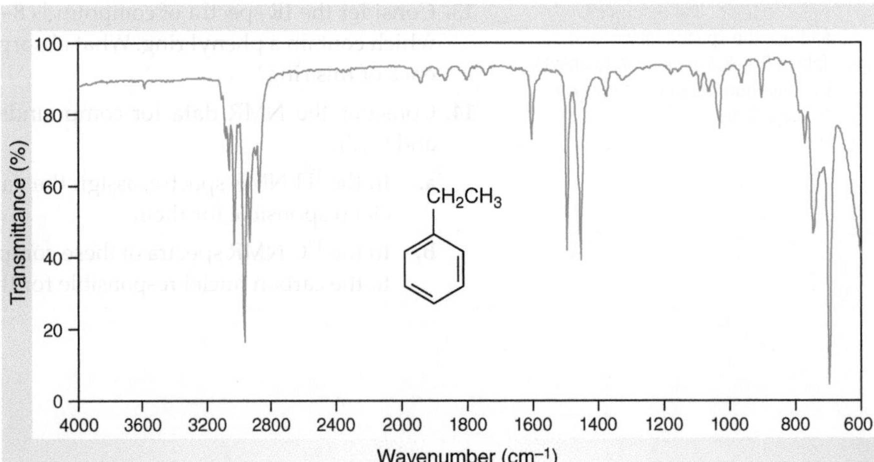

Figure 9.8
IR spectrum of ethylbenzene (neat).

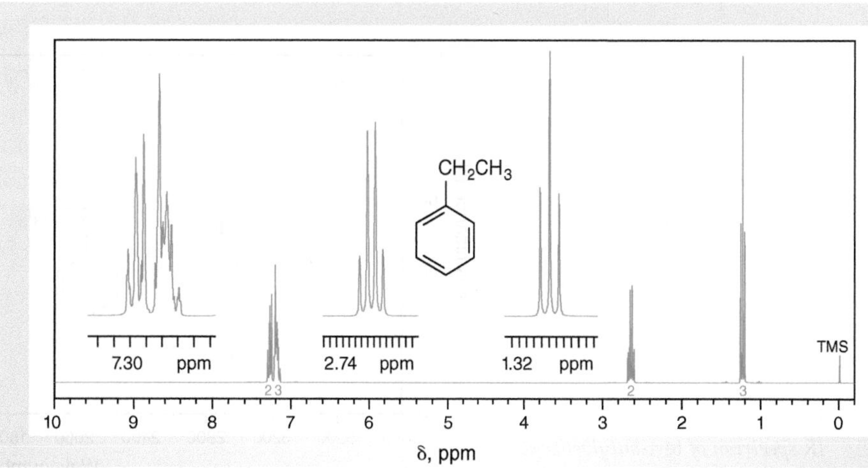

Figure 9.9
NMR data for ethylbenzene ($CDCl_3$).

(a) ^{1}H NMR spectrum (300 MHz).
(b) ^{13}C NMR data: δ 15.6, 29.1, 125.7, 127.9, 128.4, 144.2.

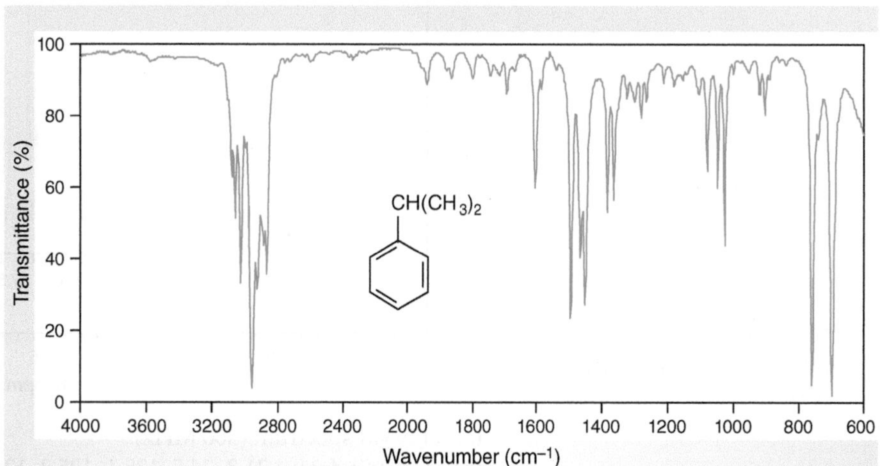

Figure 9.10
IR spectrum of isopropylbenzene (neat).

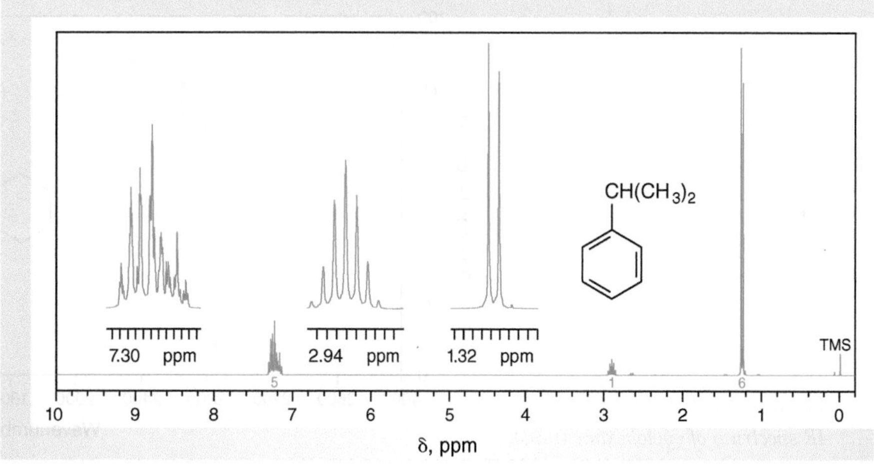

Figure 9.11
NMR data for isopropylbenzene ($CDCl_3$).

(a) ^{1}H NMR spectrum (300 MHz).
(b) ^{13}C NMR data: δ 24.1, 34.2, 125.8, 126.4, 128.4, 148.8.

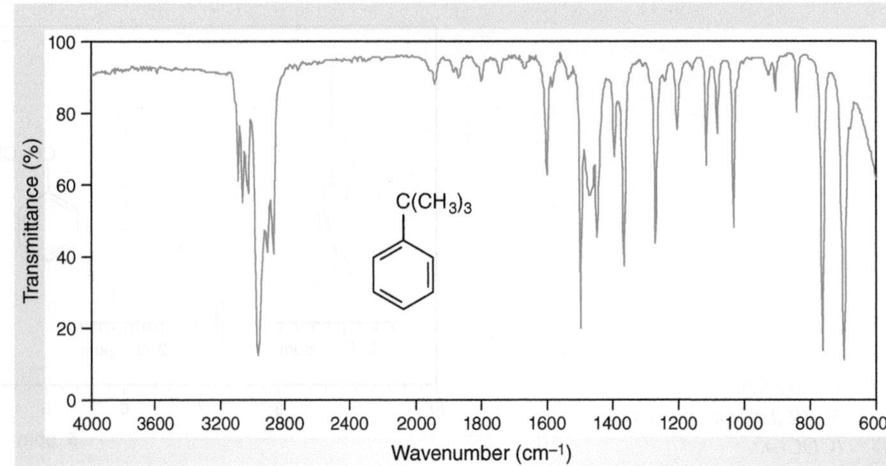

Figure 9.12
IR spectrum of tert-*butylbenzene (neat).*

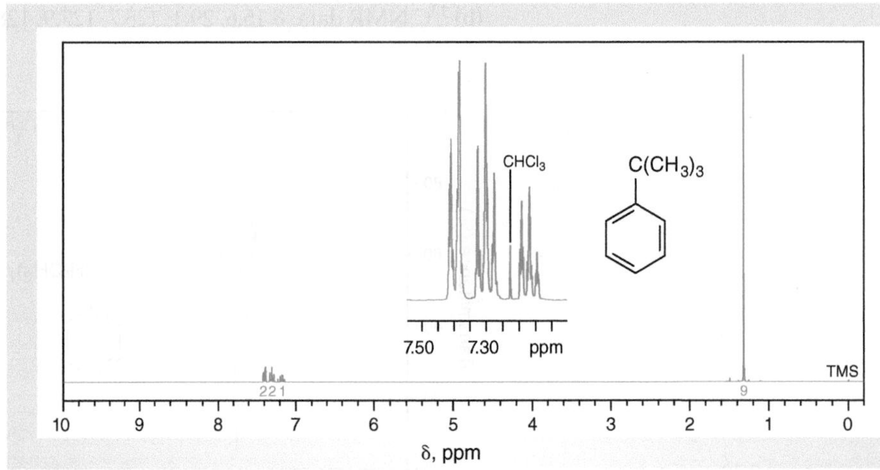

Figure 9.13
NMR data for tert-*butylbenzene ($CDCl_3$).*

(a) ^{1}H NMR spectrum (300 MHz).
(b) ^{13}C NMR data: δ 31.3, 34.5, 125.1, 125.3, 128.0, 150.8.

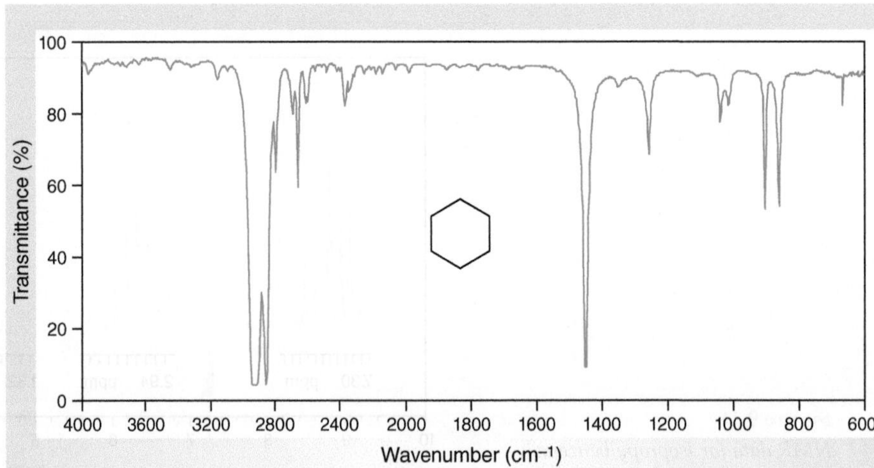

Figure 9.14
IR spectrum of cyclohexane (neat).

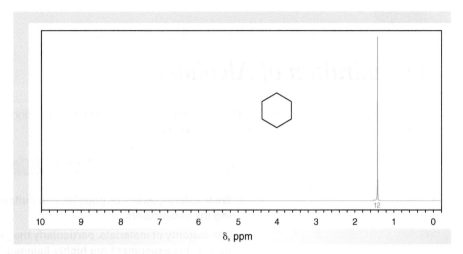

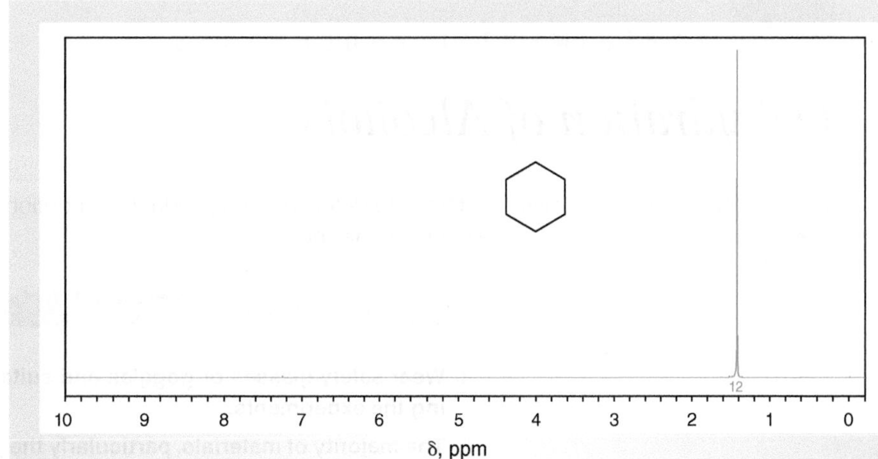

Figure 9.15
NMR data for cyclohexane ($CDCl_3$).

(a) ^{1}H NMR spectrum (300 MHz).
(b) ^{13}C NMR datum: δ 27.3.

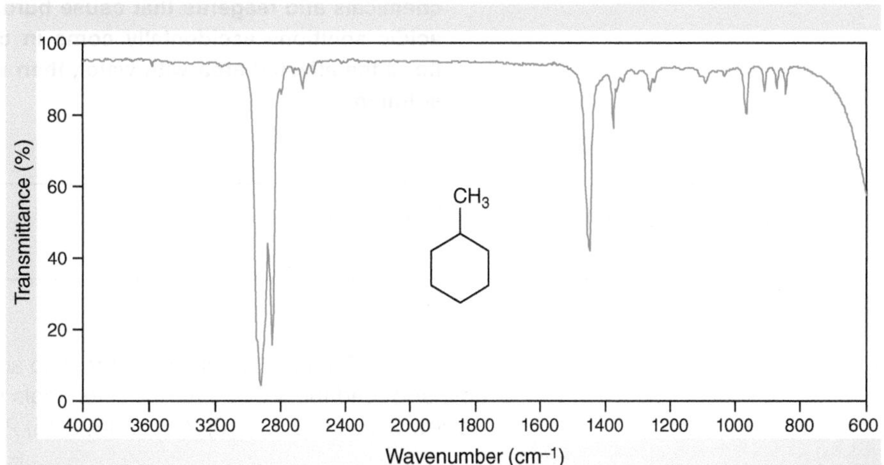

Figure 9.16
IR spectrum of methylcyclohexane (neat).

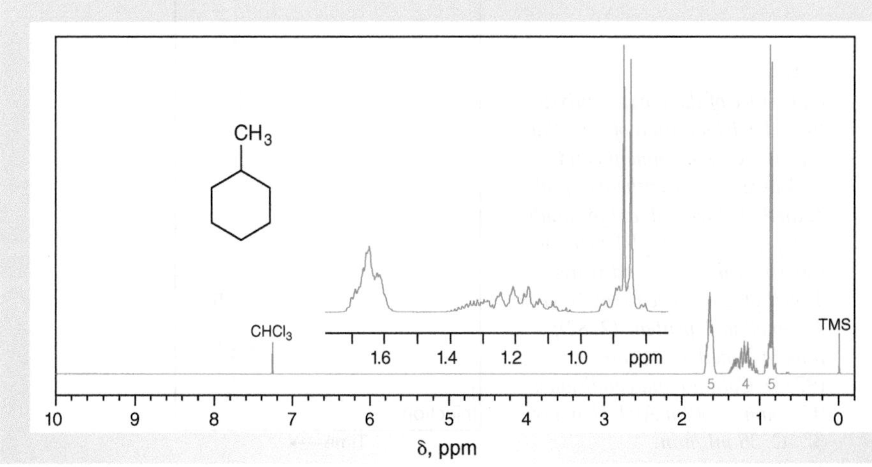

Figure 9.17
NMR data for methylcyclohexane ($CDCl_3$).

(a) ^{1}H NMR spectrum (300 MHz).
(b) ^{13}C NMR data: δ 22.9, 26.6, 26.7, 33.0, 35.6.

EXPERIMENTAL PROCEDURES

Dehydration of Alcohols

Discovery Experiment

Purpose To determine the product distribution in the acid-catalyzed dehydration of alcohols to alkenes.

SAFETY ALERT

1. **Wear safety glasses or goggles and suitable protective gloves while performing the experiments.**
2. **The majority of materials, particularly the product alkenes, that will be handled during this experiment are highly flammable, so use *flameless* heating and be certain that there are no open flames in your vicinity.**
3. **Several experimental operations require pouring, transferring, and weighing chemicals and reagents that cause burns on contact with your skin. Should acidic solutions accidentally come in contact with your skin, immediately flood the affected area with water, then wash it with 5% sodium bicarbonate solution.**

B ▪ *Dehydration of Cyclohexanol*

MINISCALE PROCEDURE

Preparation Refer to the online resources to answer Pre-Lab Exercises, access videos, and read the MSDSs for the chemicals used or produced in this procedure. Review Sections 2.9, 2.10, 2.11, 2.13, 2.14, 2.22, 2.27, and 6.4.

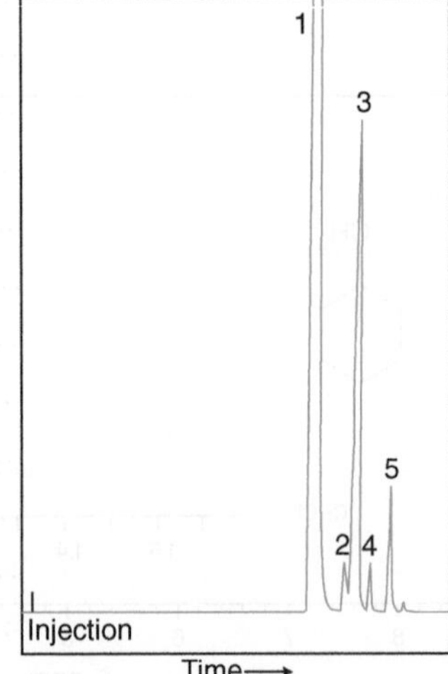

Figure 10.10
GLC trace of the product mixture from the dehydration of 4-methyl-2-pentanol. Assignments and peak areas (in parentheses): peak 1: diethyl ether (solvent for analysis); peak 2: 4-methyl-1-pentene (3030); peak 3: cis- *and* trans-*4-methyl-2-pentene (51693); peak 4: 2-methyl-1-pentene (2282); peak 5: 2-methyl-2-pentene (9733). Column and conditions: 0.25-mm × 30-m APT-Hep-Tex; 37 °C, 35 mL/min.*

Apparatus A 25-mL and two 10-mL round-bottom flasks, drying tube, ice-water bath, apparatus for simple and fractional distillation, magnetic stirring, and *flameless* heating.

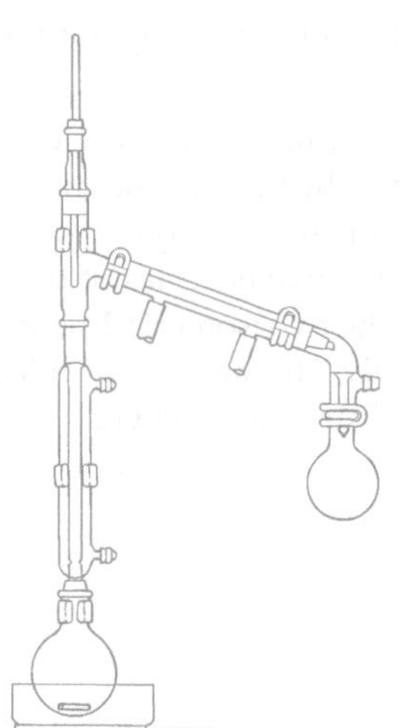

Setting Up Place a stirbar and 5.0 mL of cyclohexanol in the 25-mL round-bottom flask. Add 2.5 mL of 9 *M* sulfuric acid and thoroughly mix the liquids by gently swirling the flask. Equip the flask for fractional distillation and use an ice-water bath to cool the receiving flask.

Elimination and Isolation Follow the same protocol as provided in Part **A**, with the *single exception* that the product should be collected over the range of 80–85 °C (760 torr). Note that water and cyclohexene form a **minimum-boiling azeotrope**, which is a mixture of the two compounds that distills *below* the boiling point of either pure compound (see Figure 10.4). This makes it vital that the crude product be dried *thoroughly* prior to the simple distillation.

Analysis Weigh the distillate and, assuming that it is pure cyclohexene, determine the yield of product. Test the distillate for unsaturation using the bromine and Baeyer tests (Secs. 4.7A1 and 4.7A2, respectively). Analyze your distillate by GLC or submit a sample of it for analysis. Obtain IR and ^{1}H NMR spectra of your starting material and product and compare them with those of authentic samples (Figs. 10.23–10.26).

WRAPPING IT UP

Dilute the *residue remaining in the stillpot* with water, carefully neutralize it with sodium carbonate, and flush it down the drain with large quantities of water. Dry the *potassium carbonate* on a tray in the hood and flush it down the drain or place it in a container for nonhazardous solids. Pour the *dichloromethane solution* from the bromine test for unsaturation in a container for halogenated organic liquids, and put the *manganese dioxide* from the Baeyer test for unsaturation in a container for heavy metals.

EXERCISES

General Questions

1. Create a reaction profile (potential energy diagram) analogous to that in Figure 13.1, making it consistent with the information provided regarding the relative amounts of **18** and **19** (Eq. 10.11) and the relative energies of **20** and **21**.
2. Define the Le Châtelier principle.
3. Why is the boiling point of the parent alcohol higher than that of the product alkene?
4. Why are the distillates obtained in the initial step of the dehydration reaction dried over *anhydrous* potassium carbonate?
5. Why is the head temperature kept below 90 °C in the initial step of the dehydration reaction?

6. Why is it necessary to separate a dried organic solution from the drying agent prior to distilling the solution?

7. In principle, the equilibrium in the dehydration of an alcohol could be shifted to the right by removal of water. Why is this tactic not a good option for the dehydration of 4-methyl-2-pentanol and cyclohexanol?

8. The loss of a proton from suitably substituted carbocations can provide both the *trans*- and *cis*-isomers of the resulting alkene, but the *trans*-isomer normally predominates. For example, deprotonation at C3 of the 2-pentyl carbocation produces mainly *trans*-pentene. By analyzing the relative energies of the conformational isomers of the carbocation that lead to the two isomeric 2-pentenes, explain why the *trans*-isomer is formed preferentially. This analysis is aided by the use of Newman projections based on the partial structure shown.

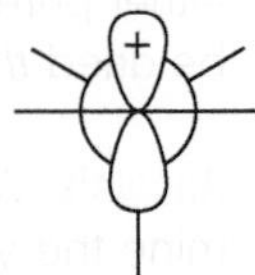

9. Why is it proposed that the alcohol functional group is protonated by acid before dehydration can occur via either an E1 or an E2 mechanism?

10. List two of the major differences in the dehydration of an alcohol by an E1 and E2 reaction mechanism.

11. What is the driving force for the rearrangement of intermediate carbocations during the dehydration of alcohols via the E1 mechanism?

12. Give a detailed mechanism for the dehydration reaction shown. Use curved arrows to symbolize the flow of electrons.

CH_3 CH_3 OH $\xrightarrow[-H_2O]{H_2SO_4(\text{cat.})}$ CH_3 CH_3

Questions for Part B

25. Define the term *minimum-boiling azeotrope* and explain why it is impossible to separate an azeotropic mixture completely by distillation.

26. Why is it particularly important that the crude cyclohexene be dry prior to its distillation?

27. Give the structure, including stereochemistry, of the product of addition of bromine (refer to Sec. 10.6) to cyclohexene. Should it be possible, at least in principle, to resolve this dibromide into separate enantiomers? Explain your answer.

28. Provide a detailed mechanism for the acid-catalyzed dehydration of cyclohexanol. Use curved arrows to symbolize the flow of electrons.

29. Cyclohexyl carbocation undergoes attack by nucleophiles. With this in mind, propose a mechanism whereby cyclohexene might form the dimer **31** in the

presence of H_3O^+. Note that this type of reaction leads to polymerization of cyclohexene.

31

Refer to the online resources and use the spectra viewer and Tables 8.1–8.8 as needed to answer the blue-numbered questions on spectroscopy.

30. Consider the spectral data for cyclohexanol (Figs. 10.23 and 10.24).
    - **a.** In the functional group region of the IR spectrum, specify any absorptions associated with the alcohol function.
    - **b.** In the ^{1}H NMR spectrum, assign the various resonances to the hydrogen nuclei responsible for them.
    - **c.** For the ^{13}C NMR data, assign the various resonances to the carbon nuclei responsible for them.

31. Consider the spectral data for cyclohexene (Figs. 10.25 and 10.26).
    - **a.** In the IR spectrum, specify the absorptions associated with the carbon-carbon double bond and with the vinylic hydrogen atoms.
    - **b.** In the ^{1}H NMR spectrum, assign the various resonances to the hydrogen nuclei responsible for them.
    - **c.** For the ^{13}C NMR data, assign the various resonances to the carbon nuclei responsible for them.

32. Discuss the differences observed in the IR and NMR spectra of cyclohexanol and cyclohexene that are consistent with dehydration occurring in this experiment.

SPECTRA

Starting Materials and Products

The ^{1}H NMR spectrum of 4-methyl-1-pentene is provided in Figure 8.25.

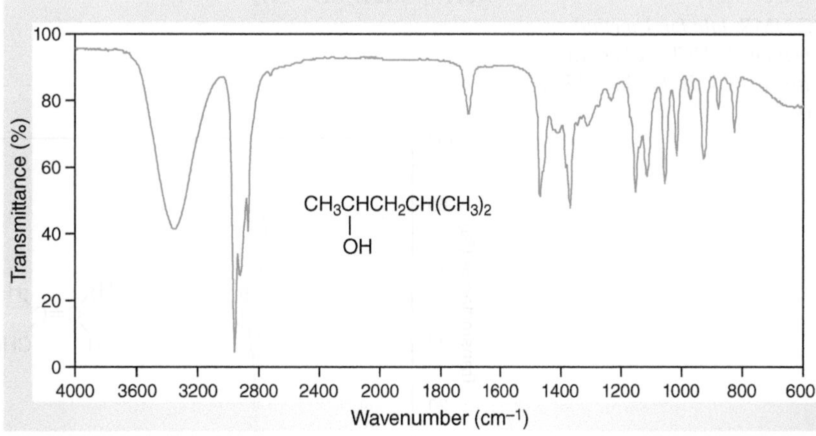

Figure 10.11
IR spectrum of 4-methyl-2-pentanol (neat).

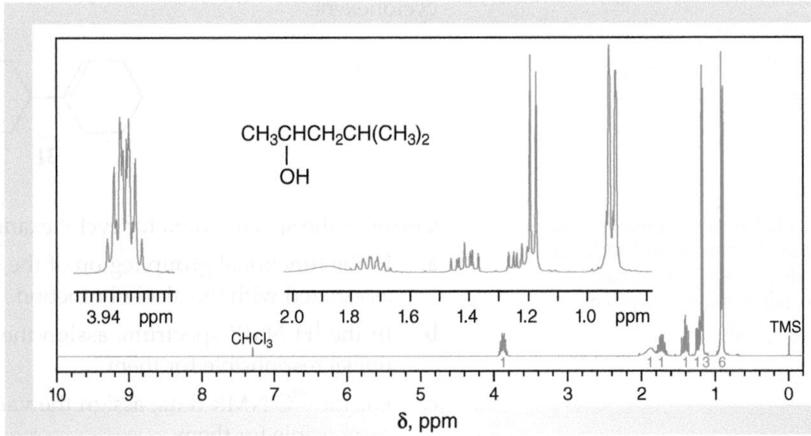

Figure 10.12
NMR data for 4-methyl-2-pentanol ($CDCl_3$).

(a) ^{1}H NMR spectrum (300 MHz).
(b) ^{13}C data: δ 22.5, 23.2, 23.9, 24.9, 48.8, 65.8.

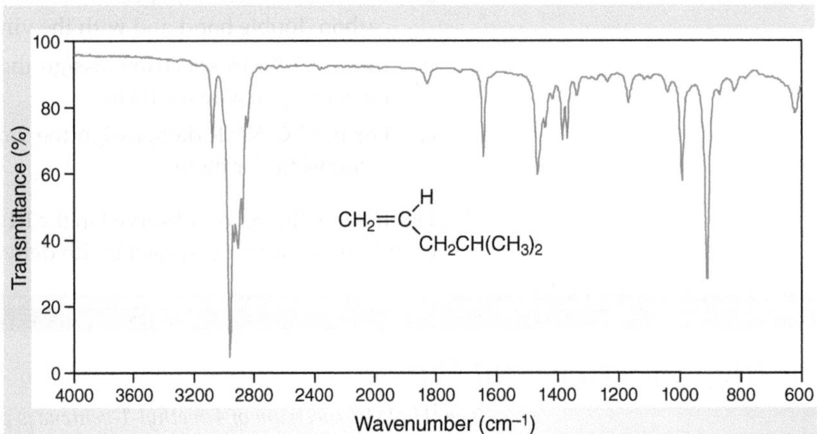

Figure 10.13
IR spectrum of 4-methyl-1-pentene (neat).

Figure 10.14
^{13}C NMR data for 4-methyl-1-pentene ($CDCl_3$). Chemical shifts: δ 22.3, 28.1, 43.7, 115.5, 137.8.

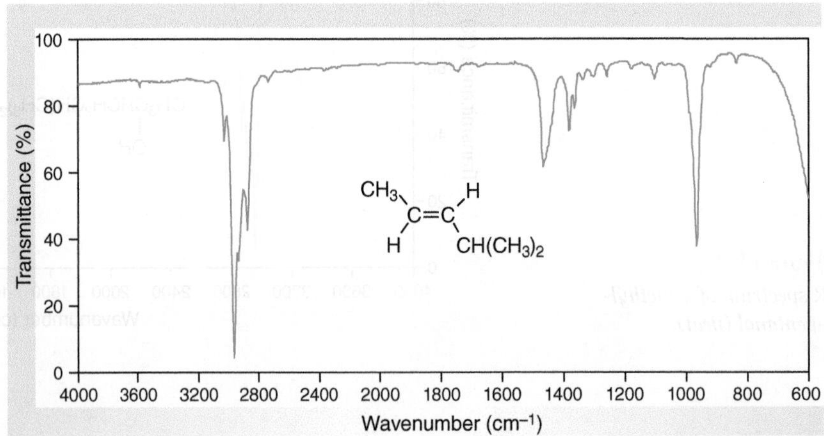

Figure 10.15
IR spectrum of trans-*4-methyl-2-pentene (neat).*

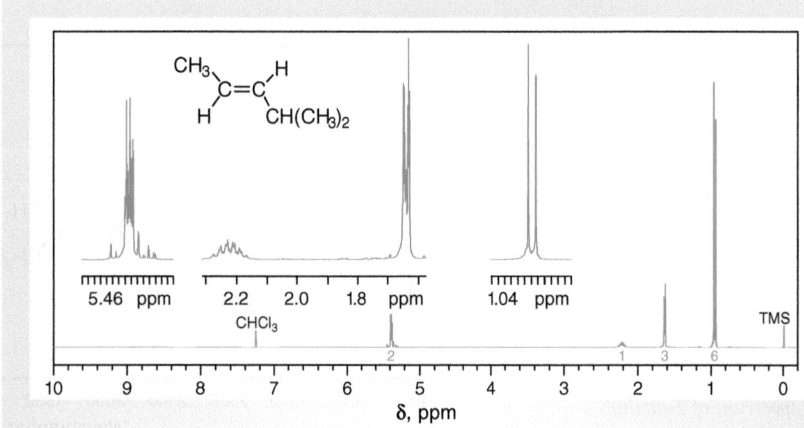

Figure 10.16
NMR data for trans-*4-methyl-2-pentene ($CDCl_3$).*

(a) ^{1}H NMR spectrum (300 MHz).
(b) ^{13}C data: δ 17.6, 22.7, 31.5, 121.6, 139.4.

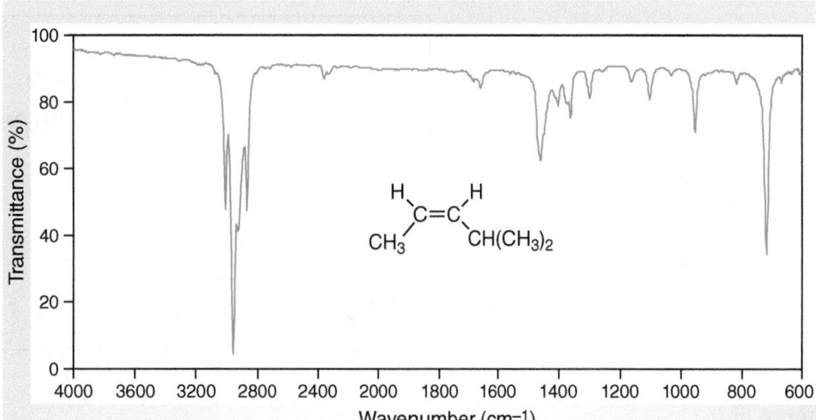

Figure 10.17
IR spectrum of cis-*4-methyl-2-pentene (neat).*

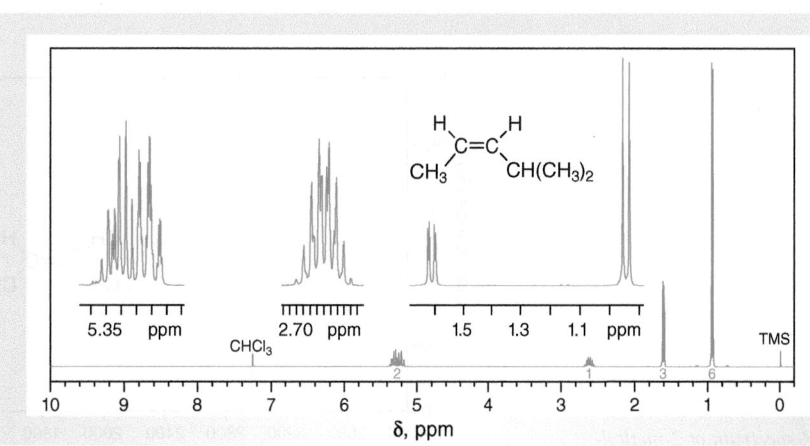

Figure 10.18
NMR data for cis-*4-methyl-2-pentene ($CDCl_3$).*

(a) ^{1}H NMR spectrum (300 MHz).
(b) ^{13}C data: δ 12.7, 23.1, 26.4, 121.4, 138.6.

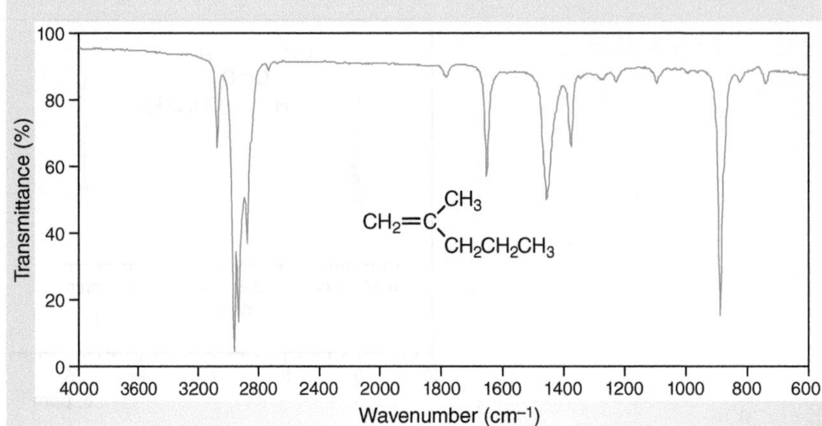

Figure 10.19
IR spectrum of 2-methyl-1-pentene (neat).

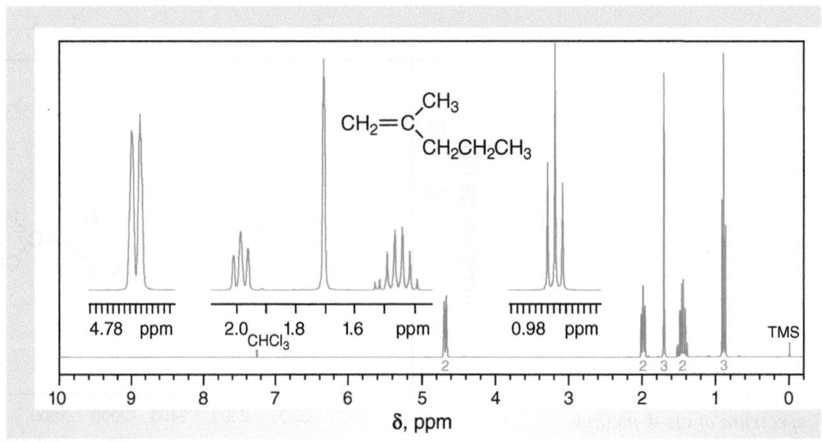

Figure 10.20
NMR data for 2-methyl-1-pentene ($CDCl_3$).

(a) ^{1}H NMR spectrum (300 MHz).
(b) ^{13}C data: δ 13.8, 20.8, 22.3, 40.0, 109.7, 146.0.

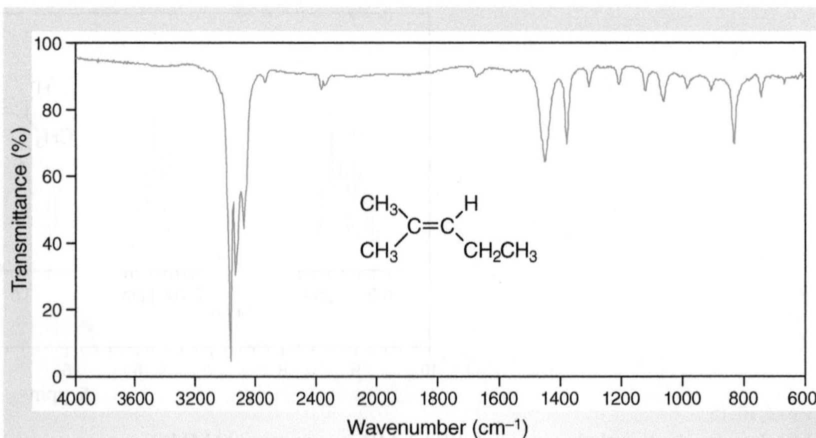

Figure 10.21
IR spectrum of 2-methyl-2-pentene (neat).

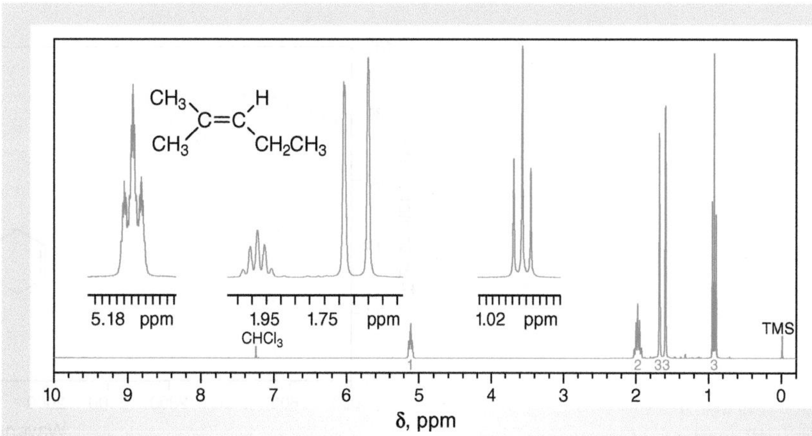

Figure 10.22
NMR data for 2-methyl-2-pentene ($CDCl_3$).

(a) ^{1}H NMR spectrum (300 MHz).
(b) ^{13}C data: δ 14.5, 17.5, 21.6, 25.7, 126.9, 130.6.

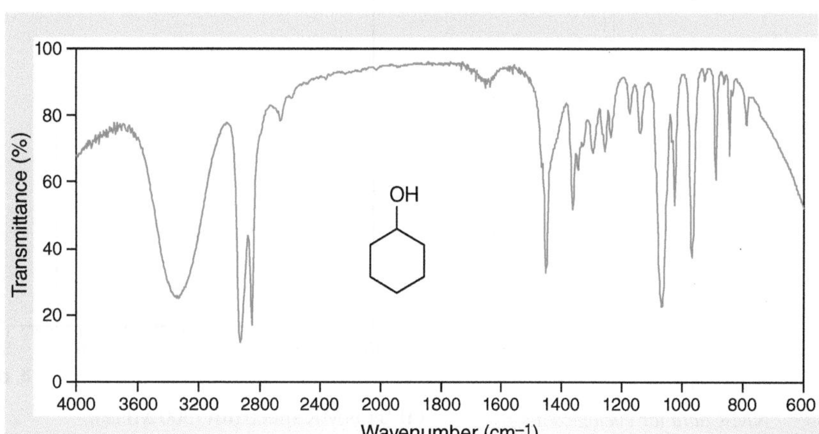

Figure 10.23
IR spectrum of cyclohexanol (neat).

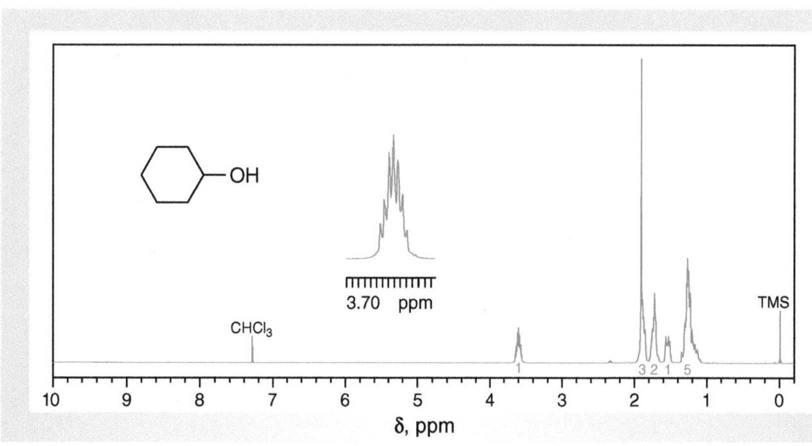

Figure 10.24
NMR data for cyclohexanol ($CDCl_3$).

(a) ^{1}H NMR spectrum (300 MHz).
(b) ^{13}C data: δ 24.5, 25.9, 35.5, 70.1.

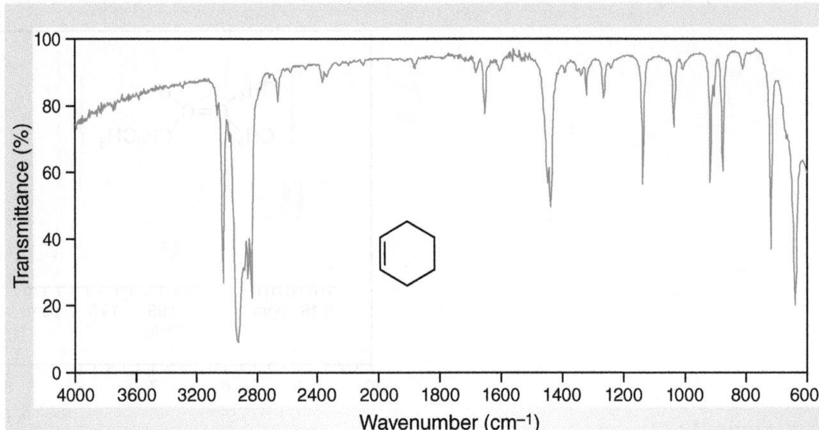

Figure 10.25
IR spectrum of cyclohexene (neat).

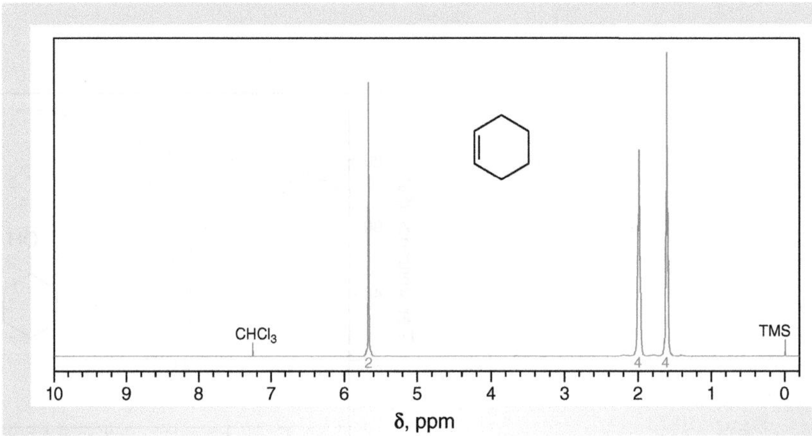

Figure 10.26
NMR data for cyclohexene ($CDCl_3$).

(a) ^{1}H NMR spectrum (300 MHz).
(b) ^{13}C data: δ 22.9, 25.2, 127.3.

EXPERIMENTAL PROCEDURE

Hydration of Norbornene

Purpose To study the acid-catalyzed addition of water to an alkene.

SAFETY ALERT 

1. **Wear safety glasses or goggles and suitable protective gloves while performing the experiment.**
2. **Norbornene is a volatile solid. Perform all weighings in a hood if possible.**
3. **If the acidic solution used in the first part of the experiment comes in contact with your skin, immediately flood the affected area with water and thoroughly rinse it with 5% sodium bicarbonate solution.**
4. **If the basic solution used in this experiment comes in contact with your skin, immediately flood the affected area with water and thoroughly rinse the area with a dilute solution (1%) of acetic acid.**

MINISCALE PROCEDURE

Preparation Refer to the online resources to answer Pre-Lab Exercises, access videos, and read the MSDSs for the chemicals used or produced in this procedure. Review Sections 2.7, 2.20, 2.21, and 2.29.

Apparatus A 25-mL Erlenmeyer flask, separatory funnel, ice-water bath, apparatus for simple distillation, magnetic stirring, sublimation, and *flameless* heating.

Setting Up Slowly add 2 mL of *concentrated* sulfuric acid to 1 mL of water in a 25-mL Erlenmeyer flask containing a stirbar and cool the solution to room temperature.

Hydration Working at the hood, add 1.0 g of norbornene in small pieces to the stirred solution of aqueous sulfuric acid. Continue stirring the mixture until all of the norbornene dissolves. Cool the flask *briefly* in an ice-water bath if the mixture becomes noticeably warm, but *do not cool the contents of the flask below room temperature.* Stir this solution for 15–30 min. Prepare a solution of 1.5 g of potassium hydroxide in 7.5 mL of water.

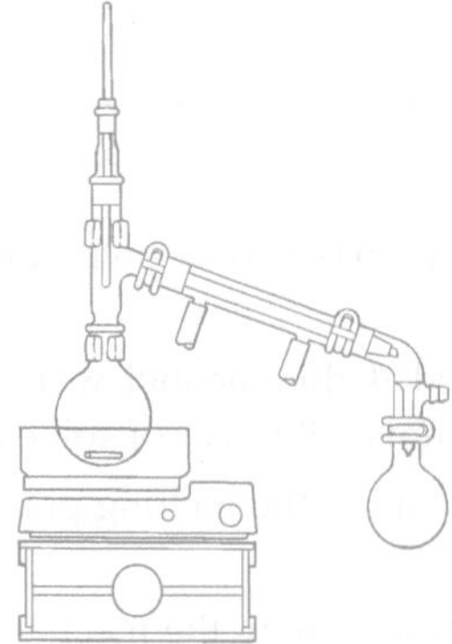

Work-Up and Isolation Cool both solutions in an ice-water bath and slowly add the base to the acidic reaction mixture to partially neutralize the acid. Be sure that the resulting mixture is at room temperature or below, then transfer it to a small separatory funnel, and add 15 mL of diethyl ether. If any solid is present in the bottom of the separatory funnel, add 1–2 mL of water to dissolve it. After shaking the funnel, *periodically venting it to release pressure*, separate the aqueous layer (*Save!*) and pour the ethereal solution into an Erlenmeyer flask. Return the aqueous layer to the separatory funnel, and extract again with a fresh 10-mL portion of diethyl ether. Separate the aqueous layer, and combine the two ethereal extracts in the separatory funnel.

Wash the combined extracts with 5 mL of water. Separate the aqueous layer, and wash the ethereal solution sequentially with 5-mL portions of saturated sodium bicarbonate solution and saturated sodium chloride solution; *periodically vent the separatory funnel* to release pressure that may develop. Separate the layers, place the ethereal solution in a dry 50-mL Erlenmeyer flask, and dry it over several spatula-tips full of *anhydrous* sodium sulfate with occasional swirling for 10–15 min.★ Add additional portions of *anhydrous* sodium sulfate if the liquid remains cloudy.

Transfer the dried ethereal solution to a 50-mL round-bottom flask equipped for simple distillation and concentrate the solution by distillation. Alternatively, rotary evaporation or other techniques may be used to concentrate the solution. Transfer the residue to a 25- or 50-mL filter flask.

Sublimation Equip the filter flask with a filter adapter or rubber stopper containing a centrifuge tube or a 13-mm × 120-mm test tube that extends to within about 2 cm of the bottom of the flask (Fig. 2.58b). The adapter or stopper should be lightly greased to prevent water from entering the sublimation chamber. Evacuate the flask using a water aspirator equipped with a trap and *then* half-fill the centrifuge tube or test tube with tightly packed chipped ice. *Gently* heat the flask using a steam bath or the sweeping motion of a heat gun or small flame. Add ice as necessary to the cold finger on which the sublimed alcohol collects. When the alcohol has completely sublimed, cool the flask, break the vacuum to the aspirator, and disconnect the flask from the vacuum hose. Carefully decant the water out of the cold finger. Carefully remove the cold finger from the flask, while maintaining the cold finger in a horizontal or slightly inverted position. Scrape the soft crystalline product from the test tube.

Analysis Weigh the purified solid and determine the yield. Measure the melting point by placing the sample in a capillary tube that has been sealed about 2 cm from the open end. Obtain IR and ^{1}H NMR spectra of your starting material and product and compare them with those of authentic samples (Figs. 10.42–10.45).

WRAPPING IT UP

Slowly combine the *aqueous layers and washes*. If necessary, neutralize them with sodium carbonate, and flush them down the drain with excess water. Pour any *diethyl ether* obtained during the concentration step into a container for flammable organic solvents. After the diethyl ether has evaporated from the *sodium sulfate* in the hood, place the solid in a container for nonhazardous solids.

EXERCISES

1. What purpose is served by washing the ethereal solution of product with bicarbonate solution? Saturated brine?
2. How would the yield of *exo*-norborneol be affected if this alcohol were left under vacuum for an excessive period of time to remove all traces of solvent?
3. Why is it necessary to seal the capillary tube before taking the melting point of *exo*-norborneol?
4. Using curved arrows to symbolize the flow of electrons, show the mechanism by which the classical cations **60a** and **60b** can be interconverted.

5. What is the significance of the dashed bonds in the structure of the nonclassical cation **61**? What is "nonclassical" about this cation (i.e., how is **61** different from a classical carbocation)?

6. *Exo*-Norborneol (**59**) contains three centers of chirality, but the product obtained from the hydration of norbornene (**58**) in this experiment is optically inactive.
   - **a.** Is norbornene chiral? Explain your answer by showing why it is or is not.
   - **b.** Identify the three chiral centers in **59** with asterisks.
   - **c.** Write the chemical structure for the stereoisomer of **59** that is produced by the hydration of **58** and show how it is formed from intermediate **61**. Are **59** and this stereoisomer enantiomers or diastereomers?

7. Why is sulfuric acid a superior acid to HCl for effecting the acid-catalyzed hydration of alkenes?

8. *Exo*-norborneol undergoes reaction with *concentrated* HBr to form a single diastereomer. Write the structure of this bromide and propose a stepwise mechanism for its formation, using curved arrows to symbolize the flow of electrons. Why is only one diastereomer produced?

9. For each of the alkenes **a–e**, write the structure of the alcohol that should be the major product of acid-catalyzed hydration.

a. CH_3 CH_3 CH_3 **b.** CH_3 **c.** CH_3

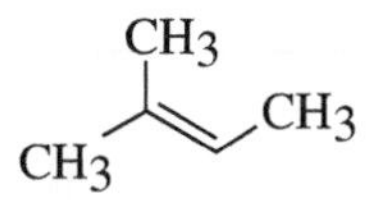

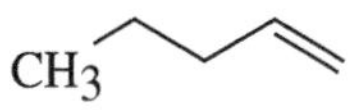

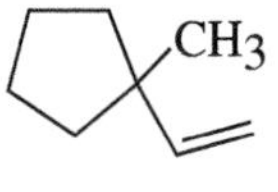

d. CH_3 **e.** NO_2 CH_3O

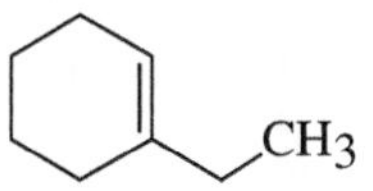

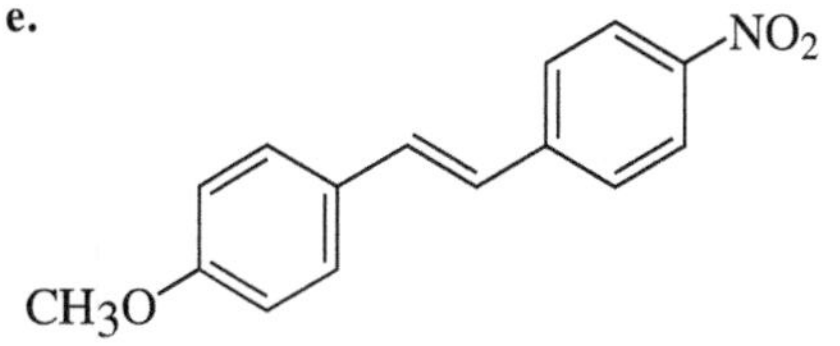

Refer to the online resources and use the spectra viewer and Tables 8.1–8.8 as needed to answer the blue-numbered questions on spectroscopy.

10. Consider the spectral data for norbornene (Figs. 10.42 and 10.43).
    - **a.** In the functional group region of the IR spectrum, identify any absorptions associated with the carbon-carbon double bond.
    - **b.** In the ^1H NMR spectrum, assign the various resonances to the hydrogen nuclei responsible for them.
    - **c.** For the ^{13}C NMR data, assign the various resonances to the carbon nuclei responsible for them. Explain why there are only four resonances in the spectrum.

11. Consider the spectral data for *exo*-norborneol (Figs. 10.44 and 10.45).
    - **a.** In the functional group region of the IR spectrum, specify any absorptions associated with the alcohol function.
    - **b.** In the ^1H NMR spectrum, assign the various resonances to the hydrogen nuclei responsible for them.
    - **c.** For the ^{13}C NMR data, assign the various resonances to the carbon atom responsible for them.

12. Discuss the differences observed in the IR and NMR spectra of norbornene and *exo*-norborneol that are consistent with the addition of water occurring in this experiment.

SPECTRA

Starting Materials and Products

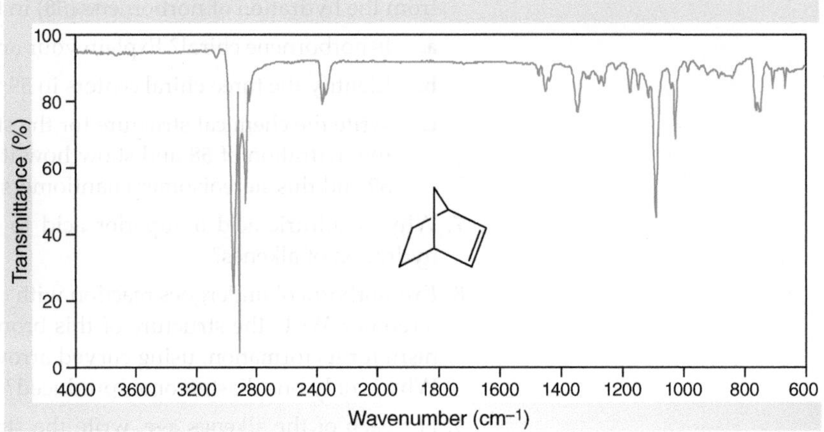

Figure 10.42
IR spectrum of norbornene (IR card).

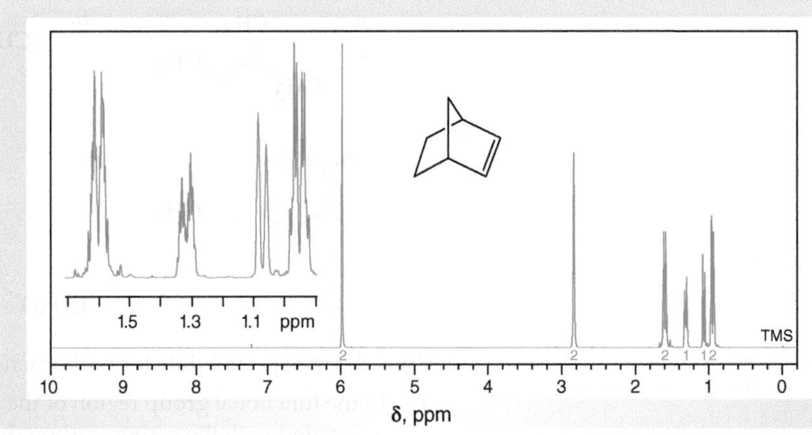

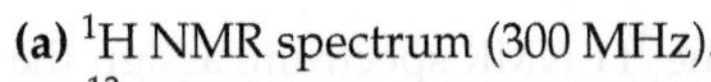

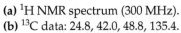

Figure 10.43
NMR data for norbornene ($CDCl_3$).

(a) ^{1}H NMR spectrum (300 MHz).
(b) ^{13}C data: 24.8, 42.0, 48.8, 135.4.

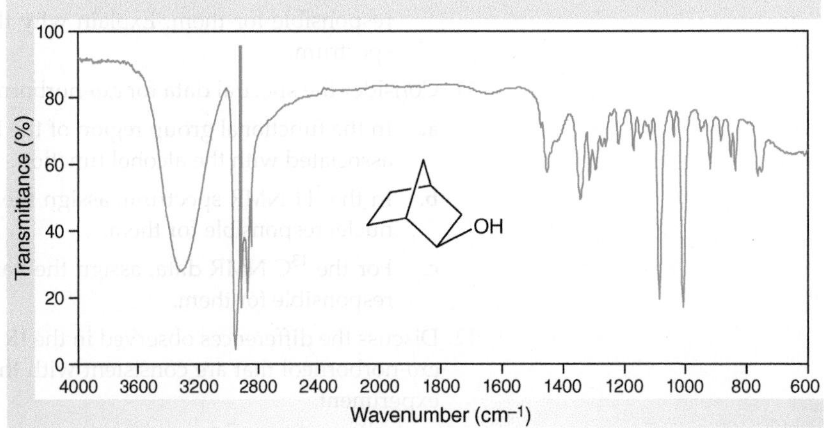

Figure 10.44
IR spectrum of exo-norborneol (IR card).

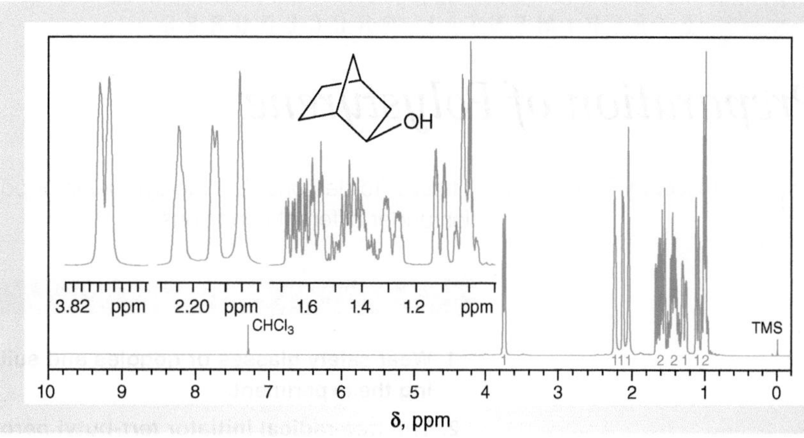

Figure 10.45
NMR data for exo-norborneol (CDCl3).

(a) ^{1}H NMR spectrum (300 MHz).
(b) ^{13}C data: δ 24.7, 28.4, 34.5, 35.5, 42.2, 44.2, 74.6.

EXPERIMENTAL PROCEDURES

Preparation of Polystyrene

Discovery Experiment

Purpose To demonstrate the synthesis of polystyrene by free-radical polymerization under different conditions.

SAFETY ALERT

1. **Wear safety glasses or goggles and suitable protective gloves while performing the experiment.**
2. **The free-radical initiator *tert*-butyl peroxybenzoate is a safe material to use in this experiment because it decomposes at a moderate rate when heated. Nonetheless, do not heat this catalyst excessively when performing the polymerization.**

MINISCALE PROCEDURE

Preparation Refer to the online resources to answer Pre-Lab Exercises, access videos, and read the MSDSs for the chemicals used or produced in this procedure. Review Sections 2.9, 2.17, 2.19, 2.21, and 2.22.

Apparatus A separatory funnel, small soft-glass test tube, 25-mL round-bottom flask, microburner, apparatus for magnetic stirring, heating under reflux, and *flameless* heating.

C ▪ *Solution Polymerization of Styrene*

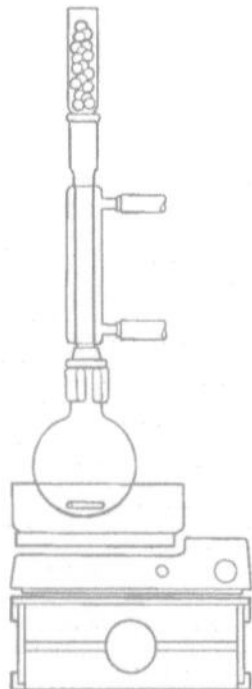

Place about 2 mL of dry styrene and 5 mL of xylene in a 25-mL round-bottom flask and add 7 drops of *tert*-butyl peroxybenzoate from a Pasteur pipet. Assemble the apparatus for heating under reflux and heat the mixture under reflux for 20 min. Cool the solution to room temperature and then pour about *half* of it into 25 mL of methanol. Collect the white precipitate of polystyrene that forms by decantation or by vacuum filtration if decantation is not practical. Resuspend the polystyrene in fresh methanol and stir it vigorously. Collect the polystyrene by filtration and allow it to dry in the hood.

Pour the remaining *half* of the polystyrene solution onto a watchglass or the bottom of a large inverted beaker and allow the solvent to evaporate. A clear film of polystyrene should form.

WRAPPING IT UP

Place the *filtrate* containing a mixture of xylene and methanol in the container for nonhalogenated organic liquids. Flush the *methanolic filtrate* obtained after resuspension of the polystyrene down the drain.

Optional Discovery Experiments

Two of the following experiments allow you to explore whether polystyrene is stable toward different organic solvents and to assess the interaction between an ionic polymer, sodium polyacrylate (**27**), and water. The third lets you investigate the change in the properties of a polymer when it is cross-linked with other strands of itself or other polymers.

Discovery Experiment

Stability of Polystyrene toward Organic Solvents

Styrofoam is a "puffed-up" form of **24** that is produced by polymerizing styrene in the presence of a "blowing agent" like pentane. The heat of the polymerization causes the agent to vaporize, and it is temporarily trapped in the polymerizing material, forming a bubble or cell if the viscosity of the material is high enough to prevent the gases from escaping. The final polymer has many of these cells, resulting in a foam-like material. The foam is a good semirigid shock absorber and also serves as an insulator because air is not very effective at transferring heat or cold. As a consequence of these physical properties, Styrofoam may be used in a variety of ways, ranging from packaging materials to ice chests.

Work in groups of at least two on this experiment and carefully observe what happens as you perform it. All of the results should be compiled and separately interpreted by each member of the team.

Working at the fume hood and away from any flames and hot plates, fill a petri dish about half-full with an organic solvent. Place a Styrofoam cup bottom-down in the solvent and record what happens. Use a glass stirring rod to explore what remains of the cup. Some solvents that might be tested are acetone, 95% ethanol, dichloromethane, and toluene. Properly dispose of all liquids and solids remaining at the completion of this experiment.

Discovery Experiment

Polymers and Water

Most polymers are water-insoluble even though they may contain polar, but neutral, substituents along the carbon backbone. Sodium polyacrylate, however, is a cross-linked ionic polymer that is water-soluble or, equivalently, is a solid polymer in which water is soluble. It is used in products as diverse as disposable diapers and as a replacement for plant soil. Just what happens when this polymer and water are combined is the subject of this experiment.

$$-\!\!\left(CH_2-\underset{\displaystyle CO_2^-\,Na^+}{\underset{|}{CH}}\right)_{\!n}\!\!-$$

Sodium poly(acrylate)

Weigh out approximately 0.5 g of sodium polyacrylate and transfer it to a *dry* 250-mL Erlenmeyer flask. Add 100 mL of water and immediately stir the mixture. Record your observations.

Discovery Experiment

Cross-Linking of Polymers

Poly(vinyl alcohol), like sodium poly(vinyl acrylate), is another water-soluble polymer and is composed of repeating units of vinyl alcohol. In contrast to the acrylate, however, the solubility is not due to a charged polar functionality; rather, extensive hydrogen-bonding involving the hydroxyl groups accounts for the water solubility.

$$\text{-}\!(CH_2\text{—}\underset{\displaystyle OH}{\underset{|}{CH}})_n\text{-}$$

Poly(vinyl alcohol)

When sodium tetraborate is dissolved in water, an equilibrium is established according to the equation below, resulting in the formation of a buffer having a pH of about 9. The protonated borate ion reacts with the hydroxyl groups of one strand of the poly(vinyl alcohol) and subsequently with the hydroxyl groups of another strand, possibly with the elimination of water. The resulting array may be represented in a general way as shown below. By joining strands of the polymer through such cross-links, a measure of rigidity is imparted to the molecular array that has been formed. In addition to the cross-links, the molecules have extensive intra- and intermolecular hydrogen-bonding, which also effects a form of cross-linking, albeit a weak one. Breaking and reforming of the hydrogen bonds presumably accounts for the viscoelastic properties of the material that is produced. This material can be formed into a ball, but you should see what happens when it is left untouched.

$$B_4O_7^{2-}{}_{(aq)} + H_2O \rightleftharpoons HB_4O_7^{-}{}_{(aq)} + HO^{-}{}_{(l)}$$

$$\text{-}\!(CH_2\text{—}CH)_n\text{-} \quad \text{O—}\bar{B}\text{—O} \quad (CH\text{—}CH_2)_n\text{-}$$

Apparatus A 100-mL and a 250-mL beaker, thermometer, glass stirring rod, and apparatus for magnetic stirring and *flameless* heating.

Setting Up Add 50 mL of distilled water into the 250-mL beaker equipped with a stirbar. Heat the water with stirring but do *not* exceed a temperature of 90 °C.

Gel Formation With continued stirring and warming, slowly sprinkle 2 g of poly(vinyl alcohol) having an average molar mass of at least 10^5 g/mol onto the surface of the water; this procedure prevents the formation of a sticky mass of polymer that is difficult to dissolve. Combine the poly(vinyl alcohol) solution and 5 mL of a 4%

(by mass) aqueous solution of sodium tetraborate, $Na_2B_4O_7$, in the 100-mL beaker, and stir the mixture vigorously with the glass rod. A material that you may consider to be "slime" should form almost immediately.

This cross-linked polymer is a gel that has interesting physical properties. You may explore some of them by forming your material into a ball and then seeing what happens when you carefully tip it in the palm of your hand. If a long column of polymer forms, jerk it abruptly and record the result. Be creative and test the properties of the gel in other ways!

WRAPPING IT UP

Clean the *beaker* and *stirring rod* used to prepare the gel with soap and water. Mix the *solution of polymer* with a copious amount of water and flush the *mixture* down the drain. Discard the *gel* itself in the container for nonhazardous waste.

EXERCISES

1. *tert*-Butylcatechol (**25**) is capable of reacting with *two* equivalents of a radical, $R^\bullet$, to produce two moles of RH and a stable nonradical oxidation product of **25**. Propose a structure for this product and write a stepwise reaction mechanism for its formation. Use curved "fish-hook" arrows to symbolize the flow of electrons.
2. The use of phenols such as *tert*-butylcatechol as free-radical scavengers is based on the fact that phenolic hydrogens are readily abstracted by radicals, producing relatively stable phenoxyl radicals that interrupt chain processes of oxidation and polymerization. Alcohols such as cyclohexanol, on the other hand, do *not* function as radical scavengers. Explain why the two types of molecules differ in their abilities to donate a hydrogen atom to a radical, $R^\bullet$.
3. Write an equation for the reaction involved in the removal of *tert*-butylcatechol from styrene by extraction with sodium hydroxide.
4. Why is it necessary to remove *tert*-butylcatechol from commercially available styrene prior to preparing polystyrene?
5. Why is *tert*-butyl peroxybenzoate a good radical initiator?
6. Explain why only a catalytic amount of the radical initiator is required in a free-radical-chain polymerization reaction.
7. Why is the polymerization of styrene an exothermic reaction? Explain in terms of a calculation based on the following equation using these bond dissociation energies: PhCH(R)–H, 83 kcal/mol; CH_2=CHPh, 53 kcal/mol (π-bond only); $PhCH_2CH_2$–$CH(CH_3)Ph$, 73 kcal/mol

$$\underset{\displaystyle CH_3}{PhCH}\text{—H} + CH_2\text{=}\underset{\displaystyle Ph}{CH} \longrightarrow \underset{\displaystyle CH_3}{PhCH}\text{—}CH_2\underset{\displaystyle H}{CHPh}$$

8. Explain why polystyrene is soluble in xylene but insoluble in methanol.
9. What effect would using a smaller proportion of catalyst to styrene have on the average molar mass of polystyrene?
10. In principle, radicals could add to styrene at the carbon atom bearing the phenyl group rather than the other one, yet they do not. Explain the basis of this selectivity for the addition reaction.
11. Specify whether polystyrene is a condensation polymer, a homopolymer, a copolymer, or a block polymer.
12. Some monomers polymerize to produce a polymer having centers of chirality (Chap. 7). If there is no preference for one configuration over another, the configuration of the centers will be random throughout the polymer. This type of polymer is called *atactic.* When the stereocenters are nonrandom, the polymer may be either *syndiotactic* or *isotactic* (see your lecture textbook for a definition of these terms).
    a. Write a portion of polystyrene containing two monomeric units and circle any stereocenters that are present.
    b. Would you expect the polystyrene generated in this experiment to be *atactic, syndiotactic,* or *isotactic?*
13. Circle the monomeric unit in the polysaccharide shown below.

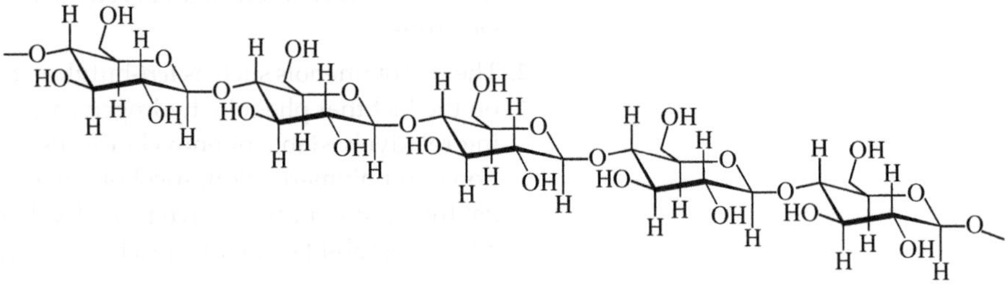

14. Teflon is produced from the polymerization of tetrafluoroethene. Write the structure of Teflon showing the monomeric unit in parentheses.
15. Why does the nucleophilic attack of isobutylene on the $(CH_3)_3C^+$ cation in Equation 22.6 form a new carbon-carbon bond at C(2) of isobutylene instead of C(1)?
16. Super Glue is a polymer formed via an anionic polymerization of methyl cyanoacrylate, $CH_2{=}(C{\equiv}N)CO_2CH_3$. Predict the structure of this glue.

Refer to the online resources and use the spectra viewer and Tables 8.1-8.8 as needed to answer the blue-numbered questions on spectroscopy.

17. Consider the spectral data for styrene (Figs. 22.1 and 22.2).
    a. In the functional group region of the IR spectrum, specify the absorptions associated with the carbon-carbon double bond and the aromatic ring. Also specify the absorptions in the fingerprint region that are characteristic for the terminal vinyl group.
    b. In the ^1H NMR spectrum, assign the various resonances to the hydrogen nuclei responsible for them.
    c. For the ^{13}C NMR data, assign the various resonances to the carbon nuclei responsible for them.

18. Consider the IR spectrum of polystyrene (Fig. 8.10). In the functional group region of the spectrum, specify the range of absorptions associated with C–H stretching vibrations for the hydrogen atoms attached to the aromatic ring and for those of the methylene groups. Also specify the absorption associated with the carbon-carbon double bond of the aromatic rings.
19. Discuss the differences in the IR spectrum of styrene and polystyrene that are consistent with the loss of the vinyl group during the polymerization of styrene in this experiment. The IR spectrum of polystyrene is presented in Figure 8.10.

SPECTRA

Starting Material and Product

The IR spectrum of polystyrene is provided in Figure 8.10.

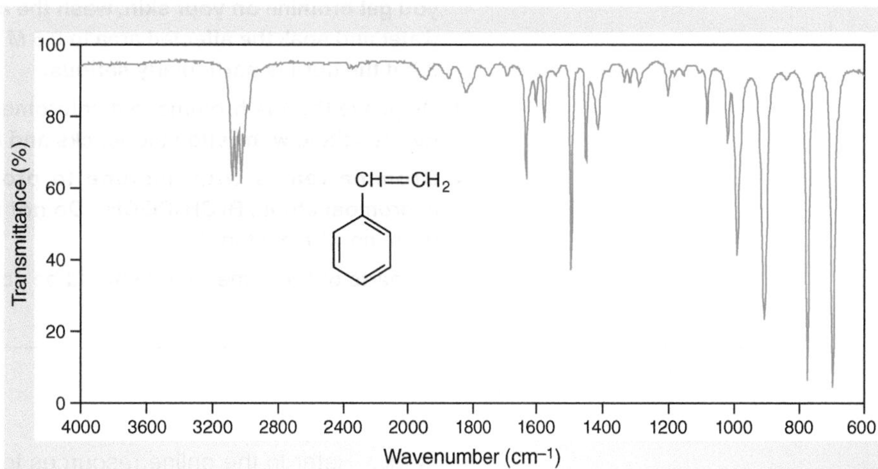

Figure 22.1
IR spectrum of styrene (neat).

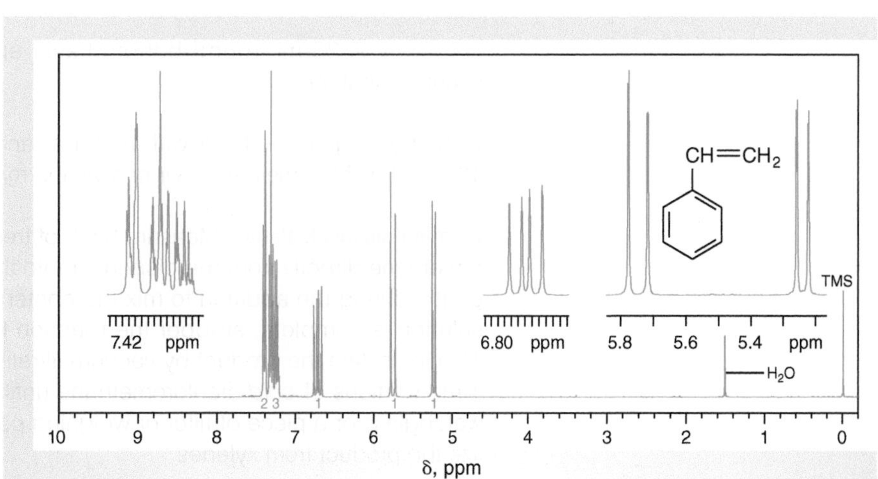

Figure 22.2
NMR data for styrene ($CDCl_3$).

(a) ^{1}H NMR spectrum (300 MHz)
(b) ^{13}C NMR data: δ 113.5, 126.2, 127.8, 128.5, 137.0, 137.7.

EXPERIMENTAL PROCEDURES

A. Bromination of (E)-Stilbene

Discovery Experiment

Purpose To determine the stereochemistry of the electrophilic addition of bromine to an alkene.

SAFETY ALERT

1. **Wear safety glasses or goggles and suitable protective gloves while performing the experiments.**
2. ***Bromine is a hazardous chemical that may cause serious chemical burns.* Do not breathe its vapors or allow it to come into contact with the skin. Perform all operations involving the transfer of the pure liquid or its solutions at a hood. If you get bromine on your skin, wash the area immediately with soap and warm water and soak the affected area in 0.6 *M* sodium thiosulfate solution, for up to 3 h if the burn is particularly serious.**
3. **Dispense the 1 *M* bromine in dichloromethane solution from burets or similar devices fitted with Teflon stopcocks and located in hoods.**
4. **Bromine reacts with acetone to produce the powerful lachrymator α-bromoacetone, $BrCH_2COCH_3$. Do *not* rinse glassware containing residual bromine with acetone!**
5. **All parts of this experiment should be conducted in a hood if possible.**

MINISCALE PROCEDURE

Preparation Refer to the online resources to answer Pre-Lab Exercises, access videos, and read the MSDSs for the chemicals used or produced in this procedure. Review Sections 2.7, 2.11, and 2.17.

Apparatus A 25-mL round-bottom flask, apparatus for magnetic stirring and vacuum filtration.

Setting Up Equip the flask with a stirbar and add to it 0.9 g of (*E*)-stilbene and 10 mL of dichloromethane. Stir or swirl the mixture to effect dissolution.

Bromination and Isolation Measure 5 mL of freshly prepared 1 *M* bromine in dichloromethane directly from the dispenser into the round-bottom flask. Swirl the flask gently during the addition to mix the contents. After the addition of the bromine solution is complete, stopper the reaction flask loosely and stir the mixture for 15 min. Isolate the product by vacuum filtration. Wash the product with one or two 1-mL portions of *cold* dichloromethane until it is white. Transfer the product to a watchglass or a piece of filter or weighing paper and allow it to air-dry. Recrystallize the product from xylenes.

Analysis Weigh the product and determine the yield. Measure the melting point to determine the stereochemistry of the bromination. *Caution:* Do *not* use mineral oil as the heating fluid for this determination! Obtain IR and ^{1}H NMR spectra of your starting material and product and compare them with those of authentic samples (Figs. 10.34–10.37).

WRAPPING IT UP

If necessary, add 10% aqueous sodium bisulfite to decolorize the *filtrate* and discard the mixture in a container for *aqueous acids*.

EXERCISES

General Questions

1. What does the "E" in (*E*)-stilbene or (*E*)-cinnamic acid stand for and what does it mean?
2. Write the expected products for the addition of bromine to the following alkenes.

   a. $CH_3CH_2CH{=}CH_2$ b. 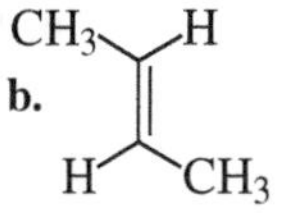 (structure: CH_3, H / H, CH_3 alkene) c. 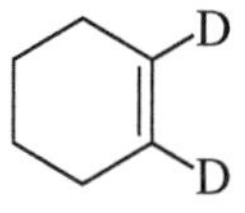 (structure: 1,2-dideuterocyclohexene, D, D)

3. Write the structure of the product obtained when cyclohexene is used to decolorize bromine-containing solutions.
4. Draw structural formulae for the alkenes that give the following products upon bromination.

   a. 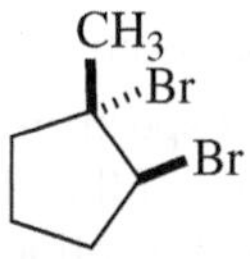 (structure: CH_3, Br, Br on cyclopentane) b. 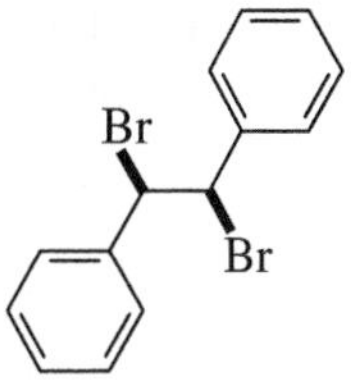 (structure: Br, Br, two phenyl rings) c. 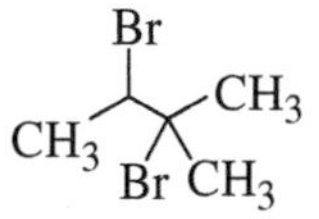 (structure: Br, CH_3, CH_3, Br, CH_3)

Questions for Part A

5. Is *meso*-stilbene dibromide optically active? What symmetry element is present in this molecule that precludes the existence of an enantiomer?
6. Explain why, in contrast to *meso*-stilbene dibromide, the dibromide **49** exists in two enantiomeric forms.
7. For the procedure in which a solution of bromine is used, why does solid not separate immediately after you begin adding the solution to that containing (*E*)-stilbene?
8. In the procedure involving *in situ* generation of bromine, what is the solid that appears when the *concentrated* hydrogen bromide is added?
9. What is the source of color that is produced upon addition of aqueous hydrogen peroxide to the reaction mixture?

10. Why should mineral oil not be used as the heating fluid for determining the melting point of *meso*-stilbene dibromide (**48**) or of the 2,3-dibromopropanoic acid (**53**) or (**54**)?
11. Using suitable stereochemical structures, write the mechanism for the addition of bromine to (*E*)-stilbene to give *meso*-stilbene dibromide via the intermediate cyclic bromonium ion **50.** Use curved arrows to symbolize the flow of electrons.
12. To what general class of mechanisms does the attack of bromide ion, Br^-, on the cyclic bromonium ion **50** belong? Does this ring-opening step follow first- or second-order kinetics?
13. How many centers of chirality are present in the bromonium ion **50** and in the isomeric carbocation **51**?
14. Draw suitable three-dimensional structures of the two products obtained by attack of bromide ion at both of the carbon atoms in the cyclic bromonium ion **50** and show that they are identical.
15. Based upon the mechanism you provided in Exercise 11, predict the major product of the addition of bromine to (*Z*)-stilbene.
16. Demonstrate that attack of bromide ion, Br^-, on the carbocation **51** can provide *both dl-* and *meso*-stilbene dibromide.
17. The reaction of bromine with cyclopentene according to Equation 10.18 is stereospecific and proceeds by *anti* addition. On the other hand, the addition of bromine to (*E*)-stilbene gives both *meso*-stilbene dibromide (**48**) and *dl*-stilbene dibromide **(49).** Rationalize this difference by comparing the relative stabilities of the carbocations resulting from ring-opening of the cyclic bromonium ions **38** and **50.**
18. How do the results of this experiment support the hypothesis that the addition of bromine to (*E*)-stilbene proceeds primarily through **50** rather than **51**?

Refer to the online resources and use the spectra viewer and Tables 8.1–8.8 as needed to answer the blue-numbered questions on spectroscopy.

19. Consider the spectral data for (*E*)-stilbene (Figs. 10.34 and 10.35).
    a. In the IR spectrum, identify the absorption(s) consistent with the *trans* relationship of the vinylic hydrogen atoms and explain the absence of a significant absorption in the range of 1600–1700 cm^{-1} normally characteristic of alkenes.
    b. In the ^1H NMR spectrum, assign the various resonances to the hydrogen nuclei responsible for them.
    c. For the ^{13}C NMR data, assign the various resonances to the carbon nuclei responsible for them.
20. Consider the ^1H NMR spectrum of *meso*-stilbene dibromide (Fig. 10.37a).
    a. In the ^1H NMR spectrum, assign the various resonances to the hydrogen nuclei responsible for them.
    b. For the ^{13}C NMR data, assign the various resonances to the carbon nuclei responsible for them.
21. Discuss the differences observed in the IR (Fig. 10.36) and NMR spectra of (*E*)-stilbene and *meso*-stilbene dibromide that are consistent with addition of Br_2 occurring in this experiment.

SPECTRA

Starting Materials and Products

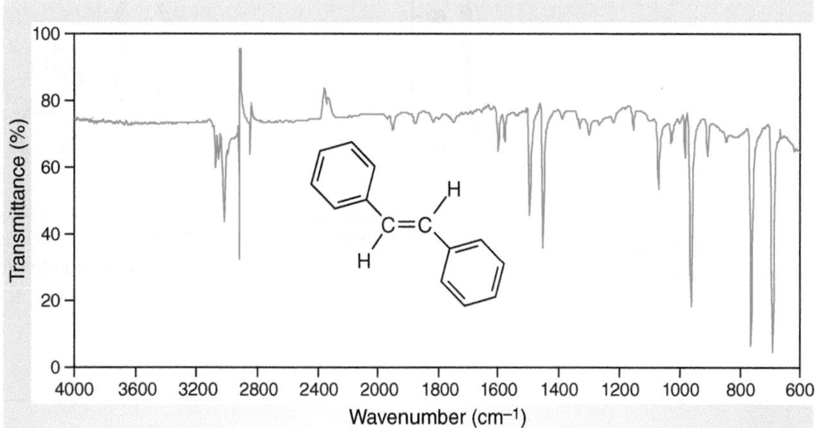

Figure 10.34
IR spectrum of (E)-stilbene (IR card).

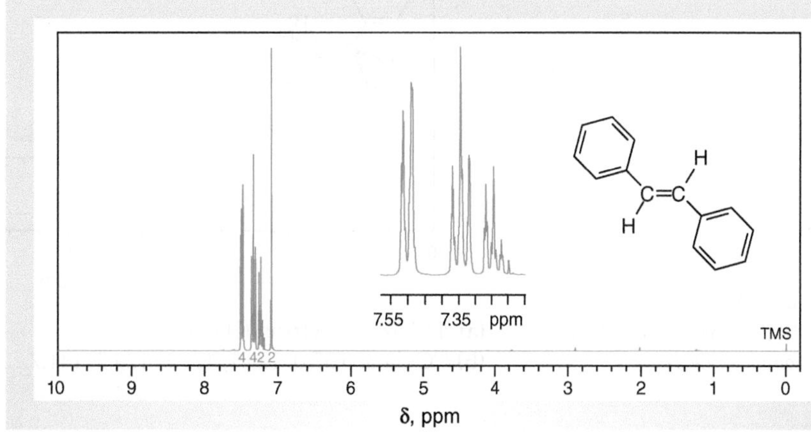

Figure 10.35
NMR data for (E)-stilbene ($CDCl_3$).

(a) ^{1}H NMR spectrum (300 MHz).
(b) ^{13}C data: δ 126.3, 127.8, 128.9, 129.0, 137.6.

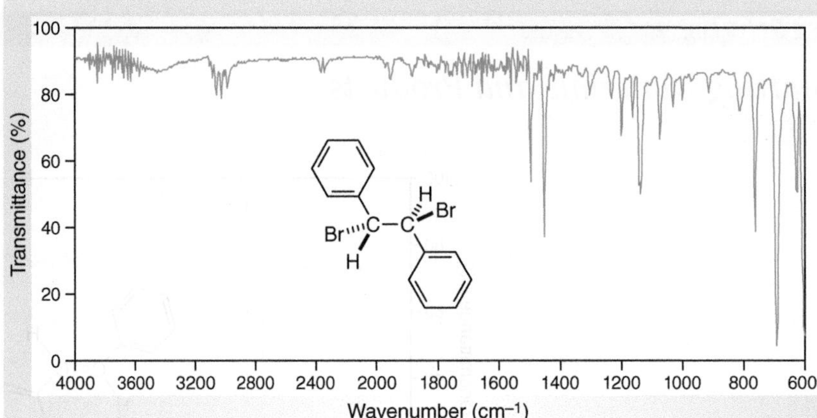

Figure 10.36
IR spectrum of meso-*stilbene dibromide (IR card).*

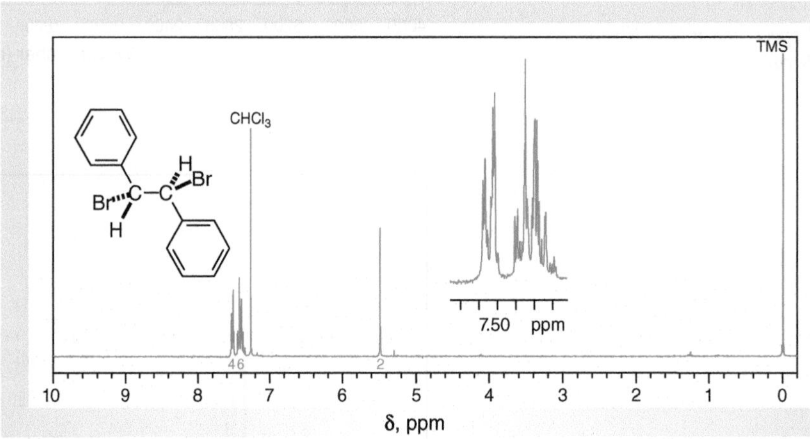

Figure 10.37
NMR data for meso-*stilbene dibromide ($CDCl_3$).*

(a) ^{1}H NMR spectrum (300 MHz).
(b) ^{13}C data: δ 57.0, 129.1, 129.6, 129.7, 141.7.

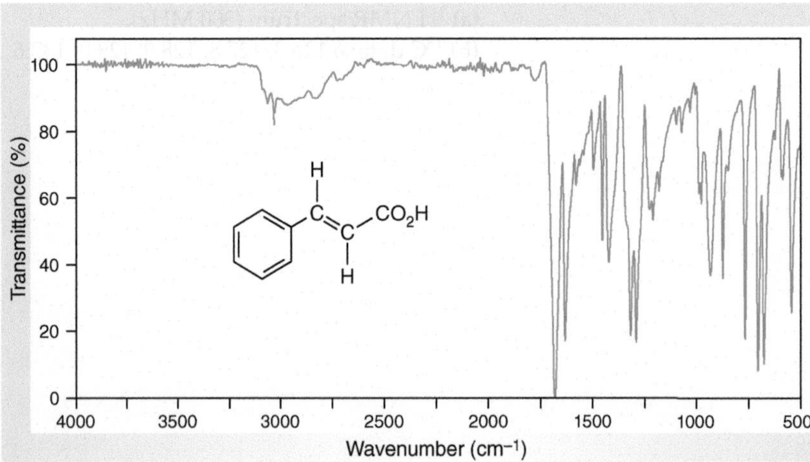

Figure 10.38
IR spectrum of (E)-*cinnamic acid.*

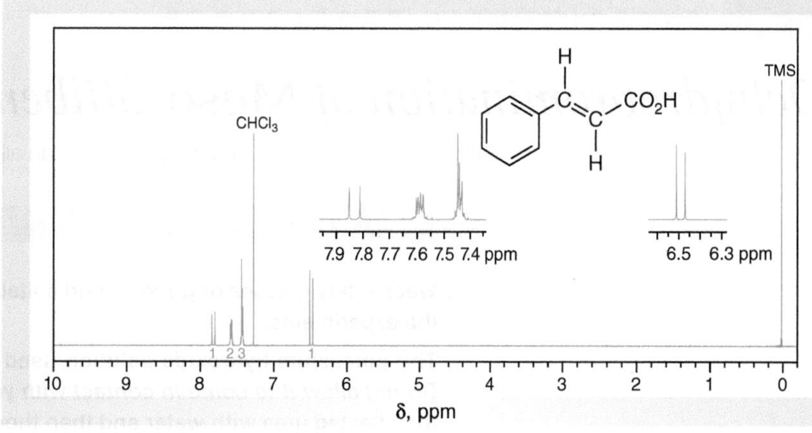

Figure 10.39
NMR data for (E)-cinnamic

(a) ^{1}H NMR (400 MHz).

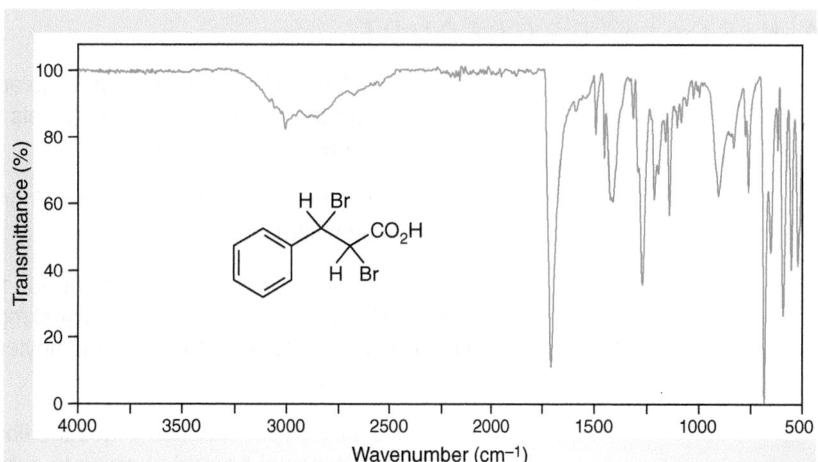

Figure 10.40
IR of 2,3-dibromo-3-phenylpropanoic acid

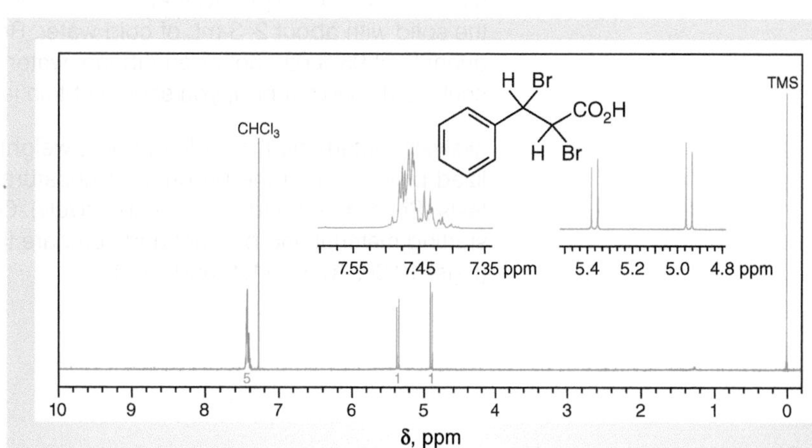

Figure 10.41
NMR data for 2,3-dibromo-3-phenylpropanoic acid

EXPERIMENTAL PROCEDURES

Dehydrobromination of Meso-*Stilbene Dibromide*

Purpose To demonstrate the preparation of an alkyne by a double dehydrohalogenation.

SAFETY ALERT

1. **Wear safety glasses or goggles and suitable protective gloves while performing the experiments.**
2. **The potassium hydroxide solution used in this experiment is *highly* caustic. *Do not allow it to come in contact with your skin.* If this should happen, flood the affected area with water and then thoroughly rinse the area with a solution of dilute acetic acid.**

MINISCALE PROCEDURE

Preparation Refer to the online resources to answer Pre-Lab Exercises, access videos, and read the MSDSs for the chemicals used or produced in this procedure. Review Sections 2.9, 2.10, and 2.17.

Apparatus A sand bath, hot plate, 25-mL Erlenmeyer flask, ice-water bath, apparatus for vacuum filtration.

Setting Up Preheat the sand bath to about 190–200 °C. Place 800 mg of *meso*-stilbene dibromide and 5 pellets (about 400 mg) of commercial potassium hydroxide in the Erlenmeyer flask. Add 4 mL of triethylene glycol and a *carborundum* boiling stone to the flask.

Dehydrobromination and Isolation Place the flask in the sand bath and heat the mixture. After potassium bromide begins to separate from solution, heat the mixture for an additional 5 min. Remove the flask from the sand bath and allow it to cool to room temperature. Add 10 mL of water and place the flask in an ice-water bath for 5 min. Collect the diphenylacetylene that precipitates by vacuum filtration. Wash the solid with about 2–3 mL of cold water. Recrystallize the product from a small quantity of 95% ethanol or an ethanol-water mixture. If the solution is allowed to cool slowly undisturbed, you should obtain large, sparlike, colorless crystals.

Analysis Determine the melting point, weight, and percent yield of the recrystallized product. Test the product for unsaturation using the bromine and Baeyer tests (Secs. 4.7A1 and 4.7A2, respectively). Obtain IR and ^{1}H NMR spectra of your starting material and product and compare them with those of authentic samples (Figs. 10.36, 10.37, 11.1, and 11.2).

MINISCALE PROCEDURE FOR MICROWAVE OPTION

Preparation Refer to the online resources to answer Pre-Lab Exercises, access videos, and read the MSDSs for the chemicals used or produced in this procedure. Review Sections 2.9, 2.10, and 2.17.

Apparatus A 10-mL pressure-rated tube with cap, stirbar, ice-water bath, apparatus for microwave heating with magnetic stirring and vacuum filtration.

Setting Up Equip the 10-mL pressure-rated tube with the stirbar and add 0.40 g of *meso*-stilbene dibromide, about 0.2 g (2 pellets) of solid potassium hydroxide, and 2 mL of methanol. Cap the pressure-rated tube and gently shake it or place it on a magnetic stirrer to facilitate initial mixing of its contents. Place the tube in the cavity of the microwave apparatus.

Dehydrobromination and Isolation Program the unit to heat the reaction mixture with stirring according to the directions provided by your instructor. Generally, the reaction temperature should be set at 150 °C and the power set at a maximum of 25 W with a 1-min ramp time and a 5-min hold time; the pressure limit should be set at 275 psi. Allow the mixture to cool to room temperature and remove the tube from the microwave apparatus. Add 5 mL of water and place the tube in an ice-water bath for 5 min. Collect the diphenylacetylene that precipitates by vacuum filtration. Wash the solid with about 2 mL of cold water. Recrystallize the product from a small quantity of 95% ethanol or an ethanol-water mixture. If the solution is allowed to cool slowly undisturbed, you should obtain large, sparlike, colorless crystals.

Analysis Determine the melting point, weight, and percent yield of the recrystallized product. Test the product for unsaturation using the bromine and Baeyer tests (Secs. 4.7A1 and 4.7A2, respectively). Obtain IR and ^{1}H NMR spectra of your starting material and product and compare them with those of authentic samples (Figs. 10.36, 10.37, 11.1, and 11.2).

WRAPPING IT UP

Combine the *filtrate* from the reaction mixture with the *mother liquor* from the recrystallization, dilute with water, and neutralize with 10% aqueous hydrochloric acid; then flush the solution down the drain. Place the *dichloromethane solution* from the bromine test for unsaturation in a container for halogenated organic liquids; put the *manganese dioxide* from the Baeyer test for unsaturation in a container for heavy metals.

EXERCISES

1. Write three-dimensional structures of *meso*-stilbene dibromide and one enantiomer of *dl*-stilbene dibromide.
2. The solvent used in the preparation of diphenylacetylene (**2**) is triethylene glycol.
   a. Write the structure of triethylene glycol; circle and label each of the functional groups in this molecule.
   b. What structural features account for the high boiling point of this solvent?
3. The functional group in alkynes is the carbon-carbon triple bond.
   a. Using a suitable drawing, show how the atomic *p*-orbitals in acetylene overlap to form π-molecular orbitals.
   b. What is the angle between these two π-orbitals?
   c. What is the angle between each of the π-orbitals and the carbon-carbon σ-bond?
4. Give a stepwise mechanism showing the base-induced formation of diphenylacetylene from *meso*-stilbene dibromide. Use curved arrows to symbolize the flow of electrons.
5. The E2 reaction of most compounds is known to proceed preferentially by removal of a proton anti-periplanar to the leaving group. Based upon this generalization, predict the geometry of the 1-bromo-1,2-diphenylethylene that is produced as the intermediate in the double dehydrobromination of *meso*-stilbene dibromide.
6. Why do you think the enthalpy of activation, $\Delta H^{\ddagger}$, for a syn-periplanar elimination is higher than that for an anti-periplanar elimination?
7. If *meso*-stilbene dibromide is treated with KOH in ethanol, it is possible to isolate the 1-bromo-1,2-diphenylethylene that is formed from the first dehydrobromination. The E2 elimination of the second molecule of hydrogen bromide from this intermediate alkene to give diphenylacetylene has a higher activation enthalpy than the first elimination and thus requires a higher reaction temperature. Explain.
8. Provide an explanation for why neither ethanol nor ethylene glycol is a suitable solvent for the second dehydrobromination.

Refer to the online resources and use the spectra viewer and Tables 8.1–8.8 as needed to answer the blue-numbered questions on spectroscopy.

9. Consider the NMR spectral data for *meso*-stilbene dibromide (Fig. 10.37).
   a. In the ^{1}H NMR spectrum, assign the various resonances to the hydrogen nuclei responsible for them.
   b. For the ^{13}C NMR data, assign the various resonances to the carbon nuclei responsible for them.
10. Consider the spectral data for diphenylacetylene (Figs. 11.1 and 11.2).
    a. In the functional group region of the IR spectrum, identify the absorptions associated with the aromatic rings. Why is there no absorption for the carbon-carbon triple bond?
    b. In the ^{1}H NMR spectrum, assign the various resonances to the hydrogen nuclei responsible for them.
    c. For the ^{13}C NMR data, assign the various resonances to the carbon nuclei responsible for them.

11. Discuss the differences observed in the NMR spectra of *meso*-stilbene dibromide and diphenylacetylene that are consistent with the double dehydrobromination in this experiment.

SPECTRA

Starting Material and Product

The IR and NMR spectra of meso-stilbene dibromide *are provided in Figures 10.36 and 10.37, respectively.*

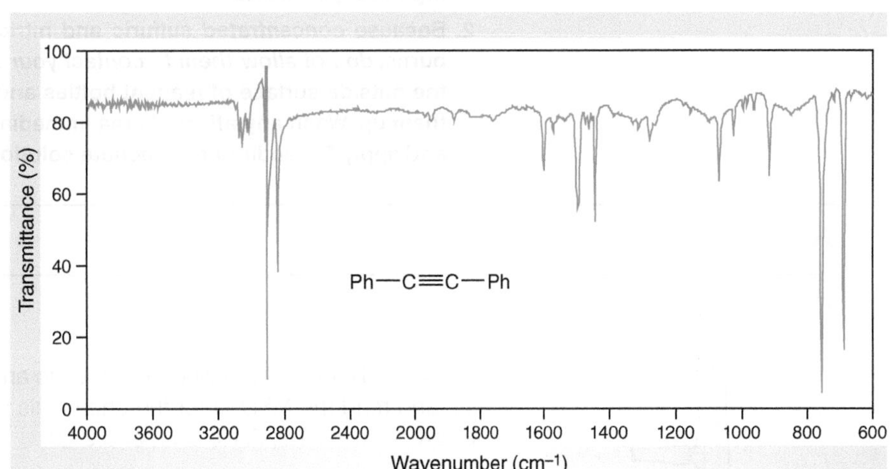

Figure 11.1
IR spectrum of diphenylacetylene (IR card).

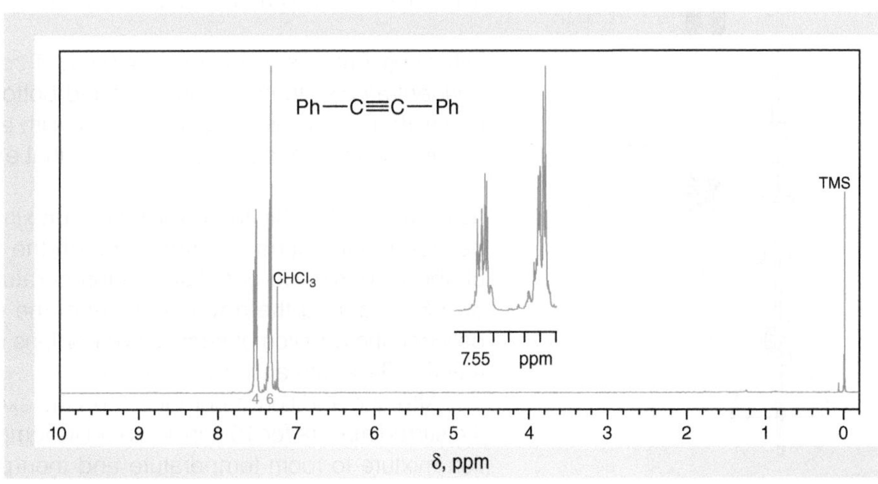

Figure 11.2
NMR data for diphenylacetylene ($CDCl_3$).

(a) ^{1}H NMR spectrum (300 MHz).
(b) ^{13}C NMR data: δ 89.6, 123.3, 128.1, 128.2, 131.6.

EXPERIMENTAL PROCEDURES

Nitration of Bromobenzene

Discovery Experiment **Purpose** To demonstrate nitration by electrophilic aromatic substitution and to test the directing effects of a bromo substituent.

SAFETY ALERT

1. **Wear safety glasses or goggles and suitable protective gloves while performing the experiments.**
2. **Because *concentrated* sulfuric and nitric acids may cause severe chemical burns, *do not allow them to contact your skin.* Wipe off any drips and runs on the outside surface of reagent bottles and graduated cylinders *before* picking them up. Wash any affected area immediately and thoroughly with cold water, and apply 5% sodium bicarbonate solution.**

A ▪ *Nitration*

MINISCALE PROCEDURE

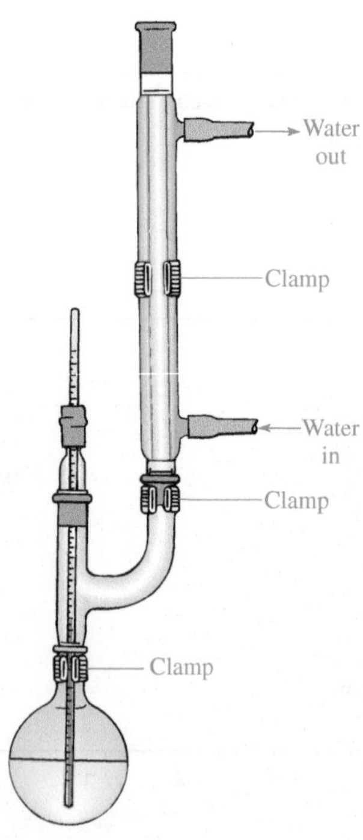

Figure 15.17
Apparatus for brominating nitrobenzene.

Preparation Refer to the online resources to answer Pre-Lab Exercises, access videos, and read the MSDSs for the chemicals used or produced in this procedure. Review Sections 2.9, 2.10, 2.11, and 2.29.

Apparatus A 25-mL round-bottom flask, Claisen adapter, thermometer, water-cooled condenser, ice-water bath, apparatus for magnetic stirring, simple distillation, vacuum filtration, and *flameless* heating.

Setting Up Prepare a solution of 4.0 mL of *concentrated* nitric acid and 4.0 mL of *concentrated* sulfuric acid in the round-bottom flask and cool it to room temperature with a water bath. Equip the flask with a stirbar and a Claisen adapter fitted with the condenser and a thermometer that extends into the flask (Fig. 15.17).

Reaction and Work-Up In portions of approximately 0.5 mL, add 4.5 mL of bromobenzene to the stirred mixture through the top of the condenser over a period of about 10 min. Do *not* allow the temperature of the reaction mixture to exceed 50–55 °C during the addition. Control the temperature by allowing more time between the addition of successive portions of bromobenzene and by cooling the reaction flask with an ice-water bath.

After the addition is complete and the exothermic reaction has subsided, heat the stirred mixture for 15 min, keeping its temperature below 60 °C.★ Cool the reaction mixture to room temperature and then pour it carefully and with stirring into 40 mL of cold water contained in a beaker.

Isolation and Purification Isolate the mixture of crude bromonitrobenzenes by vacuum filtration. Wash the filter cake thoroughly with cold water until the washes are neutral to pHydrion paper; allow the solid to drain under vacuum until nearly dry.★

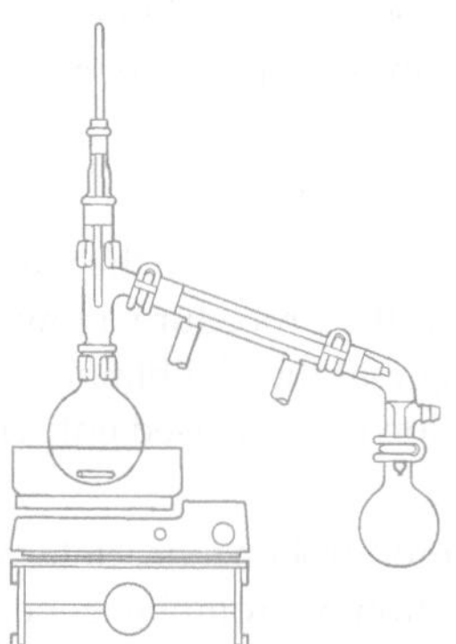

Transfer the filter cake to an Erlenmeyer flask and recrystallize the crude product from 95% ethanol. Allow the residual solution to cool slowly to room temperature; then cool it to 0 °C in an ice-water bath. Isolate the crystalline product by vacuum filtration. Wash the product with a little *ice-cold* 95% ethanol, allowing the washes to drain into the filter flask with the mother liquors. Transfer the product to a watchglass or a piece of filter paper for air-drying.

Concentrate the mother liquors to a volume of about 10 mL by simple distillation. Perform this operation in a hood to prevent release of vapors into the laboratory. Alternatively, use rotary evaporation or other techniques to concentrate the solution. Allow the residual solution to cool to room temperature to produce a second crop of 4-bromonitrobenzene. Isolate it by vacuum filtration and, after air-drying, put it in a separate vial from the first crop.

Further concentrate the mother liquors from the second crop to a volume of 3–4 mL. The resulting oil contains crude 2-bromonitrobenzene. Separate the oil from the two-phase mixture by means of a Pasteur pipet and weigh and reserve it for chromatographic analysis (Parts B and C).

Analysis Weigh both crops of product and calculate the yield. Measure the melting points of both crops. Obtain IR and NMR spectra of your starting material and product and compare them with those of authentic samples (Figs. 8.31, 15.18–15.21).

EXERCISES

1. Precipitation of the mononitration product of bromobenzene prevents dinitration from occurring. Explain how this experimental result is an application of the Le Chatelier principle.
2. How does maintaining the reaction temperature below 60 °C help suppress formation of dinitration by-products?
3. The pK_as of sulfuric and nitric acids are −3 (estimated value) and −1.3, respectively.
   a. Which of the two acids is stronger?
   b. Given your prediction in Part **a**, write a chemical equation for the equilibrium involving reaction of sulfuric and nitric acids.
   c. What is the value of K_{eq} for the acid-base reaction in Part **b**? Assume that the pK_a of the conjugate acid of nitric acid is −13.
4. Explain why 4-bromonitrobenzene (**22**) is *less* polar than 2-bromonitrobenzene (**21**).
5. Explain why the melting point of 4-bromonitrobenzene (**22**) is considerably higher than that of the 2-isomer **21**.
6. a. Provide the resonance structures that contribute to the σ-complexes **25** and **26.**
   b. Use these resonance structures to explain why the formation of 3-bromonitrobenzene (**23**) is disfavored relative to 4-bromonitrobenzene.

7. Why does 4-bromonitrobenzene (**22**) have a larger R_f-value in the TLC analysis than does the 2-isomer **21**?
8. Which isomer, 4-bromonitrobenzene or 2-bromonitrobenzene, will elute from a silica gel chromatography column first, and what physical property accounts for this order?
9. Why should a chromatography column never be allowed to go dry?
10. It is hard to measure the yield of 2-bromonitrobenzene accurately in the reaction you performed because this isomer is not purified in the procedure. However, the yield may be crudely approximated by assuming that the oil obtained from concentrating the mother liquors from recrystallization is comprised entirely of this isomer.
    a. Using the assumption that the oil is the 2-bromonitrobenzene, determine the *o*:*p* ratio of isomers formed in the mononitration of bromobenzene.
    b. Explain whether the result of your determination in Part **a** supports the hypothesis that the steric effect of the bromo substituent suppresses or augments the formation of the *o*-isomer relative to that expected statistically.
    c. A better way to assess the *o*:*p* ratio of the two bromonitro isomers would be to analyze the crude reaction mixture prior to any purification steps. Propose a way by which you might perform such an analysis. Be specific in your answer.
    d. The experimentally observed *o*:*p* ratio is reported to be 38:62.
        i. What does this ratio indicate with regard to the steric effect of the bromo substituent?
        ii. Use this ratio and the amount of 4-bromonitrobenzene actually isolated to estimate the experimental yield of mononitration in the reaction.
        iii. What errors might attend using this method to calculate the extent of mononitration?
11. The *o*:*p* ratio in the mononitration of bromobenzene has been reported to be 38:62. Use this ratio and the amount of 4-bromonitrobenzene actually isolated to estimate the experimental yield of mononitration in the reaction. What errors are there in using this method to calculate the extent of mononitration?
12. Explain why 4-bromonitrobenzene cannot be prepared efficiently by the bromination of nitrobenzene.
13. Would nitration of bromobenzene or nitration of 4-bromonitrobenzene be expected to have the higher enthalpy of activation? Explain your answer.

Refer to the online resources and use the spectra viewer and Tables 8.1–8.8 as needed to answer the blue-numbered questions on spectroscopy.

14. Consider the spectral data for bromobenzene (Figs. 15.18 and 15.19).
    a. In the IR spectrum, specify the absorption associated with the π-bonds of the aromatic ring. Indicate with what structural feature the strong absorptions at about 740 cm^{-1} and 690 cm^{-1} are associated.
    b. In the ^1H NMR spectrum, assign the various resonances to the hydrogen nuclei responsible for them.
    c. For the ^{13}C NMR data, assign the various resonances to the carbon nuclei responsible for them.

15. Consider the spectral data for 4-bromonitrobenzene (Figs. 8.31, 15.20, and 15.21).
    a. In the functional group region of the IR spectrum, specify the absorption associated with the π-bonds of the aromatic ring and indicate with what structural feature the strong absorption at 825 cm^{-1} is associated.
    b. In the ^{1}H NMR spectrum, assign the various resonances to the hydrogen nuclei responsible for them.
    c. For the ^{13}C NMR data, assign the various resonances to the carbon nuclei responsible for them.
16. Consider the spectral data for 2-bromonitrobenzene (Figs. 15.22 and 15.23).
    a. In the functional group region of the IR spectrum, specify the absorption associated with the π-bonds of the aromatic ring and indicate with what structural feature the strong absorption at about 750 cm^{-1} is associated.
    b. In the ^{1}H NMR spectrum, assign the various resonances to the hydrogen nuclei responsible for them.
    c. For the ^{13}C NMR data, assign the various resonances to the carbon nuclei responsible for them.
17. What differences in the IR and NMR spectra of bromobenzene and 4-bromonitrobenzene are consistent with the introduction of a nitro group onto the ring in this experiment?

SPECTRA

Starting Materials and Products

The ^{1}H NMR spectrum of 4-bromonitrobenzene is provided in Figure 8.31.

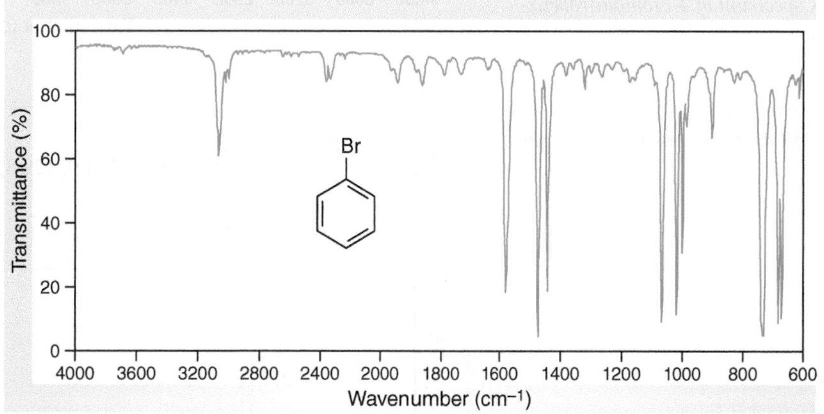

Figure 15.18
IR spectrum of bromobenzene (neat).

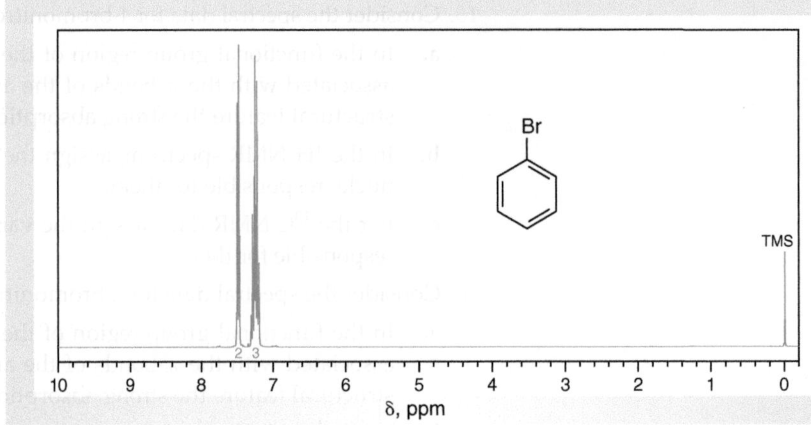

Figure 15.19
NMR data for bromobenzene ($CDCl_3$).

(a) ^{1}H NMR spectrum (300 MHz).
(b) ^{13}C NMR data: δ 122.5, 126.7, 129.8, 131.4.

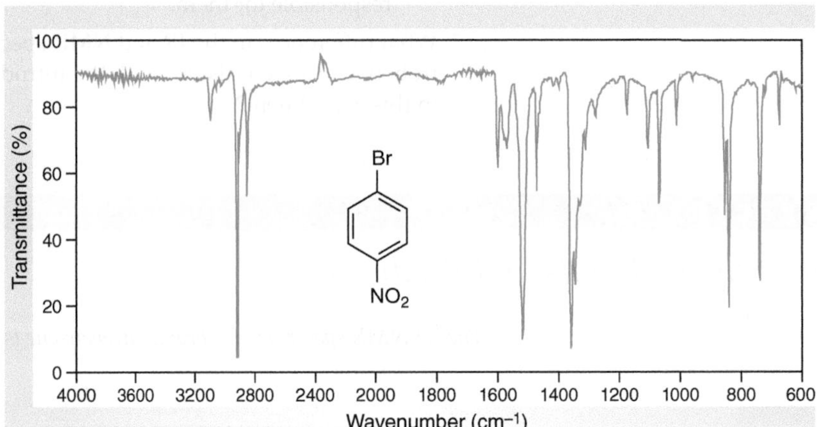

Figure 15.20
IR spectrum of 4-bromonitrobenzene (IR card).

Figure 15.21
NMR data for 4-bromonitrobenzene.

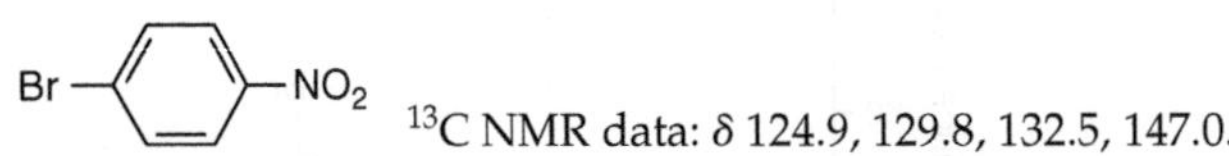

^{13}C NMR data: δ 124.9, 129.8, 132.5, 147.0.

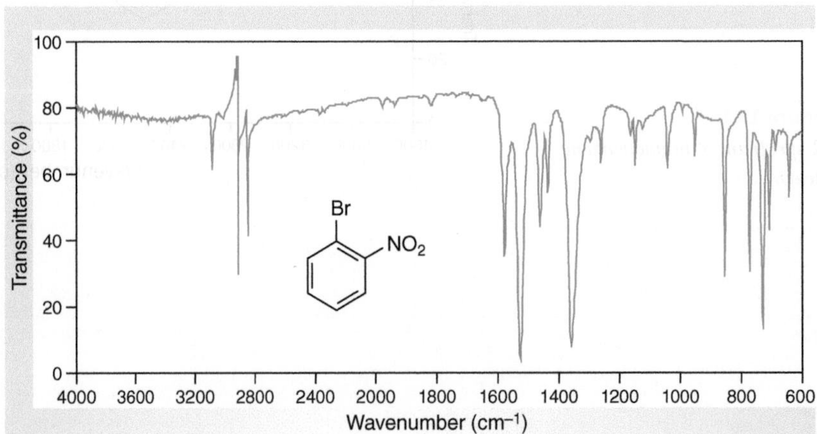

Figure 15.22
IR spectrum of 2-bromonitrobenzene (neat).

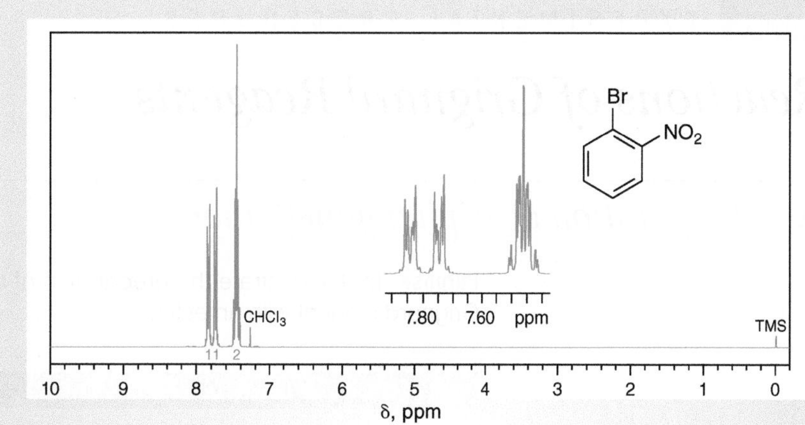

Figure 15.23
NMR data for 2-bromonitrobenzene ($CDCl_3$).

(a) ^{1}H NMR spectrum (300 MHz).
(b) ^{13}C NMR data: δ 114.1, 125.4, 128.2, 133.2, 134.8, 136.4.

EXPERIMENTAL PROCEDURES

Reactions of Grignard Reagents

A ▪ Preparation of Triphenylmethanol

Purpose To demonstrate the preparation of a tertiary alcohol by the reaction of a Grignard reagent with an ester.

SAFETY ALERT

Review the Safety Alert for Preparation of Grignard Reagents (Sec. 19.2).

MINISCALE PROCEDURE

Preparation Refer to the online resources to answer Pre-Lab Exercises, access videos, and read the MSDSs for the chemicals used or produced in this procedure. Review Sections 2.10, 2.11, 2.13, 2.17, 2.21, 2.22, and 2.29.

Apparatus Glass apparatus from the miniscale experimental procedure of Section 19.2, separatory funnel, ice-water bath, apparatus for magnetic stirring, simple distillation, vacuum filtration, and *flameless* heating.

Setting Up While the reaction mixture for the preparation of phenylmagnesium bromide (Sec. 19.2) is cooling to room temperature, dissolve 1.2 mL of methyl benzoate in about 5 mL of *anhydrous* diethyl ether, and place this solution in the separatory funnel with the *stopcock closed.* Cool the reaction flask containing the phenylmagnesium bromide in the ice-water bath.

Reaction Begin the *slow, dropwise* addition of the solution of methyl benzoate to the *stirred* solution of phenylmagnesium bromide. This reaction is *exothermic,* so you should control the rate of reaction by adjusting the rate of addition *and* by occasionally cooling the reaction flask as needed with the ice-water bath. The ring of condensate should be allowed to rise no more than one-third of the way up the reflux condenser. A white solid may form during the reaction, but this is normal. After the addition is complete and the exothermic reaction subsides, you may complete the reaction in one of two ways. Consult with your instructor to determine whether you should (1) heat the reaction mixture at reflux for 30 min or (2) stopper the flask after cooling the contents to room temperature and place it in the *hood* until the next laboratory period (no reflux required).★

Work-Up, Isolation, and Purification Place about 10 mL of cold 6 *M* sulfuric acid and about 5–10 g of crushed ice in a beaker. If the reaction mixture solidified upon cooling, add a small quantity of solvent-grade diethyl ether to the reaction flask. Pour the reaction mixture gradually with stirring into the ice-acid mixture. Rinse the round-bottom flask with 2–3 mL of solvent-grade diethyl ether and add this wash to the beaker. Continue stirring until the heterogeneous mixture is completely free of undissolved solids. It may be necessary to add a small portion of solvent-grade diethyl ether to dissolve all the organic material; the total volume of ether should be about 15–20 mL. Verify that the aqueous layer is acidic; if it is not, add cold 6 *M* sulfuric acid dropwise until the layer is acidic. If necessary, sequentially add 2- to 3-mL portions of solvent-grade diethyl ether and then water to dissolve all of the solids.

Transfer the entire mixture to a separatory funnel. Shake the funnel vigorously with venting to relieve pressure; separate the aqueous layer.★ Wash the organic layer sequentially with about 5 mL of 3 *M* sulfuric acid, two 5-mL portions of saturated aqueous sodium bicarbonate (*vent!*), and finally with one 5-mL portion of saturated sodium chloride solution. Dry the organic layer using several spatula-tips full of *anhydrous* sodium sulfate. Swirl the flask occasionally for a period of 10–15 min to facilitate drying; add further small portions of *anhydrous* sodium sulfate if the solution remains cloudy.★

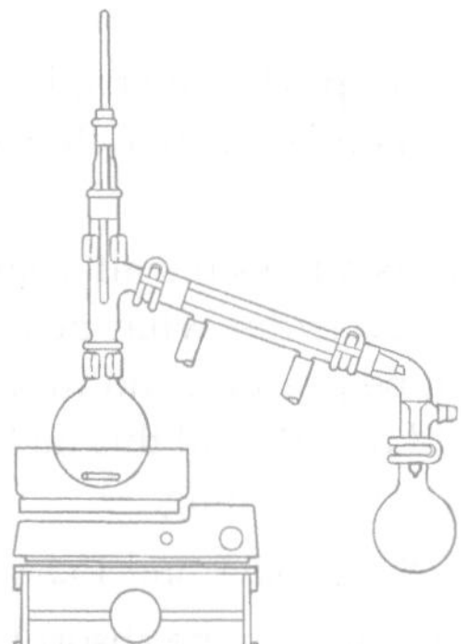

Filter or decant the solution into a 50-mL round-bottom flask and equip the flask for simple distillation. Remove the diethyl ether by simple distillation. Alternatively, use rotary evaporation or other techniques to concentrate the solution. The final traces of solvent may be removed by attaching the flask to a vacuum source and gently swirling the contents as the vacuum is applied. After the crude solid residue has dried, determine its melting range, which may be wide.★

Purify the triphenylmethanol by dissolving it in a *minimum* amount of boiling cyclohexane (ca. 10 mL/g product). Perform this operation at the hood or use a funnel that is attached to a vacuum source and inverted over the flask (Fig. 2.71b). Once all the material is in solution, evaporate the solvent *slowly* until small crystals of triphenylmethanol start to form. Allow the crystallization to continue at room temperature and then in an ice-water bath until no more crystals form. Isolate the product by vacuum filtration and air-dry it.

Analysis Weigh the triphenylmethanol and calculate the percent yield; determine its melting point. Obtain IR and ^{1}H NMR spectra of your starting materials and product, and compare them with those of authentic samples (Figs. 8.48, 15.19, 15.20, 15.33, 15.34, 19.2, and 19.3). If possible, analyze your product by GC-MS to determine if it is contaminated with benzophenone (**10**).

WRAPPING IT UP

Dilute the *combined aqueous layers and washes* with water, neutralize the solution if necessary, and flush it down the drain with excess water. Place the *ether distillate* and the *cyclohexane mother liquor* in the container for nonhalogenated organic solvents. Spread the *calcium chloride* from the drying tube and the *sodium sulfate* on a tray in the hood and, after the ether has evaporated, place them and the *filter paper* in the container for nonhazardous solids.

EXERCISES

General Questions

1. Arrange the following compounds in order of increasing reactivity toward attack of a Grignard reagent at the carbonyl carbon atom: methyl benzoate, benzoic acid, benzaldehyde, and benzophenone. Explain the basis for your decision, making use of mechanisms where needed.
2. What is (are) the product(s) of reaction of each of the carbonyl-containing compounds in Exercise 1 with *excess* Grignard reagent, RMgBr?

3. How might primary, secondary, and tertiary alcohols be prepared from a Grignard reagent and a suitable carbonyl-containing compound? Write chemical reactions for these preparations using any starting materials you wish; indicate stoichiometry where important.

Questions for Part A

4. Why is it unwise to begin addition of the solution of methyl benzoate to the Grignard reagent before the latter has cooled to room temperature and then been placed in an ice-water bath?
5. Why should anhydrous rather than solvent-grade diethyl ether be used to prepare the solution of methyl benzoate that is added to the Grignard reagent?
6. What is the solid that forms during the addition of the ester to the Grignard reagent?
7. Why is it necessary to acidify the mixture obtained after the reaction of methyl benzoate with phenylmagnesium bromide?
8. Cyclohexane is used as the recrystallization solvent to purify the triphenylmethanol by removing the biphenyl impurity. Why is this a better choice of solvent than a solvent such as isopropyl alcohol?
9. Comment on the use of steam distillation (Sec. 4.4) as a possible alternative procedure for purifying crude triphenylmethanol. Consider what possible starting materials, products, and by-products might be present, and indicate which of these should steam-distill and which should not. Would this method of purification yield pure triphenylmethanol? Give your reasoning.

Refer to the online resources and use the spectra viewer and Tables 8.1–8.8 as needed to answer the blue-numbered questions on spectroscopy.

10. Consider the spectral data for methyl benzoate (Figs. 8.48, 15.33, and 15.34).
    a. In the functional group region of the IR spectrum, identify the absorptions associated with the ester functional group and the aromatic ring.
    b. In the ^1H NMR spectrum, assign the various resonances to the hydrogen nuclei responsible for them.
    c. For the ^{13}C NMR data, assign the various resonances to the carbon nuclei responsible for them.
11. Consider the spectral data for triphenylmethanol (Figs. 19.2 and 19.3).
    a. In the functional group region of the IR spectrum, specify the absorptions due to the aromatic ring. There is a broad absorption at about 3450 cm^{-1}. What functional group is responsible for this absorption and why is the absorption broad?
    b. In the ^1H NMR spectrum, assign the various resonances to the hydrogen nuclei responsible for them.
    c. For the ^{13}C NMR data, assign the various resonances to the carbon nuclei responsible for them.
12. Discuss the differences observed in the IR and NMR spectra of methyl benzoate and triphenylmethanol that are consistent with the conversion of an ester into a tertiary alcohol in this experiment.

SPECTRA

Starting Materials and Products

The ^{13}C NMR spectrum of methyl benzoate is shown in Figure 8.48; its IR and 1H NMR spectra are provided in Figures 15.33 and 15.34, respectively. The IR and NMR spectra for 1-bromobutane, bromobenzene, and 2-methylpropanal are presented in Figures 14.2, 14.4, 15.19, 15.20, 18.17, and 18.18, respectively.

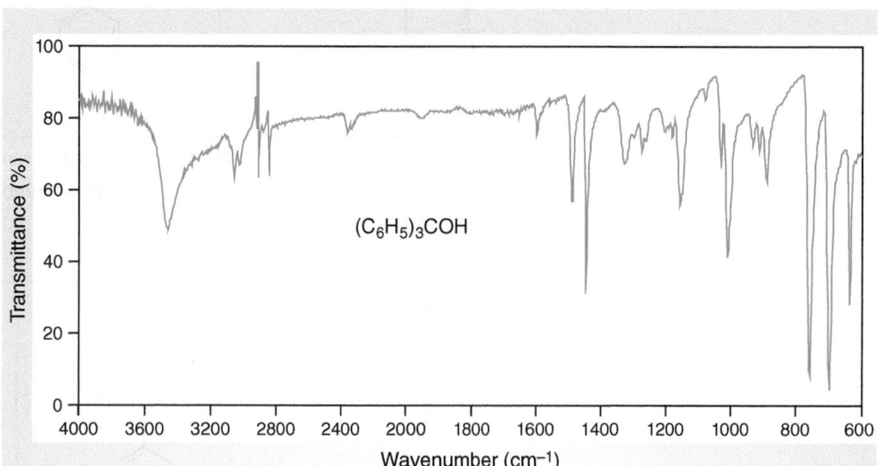

Figure 19.2
IR spectrum of triphenylmethanol (IR card).

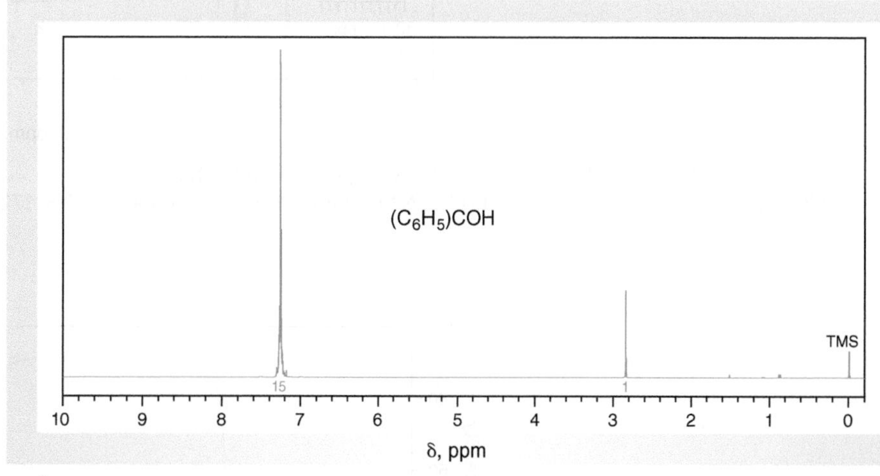

Figure 19.3
NMR data for triphenylmethanol ($CDCl_3$).

(a) ^{1}H NMR spectrum (300 MHz).
(b) ^{13}C NMR data: δ 82.0, 127.2, 127.9, 146.9.

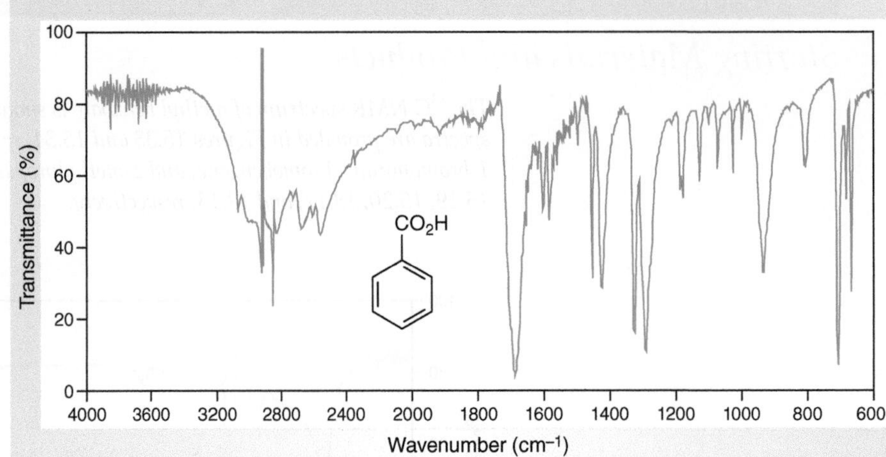

Figure 19.4
IR spectrum of benzoic acid (IR card).

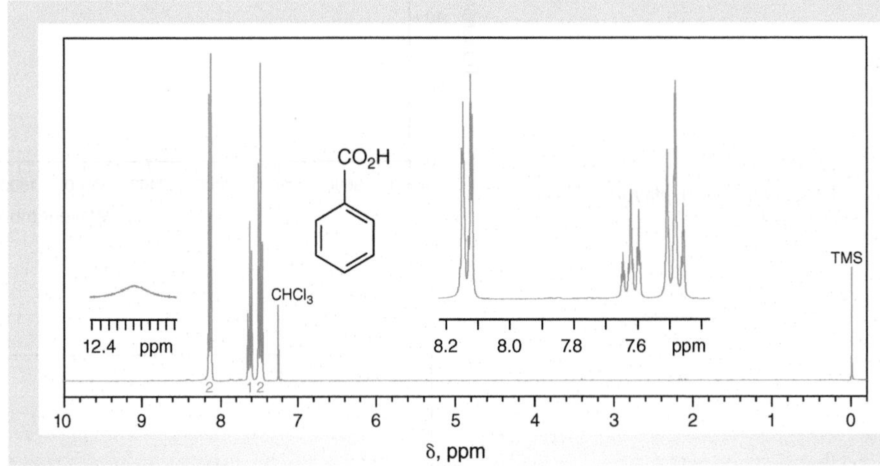

Figure 19.5
NMR data for benzoic acid ($CDCl_3$).

(a) ^{1}H NMR spectrum (300 MHz).
(b) ^{13}C NMR data: δ 128.5, 129.5, 130.3, 133.8, 172.7.

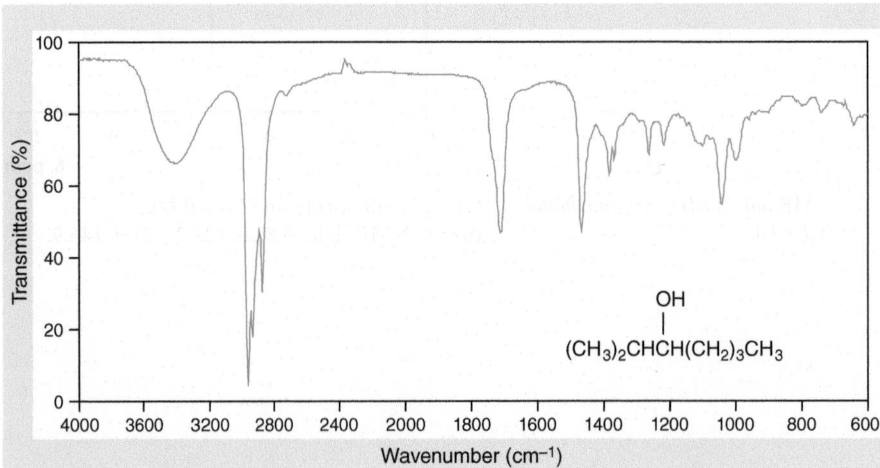

Figure 19.6
IR spectrum of 2-methyl-3-heptanol (neat).

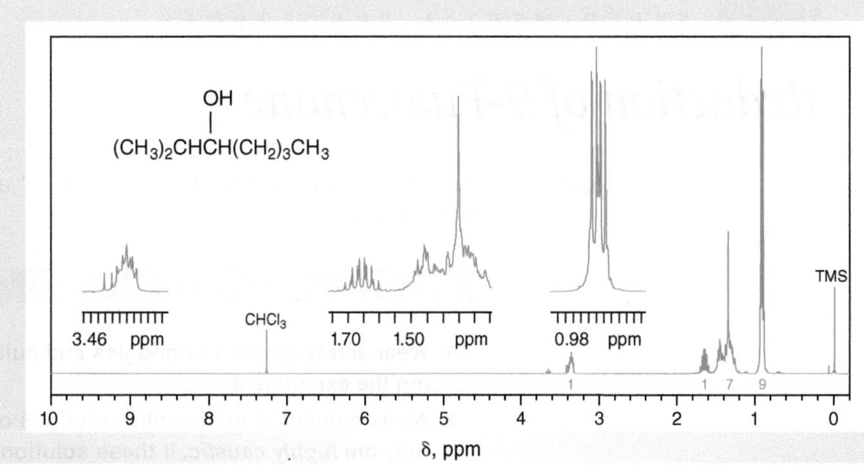

Figure 19.7
NMR data for 2-methyl-3-heptanol ($CDCl_3$).

(a) ^{1}H NMR spectrum (300 MHz).
(b) ^{13}C NMR data: δ 14.2, 17.5, 19.3, 23.1, 28.6, 33.8, 34.1, 76.6.

EXPERIMENTAL PROCEDURES

Reduction of 9-Fluorenone

Discovery Experiment

Purpose To demonstrate the reduction of a ketone to an alcohol using sodium borohydride.

SAFETY ALERT

1. **Wear safety glasses or goggles and suitable protective gloves while performing the experiment.**
2. **Avoid contact of methanolic solutions of sodium borohydride with your skin; they are *highly caustic*. If these solutions accidentally get on your skin, wash the affected area first with a 1% acetic acid solution and then with copious quantities of water.**
3. **Do *not* stopper flasks containing methanolic sodium borohydride; the solution slowly evolves dihydrogen gas, and a dangerous buildup of pressure could occur in a stoppered flask.**

MINISCALE PROCEDURE

Preparation Refer to the online resources to answer Pre-Lab Exercises, access videos, and read the MSDSs for the chemicals used or produced in this procedure. Review Sections 2.9 and 2.17.

Apparatus A 25-mL Erlenmeyer flask, ice-water bath, apparatus for vacuum filtration and *flameless* heating.

Setting Up Add 0.6 g of 9-fluorenone to the Erlenmeyer flask containing 6 mL of methanol, and swirl the flask with slight warming to dissolve the ketone. Allow the solution to cool to room temperature. *Quickly* weigh 0.05 g of sodium borohydride into a dry test tube, and stopper the test tube *immediately* to avoid undue exposure of the hygroscopic reagent to atmospheric moisture.

Reduction Add the sodium borohydride in *one* portion to the solution of 9-fluorenone in methanol, and swirl the mixture vigorously to dissolve the reagent. After all of the sodium borohydride dissolves, allow the solution to stand at room temperature for 20 min; swirl the solution occasionally. If the solution does not become colorless during this time, add an additional small portion of sodium borohydride with swirling to complete the reaction.★

Work-Up Add 2 mL of 3 *M* sulfuric acid to the reaction mixture. Heat the contents in the flask gently and intermittently for 5–10 min. Stir the mixture occasionally with a glass rod to help dissolve the solid; maintain the internal temperature just below the reflux point to *minimize the loss of solvent.* If all of the solids do not dissolve, *gradually* add methanol in about 0.5- to 1-mL portions with continued heating until a solution is obtained. When all of the precipitated solids redissolve, allow the solution to cool to room temperature, and then cool in an ice-water bath for 10–15 min.

Isolation and Purification Collect the solid product by vacuum filtration, *wash it thoroughly* with water until the filtrate is *neutral,* and air-dry the product.★ Recrystallize the 9-fluorenol by a mixed solvent recrystallization (Sec. 3.2) using methanol and water or some other suitable solvent. After cooling the solution first to room temperature and then in an ice-water bath for 10–15 min, collect and air-dry the crystals.

Analysis Weigh the product and calculate the percent yield; determine its melting point. Obtain IR and ^{1}H NMR spectra of your starting material and product, and compare them with those of authentic samples (Figs. 17.33–17.36).

WRAPPING IT UP

Dilute the combined *aqueous methanol filtrates* with water, neutralize the resulting solution with sodium carbonate, and flush the mixture down the drain with excess water.

EXERCISES

1. Determine the molar ratio of sodium borohydride to 9-fluorenone that you used in the experiment. Why is it necessary to use a greater molar ratio than theoretical?
2. After the reaction between sodium borohydride and the ketone is complete, the reaction mixture is treated with water and acid to produce the desired secondary alcohol. Explain this reaction by indicating the source of the hydrogen atom that ends up on the oxygen atom.
3. Sodium borohydride is fairly unreactive toward methanol, but adding a mineral acid to this solution results in the rapid destruction of the sodium borohydride. Explain.
4. How many molar equivalents of hydride does sodium borohydride contain?
5. Using curved arrows to symbolize the flow of electrons, write the mechanism for the steps involved in the conversion of 9-fluorenone to 9-fluorenol with sodium borohydride followed by aqueous acid according to Equation 17.19.
6. Suggest a structure for the white precipitate formed in the reaction of 9-fluorenone with sodium borohydride.
7. What gas is evolved when sulfuric acid is added to the reaction mixture?
8. 9-Fluorenone is colored, but 9-fluorenol is not. What accounts for this difference?

9. Draw the structure of the product that results from complete reduction of the following compounds by sodium borohydride.
   a. cyclohexanone
   b. 3-cyclohexen-1-one
   c. 1, 4-butanediol
   d. 4-oxohexanal
   e. acetophenone
10. Draw the structure of the product that would be formed from allowing each of the compounds in Exercise 9 to react with excess dihydrogen gas in the presence of a nickel catalyst.
11. A nitro group, a carbon-carbon double bond, a carbon-nitrogen double bond, and an aromatic ring may each be reduced under certain conditions. Rank these functional groups in order of *increasing* reactivity toward hydride reducing agents such as sodium borohydride.
12. Esters are normally unreactive toward sodium borohydride, but they react readily with lithium aluminum hydride to produce alcohols.
    a. Propose a rationale for the lack of reactivity of esters toward sodium borohydride.
    b. Propose a rationale for the greater reactivity of lithium aluminum hydride over that of sodium borohydride.
    c. Write the structures of the organic products that will be formed when methyl benzoate is treated with lithium aluminum hydride and the reaction mixture is worked up with aqueous acid.

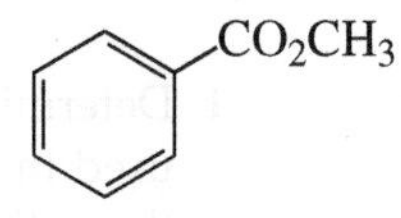

Methyl benzoate

Refer to the online resources and use the spectra viewer and Tables 8.1–8.8 as needed to answer the blue-numbered questions on spectroscopy.

13. Consider the spectral data for 9-fluorenone (Figs. 17.33 and 17.34).
    a. In the functional group region of the IR spectrum, specify the absorptions associated with the carbonyl group and with the aromatic rings.
    b. In the ^1H NMR spectrum, assign the various resonances to the hydrogen nuclei responsible for them.
    c. For the ^{13}C NMR data, assign the various resonances to the carbon nuclei responsible for them.
14. Consider the spectral data for 9-fluorenol (Figs. 17.35 and 17.36).
    a. In the functional group region of the IR spectrum, specify the functional group that is associated with the broad absorption at about 3100–3250 cm^{-1}; why is this absorption broad?
    b. In the ^1H NMR spectrum, assign the various resonances to the hydrogen nuclei responsible for them.
    c. For the ^{13}C NMR data, assign the various resonances to the carbon nuclei responsible for them.
15. Discuss the differences observed in the IR and NMR spectra of 9-fluorenone and 9-fluorenol that are consistent with the reduction of the ketone functional group in this experiment.

SPECTRA

Starting Materials and Products

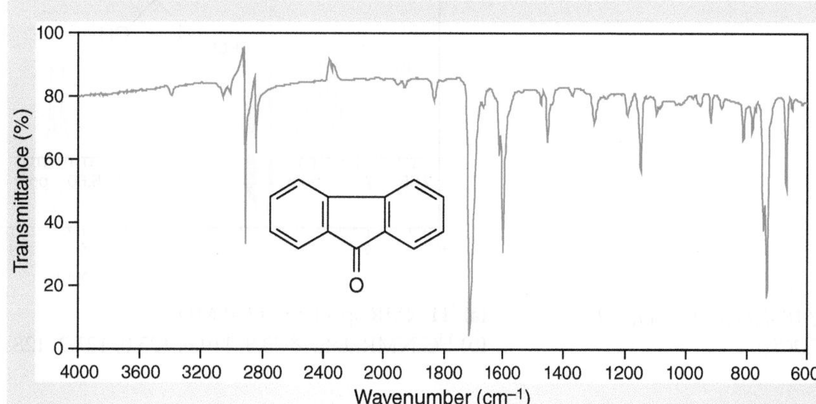

Figure 17.33
IR spectrum of 9-fluorenone (IR card).

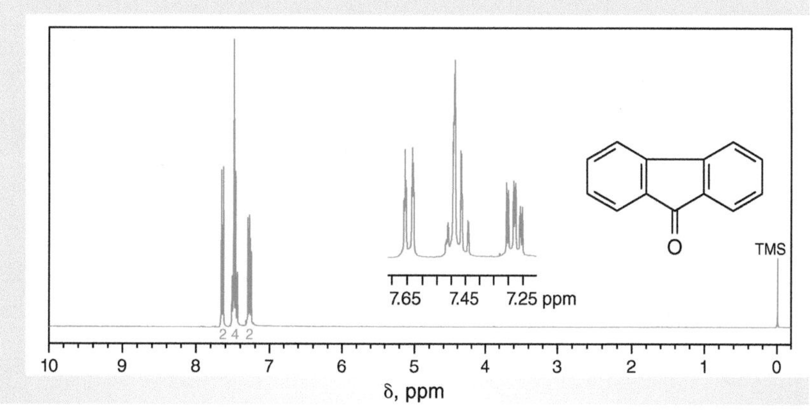

Figure 17.34
NMR data for 9-fluorenone ($CDCl_3$).

(a) ^{1}H NMR spectrum (300 MHz).
(b) ^{13}C NMR data: δ 120.1, 123.8, 128.8, 133.9, 134.4, 144.1, 193.1.

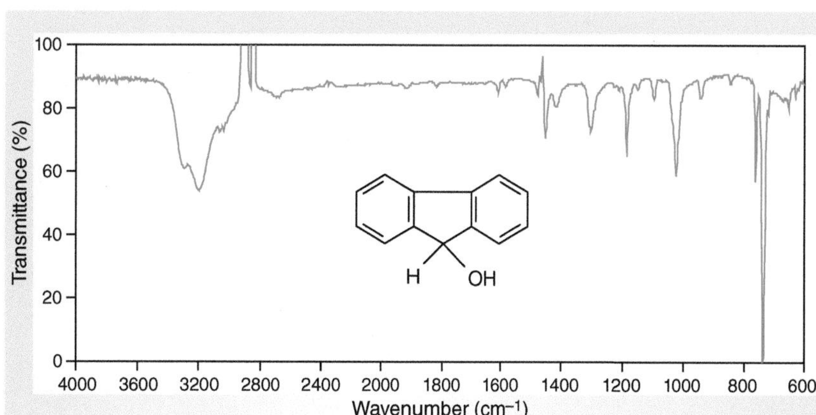

Figure 17.35
IR spectrum of 9-fluorenol (IR card).

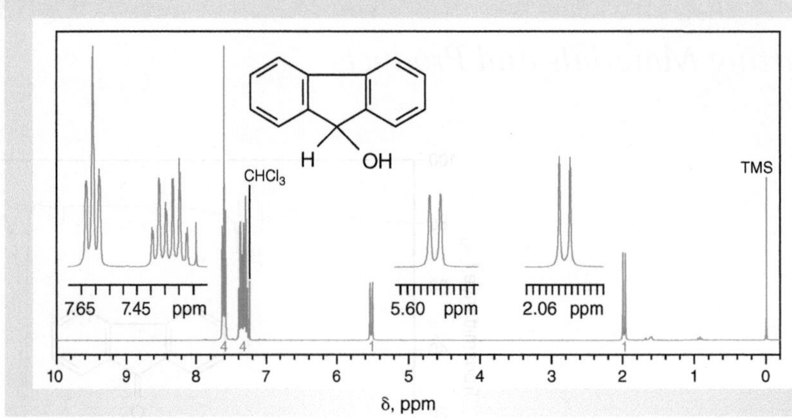

Figure 17.36
NMR data for 9-fluorenol ($CDCl_3$).

(a) ^{1}H NMR spectrum (300 MHz).
(b) ^{13}C NMR data: δ 73.8, 119.6, 125.0, 127.2, 128.2, 139.5, 146.8.

EXPERIMENTAL PROCEDURES

Fischer Esterification of Carboxylic Acids

A ▪ Preparation of Benzocaine

Purpose To demonstrate the acid-catalyzed esterification of a carboxylic acid with an alcohol.

SAFETY ALERT

1. **Wear safety glasses or goggles and suitable protective gloves while performing the experiment.**
2. ***Concentrated* sulfuric acid is *very corrosive* and may cause serious chemical burns if allowed to come into contact with your skin. When it is poured from the reagent bottle, some may run down the outside of the bottle; wipe the bottle clean with a sponge or paper towel. If any sulfuric acid comes into contact with your skin, immediately flood the affected area with cold water and then with 5% sodium bicarbonate solution.**

MINISCALE PROCEDURE

Preparation Refer to the online resources to answer Pre-Lab Exercises, access videos, and read the MSDSs for the chemicals used or produced in this procedure. Review Sections 2.9, 2.10, 2.11, 2.17, and 2.22.

Apparatus A 25-mL round-bottom flask, ice-water bath, apparatus for heating under reflux, magnetic stirring, vacuum filtration, and *flameless* heating.

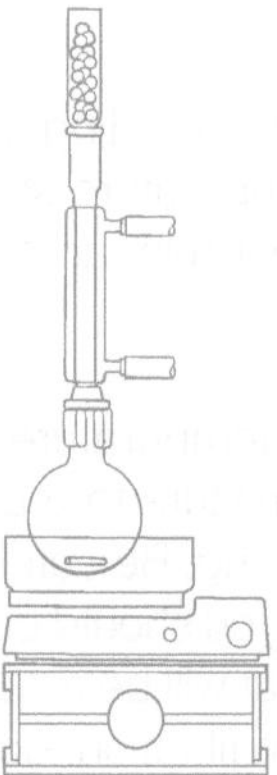

Setting Up Add 1.0 g of *p*-aminobenzoic acid and 10 mL of *absolute* ethanol to the round-bottom flask containing a spinvane. Stir the mixture until the solid is *completely* dissolved. Add 1 mL of *concentrated* sulfuric acid *dropwise* to the ethanolic solution of *p*-aminobenzoic acid, equip the flask with a condenser, and set up the apparatus for heating under reflux.

Reaction Heat the mixture under gentle reflux for 30 min. If any solid remains in the flask at this time, remove the heat source and allow the mixture to cool for 2–3 min. Add 3 mL of ethanol and 0.5 mL of *concentrated* sulfuric acid to the reaction flask and resume heating under reflux. After the reaction mixture becomes homogeneous, continue heating it under gentle reflux for another 30 min. *For the experiment to succeed, it is important that all of the solids dissolve during the period of reflux.*★

Work-Up and Isolation Allow the reaction mixture to cool to room temperature, and then pour it into a beaker containing 30 mL of water. Bring the mixture to a pH of about 8 by *slowly* adding 10% aqueous sodium carbonate with stirring. Be careful in this step, as frothing occurs during the neutralization. Beforehand, you should calculate the approximate volume of 10% aqueous sodium carbonate that will be required to neutralize the *total* amount of sulfuric acid you used. By vacuum filtration, collect the crude benzocaine that precipitates. Use three 10-mL portions of cold water to rinse the solid from the beaker and wash the filter cake, and then air-dry the product.★

Purification Weigh the crude product and transfer it to a 50-mL Erlenmeyer flask containing a stirbar and 20 mL of water. Heat the mixture with stirring to about 60 °C and then add just enough methanol to dissolve the solid (5–10 mL); do *not* add more methanol than necessary. When the solid has dissolved, allow the solution to cool to room temperature and then cool it in an ice-water bath for 10–15 min to complete crystallization. Isolate the crystals by vacuum filtration, wash them with 5–10 mL of cold water, and allow them to air-dry.

Analysis Weigh the recrystallized product and calculate the percent yield; determine its melting point. Obtain IR and ^1H NMR spectra of your starting materials and product, and compare them with those of authentic samples (Figs. 20.1–20.6).

MINISCALE PROCEDURE FOR MICROWAVE OPTION

Preparation Refer to the online resources to answer Pre-Lab Exercises, access videos, and read the MSDSs for the chemicals used or produced in this procedure. Review Sections 2.9, 2.10, 2.11, 2.17, and 2.22.

Apparatus A 10-mL pressure-rated tube with cap, stirbar, ice-water bath, apparatus for microwave heating with magnetic stirring and vacuum filtration.

Setting Up Place 0.50 g of *p*-aminobenzoic acid and a stirbar in the 10-mL tube. Add 5 mL of *absolute* ethanol. Add about 0.3 mL (6 drops) of *concentrated* sulfuric acid, seal the vial with the cap, and place it in the cavity of the microwave apparatus.

Reaction Program the unit to heat the reaction mixture with stirring according to the directions provided by your instructor. Generally, the reaction temperature should be set at 140 °C and the power set at a maximum of 300 W with a 1-min ramp time and a 5-min hold time; the pressure limit should be set at 250 psi.

Work-Up and Isolation Allow the reaction mixture to cool to room temperature and then pour it into a beaker containing 15 mL of water. Bring the mixture to a pH of about 8 by *slowly* adding 10% aqueous sodium carbonate with stirring. Be careful in this step, as frothing occurs during the neutralization. Beforehand, you should calculate the approximate volume of 10% aqueous sodium carbonate that will be required to neutralize the amount of sulfuric acid that you used. By vacuum filtration, collect the crude benzocaine that precipitates. Use three 5-mL portions of cold water to rinse the solid from the beaker and wash the filter cake, and then air-dry product.★

Purification Weigh the crude product and transfer it to a 25-mL Erlenmeyer flask containing a stirbar and 20 mL of water. Heat the mixture with stirring to about 60°C and then add just enough methanol to dissolve the solid (3–5 mL); do *not* add more methanol than necessary. When the solid has dissolved, allow the solution to cool to room temperature and then cool it in an ice-water bath for 10–15 min to complete crystallization. Isolate the crystals by vacuum filtration, wash them with 3–5 mL of cold water, and allow them to air-dry.

Analysis Weigh the recrystallized product and calculate the percentage yield; determine the melting point. Obtain IR and ^{1}H NMR spectra of your starting materials and product, and compare them with those of authentic samples (Figs. 20.1–20.6).

WRAPPING IT UP

Flush all *filtrates* down the drain.

EXERCISES

1. Why is absolute ethanol rather than 95% ethanol used in this experiment?
2. Propose a structure for the solid that separates when *concentrated* sulfuric acid is added to the solution of *p*-aminobenzoic acid in ethanol.
3. Why is it important that the solid referred to in Exercise 2 dissolve during the reaction to obtain a good yield of ethyl *p*-aminobenzoate?
4. Sodium carbonate is used to adjust the pH to 8 during the work-up of the reaction.
   a. Why is it necessary to adjust to this pH prior to extracting the aqueous mixture with diethyl ether?
   b. What undesired reaction might occur if you made the solution strongly basic with aqueous sodium hydroxide?
   c. Using curved arrows to symbolize the flow of electrons, write the stepwise mechanism for the reaction of Part **b**.
5. Consider the equilibrium for the esterification of *p*-aminobenzoic acid (**16**) to give ethyl *p*-aminobenzoate (**17**) shown in Equation 20.4.
   a. Write the mathematical expression for the equilibrium constant, K_{eq}, as a function of the concentrations of the products and reactants for this reaction.
   b. Provide two specific ways whereby the Le Chatelier principle may be applied to this equilibrium to drive the reaction completely to the ester **17**.
   c. Which one of the techniques given in Part b is used in this experiment?
6. Using curved arrows to symbolize the flow of electrons, write the stepwise mechanism for the acid-catalyzed esterification of **16** to give **17**.
7. A strong acid is generally used to catalyze the Fischer esterification of carboxylic acids. What *two* steps in the reaction are accelerated by the presence of strong acid, and what function does the acid play in each of these steps?

Refer to the online resources and use the spectra viewer and Tables 8.1–8.8 as needed to answer the blue-numbered questions on spectroscopy.

8. Consider the spectral data for *p*-aminobenzoic acid (Figs. 20.1 and 20.2).
   a. In the functional group region of the IR spectrum, specify the absorption associated with the carbonyl component of the carboxyl group. What functional group is responsible for the broad absorption in the region of about 2800 cm^{-1}, and why is the absorption broad?

b. In the ^{1}H NMR spectrum, assign the various resonances to the hydrogen nuclei responsible for them.
c. For the ^{13}C NMR data, assign the various resonances to the carbon nuclei responsible for them.

9. Consider the spectral data for ethanol (Figs. 20.3 and 20.4).
   a. What functional group accounts for the broad absorption centered at about 3350 cm^{-1} in the IR spectrum, and why it is broad?
   b. In the ^{1}H NMR spectrum, assign the various resonances to the hydrogen nuclei responsible for them.
   c. In the ^{13}C NMR spectrum, assign the various resonances to the carbon nuclei responsible for them.
10. Consider the spectral data for ethyl *p*-aminobenzoate (Figs. 20.5 and 20.6).
   a. In the functional group region of the IR spectrum, specify the absorption associated with the carbonyl component of the ester group. What functional group is responsible for the broad absorption in the region of about 3200 cm^{-1}, and why is the absorption broad?
   b. In the ^{1}H NMR spectrum, assign the various resonances to the hydrogen nuclei responsible for them.
   c. For the ^{13}C NMR data, assign the various resonances to the carbon nuclei responsible for them.
11. Discuss the differences observed in the IR and NMR spectra of *p*-aminobenzoic acid and ethyl *p*-aminobenzoate that are consistent with the formation of the latter in this procedure.

SPECTRA

Starting Materials and Products

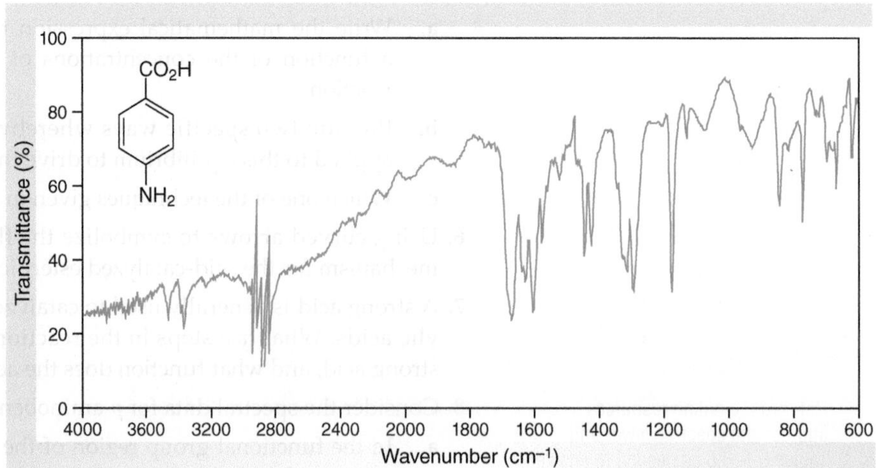

Figure 20.1
IR spectrum of p*-aminobenzoic acid (IR card).*

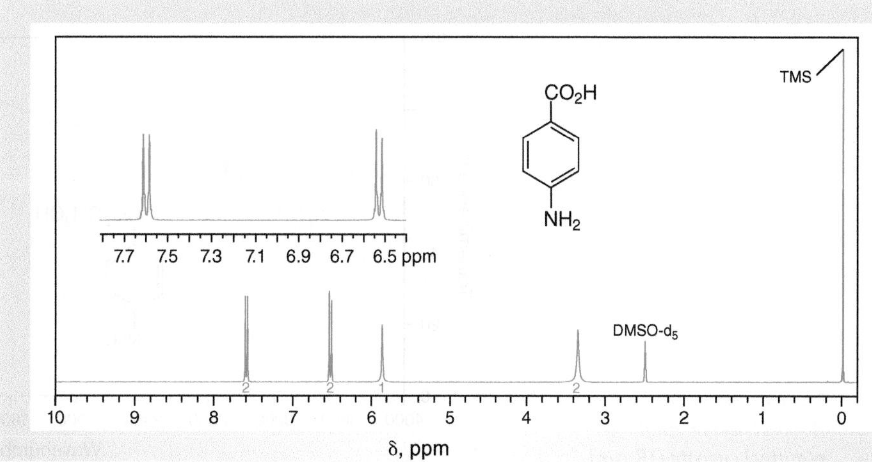

Figure 20.2
NMR data for p-aminobenzoic acid (DMSO-d_6).

(a) ^{1}H NMR spectrum (300 MHz).
(b) ^{13}C NMR data: δ 112.6, 116.9, 131.2, 153.1, 167.5.

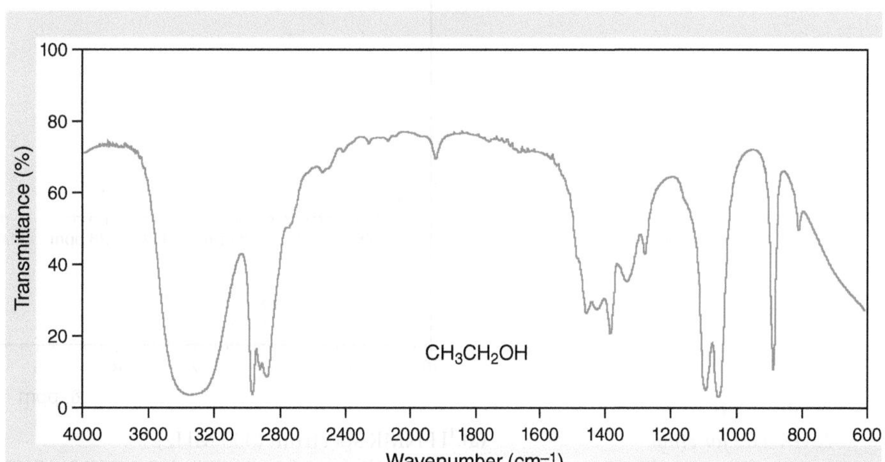

Figure 20.3
IR spectrum of ethanol (neat).

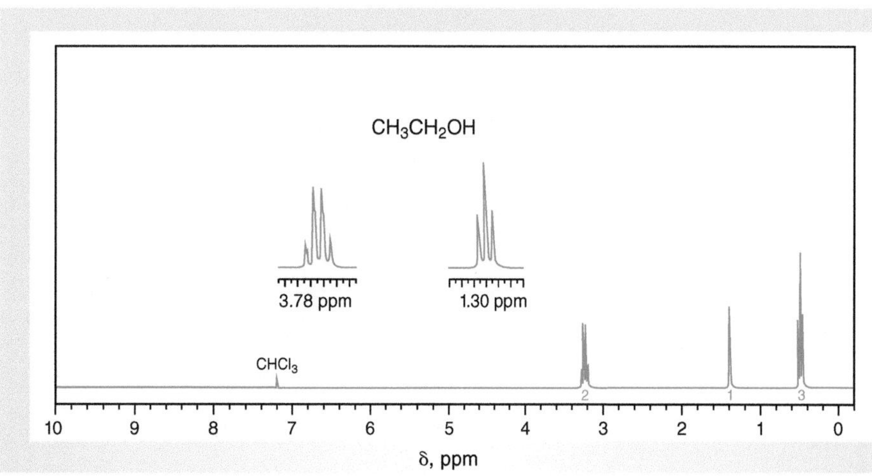

Figure 20.4
NMR data for ethanol ($CDCl_3$).

(a) ^{1}H NMR spectrum (300 MHz).
(b) ^{13}C NMR data: 18.1, 57.8.

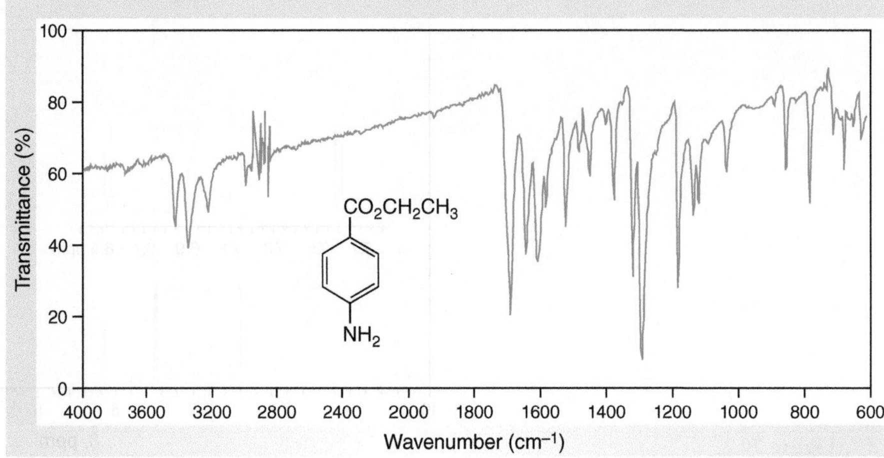

Figure 20.5
IR spectrum of ethyl p-aminobenzoate (IR card).

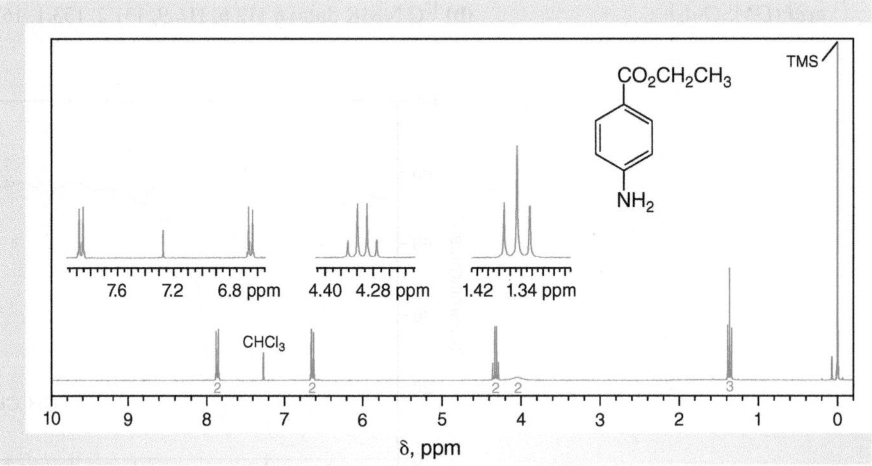

Figure 20.6
NMR data for ethyl p-aminobenzoate ($CDCl_3$).

(a) ^{1}H NMR spectrum (300 MHz).
(b) ^{13}C NMR data: δ 14.4, 60.9, 113.8, 120.2, 131.5, 150.7, 166.7.

EXPERIMENTAL PROCEDURES

Wittig and Horner-Wadsworth-Emmons Reactions

A ■ Preparation of (Z)- and (E)-Stilbenes by a Wittig Reaction

Purpose To synthesize a mixture of stilbenes by a phase-transfer Wittig reaction, to determine the major product, and to perform their geometric isomerization.

SAFETY ALERT

1. **Wear safety glasses or goggles and suitable protective gloves while performing the experiment.**
2. **The 50% (by mass) aqueous sodium hydroxide solution is *highly* caustic. *Do not allow it to come in contact with your skin.* If this should happen, wash the affected area with dilute acetic acid and then copious amounts of water.**

MINISCALE PROCEDURE

Preparation Refer to the online resources to answer Pre-Lab Exercises, access videos, and read the MSDSs for the chemicals used or produced in this procedure. Review Sections 2.9, 2.11, 2.13, 2.17, 2.21, 2.22, and 2.29.

Apparatus A 25- and a 50-mL round-bottom flask, separatory funnel, ice-water bath, apparatus for heating under reflux, magnetic stirring, simple distillation, vacuum filtration, and *flameless* heating.

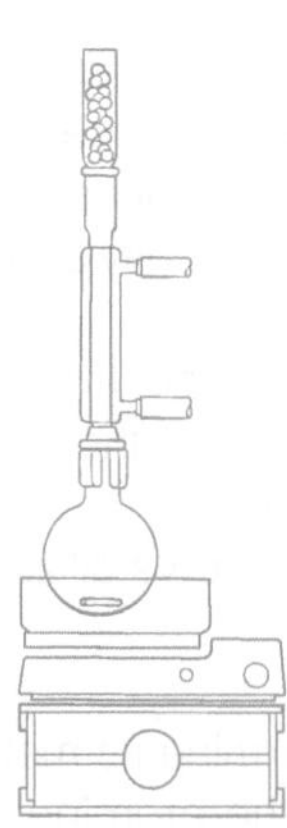

Setting Up Prepare a 50% (by mass) sodium hydroxide solution by dissolving 5.0 g of sodium hydroxide in 5 mL of water. The mixture may be heated gently to facilitate dissolution, but be sure to cool the solution to room temperature before proceeding. Add 3.8 g of benzyltriphenylphosphonium chloride and 1 mL of benzaldehyde to the 50-mL round-bottom flask containing 10 mL of dichloromethane and a stirbar. Set up the apparatus for heating under reflux. Heat the mixture with stirring until it refluxes *gently.*

Reaction Using a Pasteur pipet, add 5 mL of the 50% aqueous sodium hydroxide solution dropwise through the top of the reflux condenser to the solution, which should be stirred as *vigorously* as possible to ensure complete mixing of the phases. Try to add the solution *directly* into the flask without allowing it to touch the walls of the condenser. After the addition is complete, continue stirring under gentle reflux for 30 min.

Work-Up and Isolation of Isomeric Stilbenes Allow the reaction mixture to cool to room temperature and transfer it to a separatory funnel. Rinse the round-bottom flask with a 5-mL portion of dichloromethane and transfer the wash to the separatory funnel. Separate the layers and wash the organic layer sequentially with 10 mL of water and 15 mL of saturated aqueous sodium bisulfite. Finally, wash the organic layer with 10-mL portions of water until the pH of the wash is neutral. Transfer the organic solution to a dry Erlenmeyer flask and add several spatula-tips full of *anhydrous* sodium sulfate. Occasionally swirl the mixture over a period of 10–15 min to facilitate drying; add further small portions of *anhydrous* sodium sulfate if the solution remains cloudy.★

To determine the ratio of (*Z*)- and (*E*)-stilbene in the *crude* reaction mixture by ^1H NMR spectroscopy, use a filter-tip pipet to transfer a 0.5-mL portion of the dry organic solution to a small round-bottom flask and evaporate the dichloromethane by one of the techniques described in Section 2.29. The final traces of solvent may be removed by attaching the flask to a vacuum source and gently swirling the contents as vacuum is applied.★

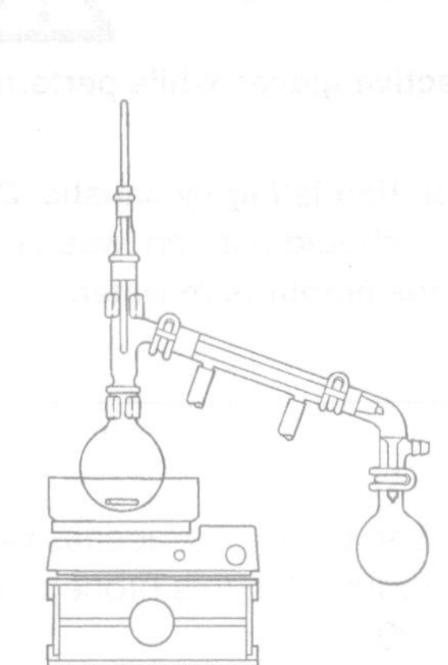

Isomerization Filter or decant the remainder of the dry dichloromethane solution into the 25-mL round-bottom flask containing a stirbar, rinse the sodium sulfate with about 1 mL of fresh dichloromethane, and transfer this wash to the round-bottom flask. Add about 75 mg of iodine to the dichloromethane solution, fit the flask with a reflux condenser, and irradiate the solution with stirring for 1 h with a 150-W lightbulb.★

Work-Up and Isolation of Stilbene Decant the solution into a separatory funnel, and wash the dichloromethane solution with a 5-mL portion of saturated aqueous sodium bisulfite; shake the mixture vigorously to decolorize the dichloromethane layer. Wash the organic solution with a 5-mL portion of saturated aqueous sodium chloride, transfer it to a dry Erlenmeyer flask, and add several spatula-tips full of *anhydrous* sodium sulfate. Occasionally swirl the mixture over a period of 10–15 min to facilitate drying; add further small portions of *anhydrous* sodium sulfate if the solution remains cloudy.★

Filter or decant the dried solution into a tared round-bottom flask, equip the flask for simple distillation, and distil the dichloromethane. Alternatively, use rotary evaporation or other techniques to concentrate the solution. The final traces of solvent may be removed by attaching the flask to a vacuum source and gently swirling the contents as vacuum is applied.★

Remove about 50 mg of the residue for analysis by ^1H NMR spectroscopy. Dissolve the remaining residue in 10–12 mL of hot 95% ethanol. Cool the resulting solution first to room temperature and then in an ice-water bath for 15–20 min to complete crystallization. Collect the precipitate and air-dry it. Recrystallize the crude stilbene from 95% ethanol or some other suitable solvent.

Analysis Weigh the product and calculate the percent yield; determine its melting point. Perform the tests for unsaturation on the product using the bromine and Baeyer tests provided in Section 4.7A. Obtain IR and ^1H NMR spectra of your starting materials, the final product, and the crude product mixtures before and after irradiation with iodine. Compare these spectra with those of authentic samples (Figs. 10.34, 10.35, 18.1–18.6) to determine the ratio of the isomeric stilbenes **9** and **10** in the crude mixture and which one is the product after irradiation.

WRAPPING IT UP

Neutralize the combined *aqueous layers and washes* with dilute hydrochloric acid, and flush them down the drain. Place the *recovered dichloromethane,* the *dichloromethane solution* from the bromine test for unsaturation, and any NMR solutions in a container for halogenated organic liquids; put the *manganese dioxide* from the Baeyer test for unsaturation in a container for heavy metals. Flush the *ethanolic filtrate* down the drain.

EXERCISES

General Questions

1. Compare the mechanism of aldol addition (Sec. 18.3) to that of the Wittig synthesis, pointing out similarities and differences.

2. Why should the aldehydes used as starting materials in Wittig syntheses be free of contamination by carboxylic acids?

3. Considering the mechanism of the Wittig reaction, speculate what the driving force for the decomposition of the oxaphosphetane intermediate might be.

4. Ylides react readily with aldehydes and ketones but slowly or not at all with esters. Explain this difference in reactivity.

5. Explain why you would expect an anion of type **5** to be more stable if one of the R groups is cyano, C≡N, rather than alkyl.

6. An ylide like **5** is a stabilized carbanion. In what way(s) does the phosphorus atom provide stability to the carbanion?

7. Write equations for the preparation of the following alkenes by the Wittig reaction or the Horner-Wadsworth-Emmons modification of the Wittig reaction. Start with any carbonyl compound and Wittig or Horner-Wadsworth-Emmons reagent together with any other organic or inorganic reagents that you require.

- **a.** $C_6H_5CH{=}C(CH_3)C_6H_5$
- **b.** $CH_2{=}CH{-}CH{=}CH{-}C_6H_5$
- **c.** $(CH_3)_2C{=}CH{-}CO_2C_2H_5$

8. Suggest *two* different routes for preparing $C_6H_5CH{=}CHCH_3$ via a Wittig reaction, using a phosphorane as the ylide precursor in both cases.

Questions for Part A

9. Suggest a method for preparing benzyltriphenylphosphonium chloride (**4**) via an S_N2 reaction.

10. Define the term *phase-transfer catalyst.*

11. Consider the step in which you washed the crude reaction mixture obtained *immediately* following the Wittig reaction with saturated aqueous sodium bisulfite.

- **a.** What potential contaminant of the final product is removed in this step?
- **b.** Write the chemical equation by which the contaminant is removed and specify whether it is being oxidized, reduced, or neither in the process.

12. Propose a mechanism for the isomerization of (*Z*)-stilbene into (*E*)-stilbene using a trace of iodine and light (Eq. 18.6). (*Hint:* The iodine-iodine bond undergoes homolysis upon irradiation with light; see also Section 7.3.)

13. Based on your experimental results, what are you able to conclude about the iodine/light-promoted isomerization of (*E*)-stilbene? Which of the stilbene isomers appears to be the more stable, and how do you rationalize this difference in stabilities?

Refer to the online resources and use the spectra viewer and Tables 8.1–8.8 as needed to answer the blue-numbered questions on spectroscopy.

14. Consider the spectral data for benzaldehyde (Figs. 18.1 and 18.2).

- **a.** In the functional group region of the IR spectrum, specify the absorptions associated with the carbonyl group and the aromatic ring.
- **b.** In the ^{1}H NMR spectrum, assign the various resonances to the hydrogen nuclei responsible for them.
- **c.** For the ^{13}C NMR data, assign the various resonances to the carbon nuclei responsible for them.

15. Consider the NMR spectral data for benzyltriphenylphosphonium chloride (Fig. 18.6). Note that ^{31}P has $I_z = 1/2$ and therefore couples with neighboring hydrogen and carbon and carbon nuclei having $I_z = 1/2$.

- **a.** In the ^{1}H NMR spectrum, assign the various resonances to the hydrogen nuclei responsible for them.
- **b.** For the ^{13}C NMR data, assign the various resonances to the carbon nuclei responsible for them.

16. Consider the spectral data for (*E*)-stilbene (Figs. 10.34 and 10.35).

- **a.** In the functional group region of the IR spectrum, specify the absorptions associated with the aromatic rings.
- **b.** In the ^{1}H NMR spectrum, assign the various resonances to the hydrogen nuclei responsible for them.
- **c.** For the ^{13}C NMR data, assign the various resonances to the carbon nuclei responsible for them.

17. Consider the spectral data for (*Z*)-stilbene (Figs. 18.3 and 18.4).

- **a.** In the functional group region of the IR spectrum, specify the absorptions associated with the aromatic rings.
- **b.** In the ^{1}H NMR spectrum, assign the various resonances to the hydrogen nuclei responsible for them.
- **c.** For the ^{13}C NMR data, assign the various resonances to the carbon nuclei responsible for them.

18. Discuss the differences observed in the IR and NMR spectra of (*Z*)-stilbene and (*E*)-stilbene that enable you to distinguish between the two isomers. What differences in the IR and NMR spectra of benzaldehyde, (*Z*)-stilbene, and (*E*)-stilbene are consistent with the conversion of benzaldehyde to a mixture of the isomeric stilbenes in this experiment?

19. By analysis of the ^{1}H NMR spectra of the crude product before *and* after irradiation in the presence of iodine, determine the approximate ratios of (*Z*)-stilbene and (*E*)-stilbene.

SPECTRA

Starting Materials and Products

The IR and NMR spectra of (E)-stilbene are provided in Figures 10.34 and 10.35, respectively.

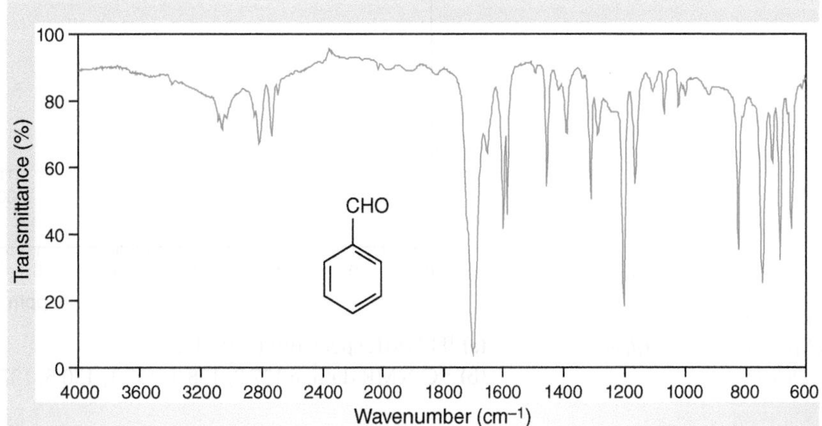

Figure 18.1
IR spectrum of benzaldehyde (neat).

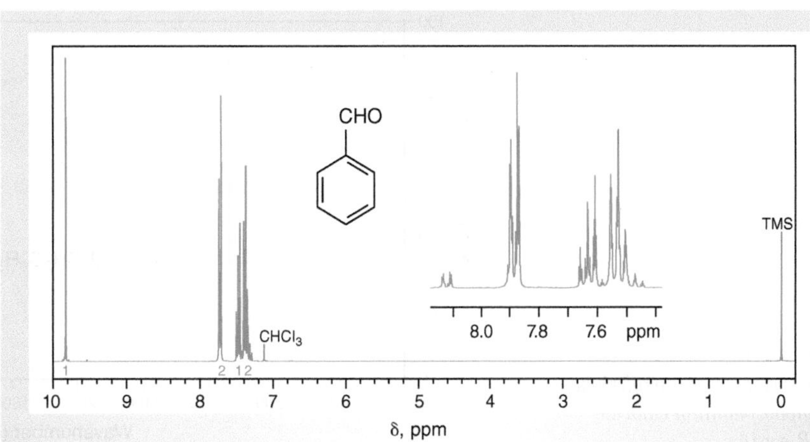

Figure 18.2
NMR data for benzaldeyde ($CDCl_3$).

(a) ^{1}H NMR spectrum (300 MHz).
(b) ^{13}C NMR data: δ 129.0, 129.7, 134.4, 136.6, 192.0.

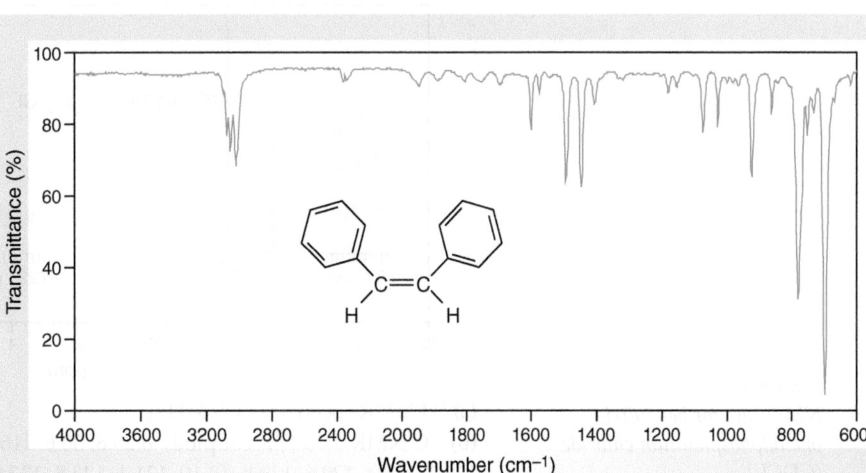

Figure 18.3
IR spectrum of (Z)-stilbene (neat).

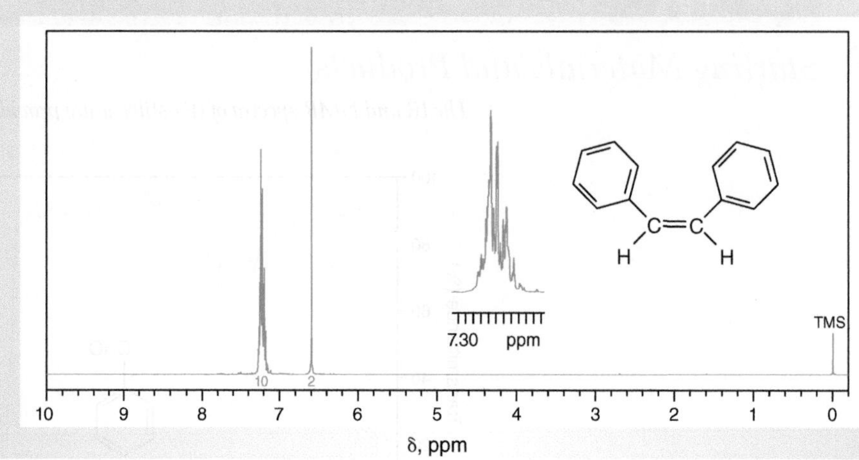

Figure 18.4
NMR data for (Z)-stilbene ($CDCl_3$).

(a) ^{1}H NMR spectrum (300 MHz).
(b) ^{13}C NMR data: δ 127.3, 128.4, 129.1, 130.5, 137.5.

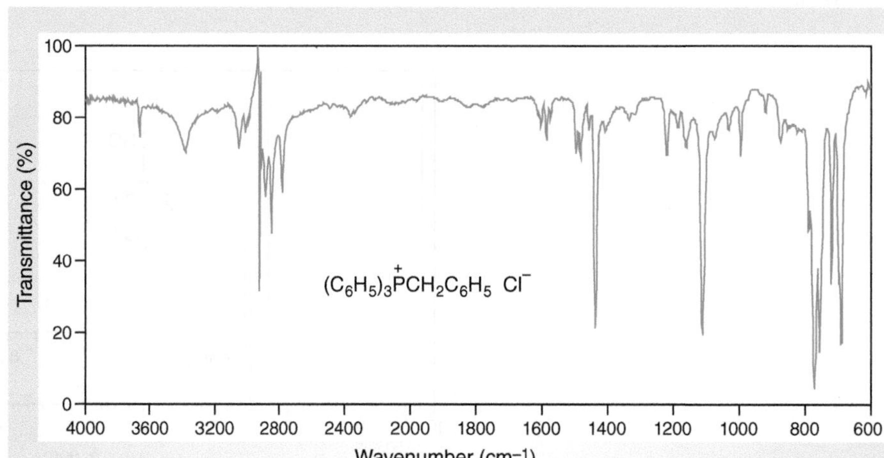

Figure 18.5
IR spectrum of benzyltriphenylphosphonium chloride (IR card).

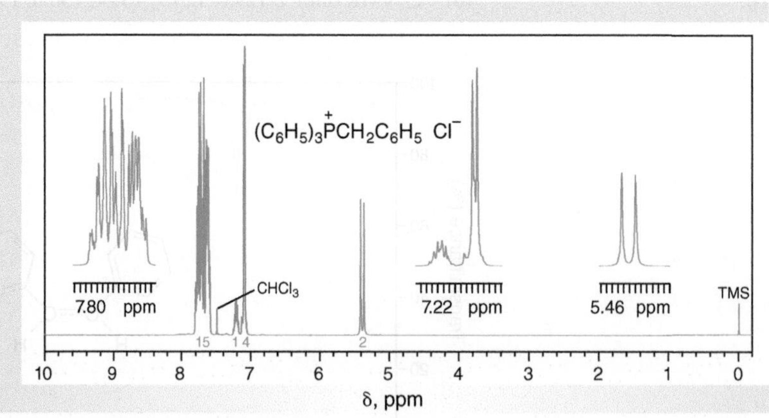

Figure 18.6
NMR data for benzyltriphenylphosphonium chloride ($CDCl_3$).

(a) ^{1}H NMR spectrum (300 MHz).
(b) ^{13}C NMR data (^{31}P-coupled): δ 29.8, 30.6, 116.6, 118.0, 126.8, 127.0, 127.9, 128.3, 128.4, 129.6, 129.8, 13.10, 131.1, 133.8, 133.9, 134.6.

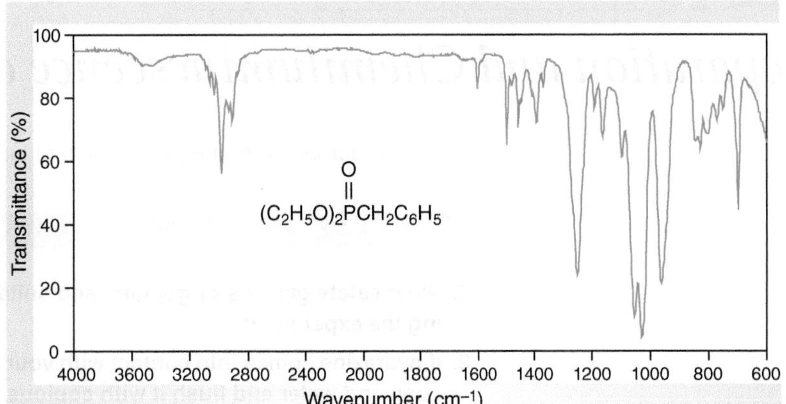

Figure 18.7
IR spectrum of diethyl benzylphosphonate (neat).

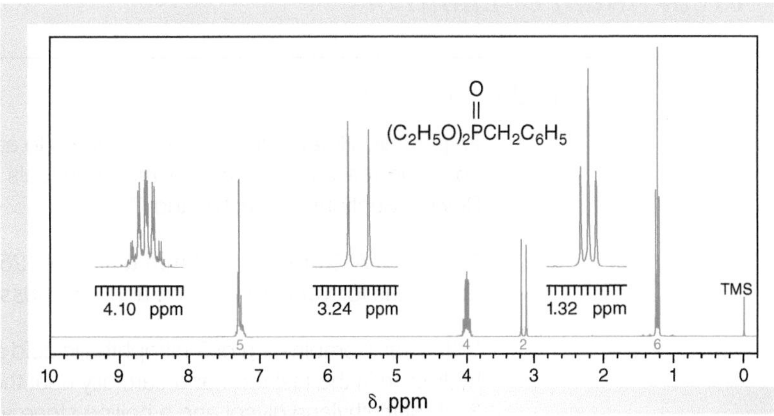

Figure 18.8
NMR data for diethyl benzylphosphonate ($CDCl_3$).

(a) ^{1}H NMR spectrum (300 MHz).

(b) ^{13}C NMR data (^{31}P-coupled): δ 15.9, 16.0, 32.2, 34.4, 61.5, 61.6, 126.3, 126.4, 128.0, 128.1, 129.3, 129.4, 131.1, 131.3.

EXPERIMENTAL PROCEDURES

Preparation and Chemiluminescence of Luminol

Purpose To demonstrate the preparation of luminol and its chemiluminescence.

SAFETY ALERT

1. **Wear safety glasses or goggles and suitable protective gloves while performing the experiment.**
2. **If hydrazine comes into contact with your skin, immediately wash the area with soap and water and flush it with copious amounts of water.**

A ▪ *Preparation of Luminol*

MINISCALE PROCEDURE

Preparation Refer to the online resources to answer Pre-Lab Exercises, access videos, and read the MSDSs for the chemicals used or produced in this procedure. Review Sections 2.9, 2.10, and 2.17.

Apparatus A 20-mm × 150-mm test tube, 25-mL Erlenmeyer flask, thermometer, apparatus for vacuum filtration and *flameless* heating.

Setting Up Combine 1 g of 3-nitrophthalic acid and 2 mL of an 8% aqueous solution of hydrazine in the test tube and carefully heat the mixture until the solid dissolves. Add 3 mL of triethylene glycol and a boiling stone and clamp the vial in a vertical position. Insert a thermometer into the solution, securing the thermometer with a clamp.

Reaction Bring the solution to a vigorous boil to remove excess water. During this time, the temperature should be around 110–120 °C. After the water has evaporated, the temperature should rise to 215 °C in a 3–4-min period. Maintain the temperature at 215–220 °C for 2 min and then remove the test tube from the heat source and allow the solution to cool to about 100 °C. While the test tube and its contents are cooling, bring about 15 mL of water to boiling in the Erlenmeyer flask. Slowly add the hot water to the test tube, stir the contents with a glass stirring rod, cool the mixture to room temperature, and collect the solid nitrohydrazide by vacuum filtration.

Return the damp solid to the uncleaned test tube, add 5 mL of 3 *M* aqueous sodium hydroxide, and mix the contents until the solid is dissolved. Add 3 g of fresh sodium hydrosulfite dihydrate to the solution, rinsing any solid adhering to the walls of the test tube into the solution with a few drops of water, and heat the resulting mixture to just below boiling for 5 min, taking care to avoid bumping.

Work-Up and Isolation Add 2 mL of *glacial* acetic acid to the reaction mixture, cool the test tube in a beaker of cold water, and collect the crude luminol by vacuum filtration. A second crop of product may separate from the filtrate upon standing, but do not combine it with the first crop, which is to be used in the chemiluminescence experiment.

Analysis If instructed to do so, recrystallize the 3-nitrophthalhydrazide and luminol, and obtain their IR and ^{1}H NMR spectra and those of 3-nitrophthalic acid; compare these spectra with those of authentic samples (Figs. 20.15–20.20).

WRAPPING IT UP

Flush the *aqueous filtrates* down the drain with excess water. Put the *filter papers* in the container for nontoxic waste.

EXERCISES

1. Define the following terms.
   - **a.** fluorescence
   - **b.** phosphorescence
   - **c.** chemiluminescence
   - **d.** intersystem crossing
2. What is the difference in electronic configuration of a singlet and a triplet state?
3. There are two carboxylic acid functions in 3-nitrophthalic acid (17). The pK_a of the acid function at the 2-position is approximately 2, whereas that at the 1-position is about 3. Which of the two is the more acidic and why?
4. Given the approximate pK_as provided, compute K_{eq} for the reaction below.

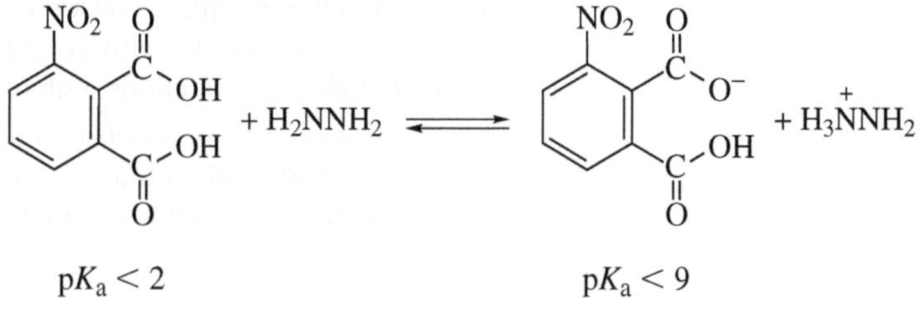

NO_2 O C OH C OH O + H_2NNH_2 ⇌ NO_2 O C O$^-$ C OH O + $H_3\overset{+}{N}NH_2$

p$K_a < 2$ p$K_a < 9$

5. Using curved arrows to symbolize the flow of electrons, propose a mechanism for the transformation shown below.

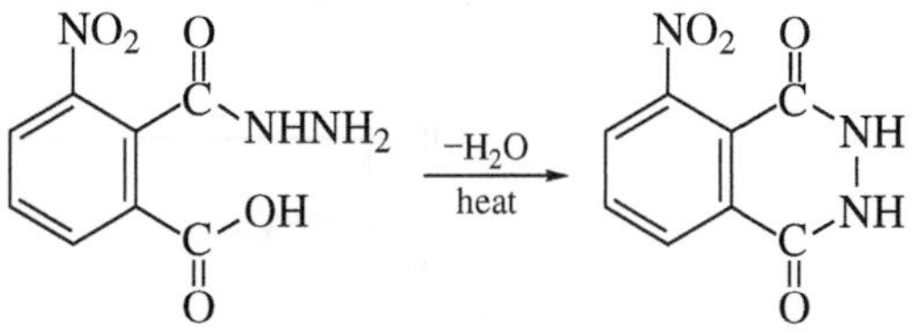

NO_2 O C NHNH$_2$ C OH O —($-H_2O$, heat)→ NO_2 O C NH NH C O

20

6. What factor(s) make the hydrogen atoms of the hydrazide moiety sufficiently acidic so that hydroxide can convert luminol to the dianion portrayed in Scheme 20.3?

Refer to the online resources and use the spectra viewer and Tables 8.1–8.8 as needed to answer the blue-numbered questions on spectroscopy.

7. Consider the spectral data for 3-nitrophthalic acid (Figs. 20.15 and 20.16).
   - **a.** In the functional group region of the IR spectrum, specify the absorptions associated with the O–H bonds and the carbonyl and nitro functions of the molecule.

b. In the ^{1}H NMR spectrum, assign the various resonances to the hydrogen nuclei responsible for them.

c. In the ^{13}C NMR spectrum, assign the various resonances to the carbon nuclei responsible for them.

8. Consider the spectral data for 3-nitrophthalhydrazide (Figs. 20.17 and 20.18).

   a. In the functional group region of the IR spectrum, specify the absorptions associated with the N–H bonds and carbonyl and nitro functions of the molecule.

   b. In the ^{1}H NMR spectrum, assign the various resonances to the hydrogen nuclei responsible for them.

   c. In the ^{13}C NMR spectrum, assign the various resonances to the carbon nuclei responsible for them.

9. Consider the spectral data for luminol (3-aminophthalhydrazide) (Figs. 20.19 and 20.20).

   a. In the functional group region of the IR spectrum, specify the absorptions associated with the N–H bonds of the hydrazide and of the amino group and that of the carbonyl functions of the molecule.

   b. In the ^{1}H NMR spectrum, assign the various resonances to the hydrogen nuclei responsible for them.

   c. In the ^{13}C NMR spectrum, assign the various resonances to the carbon nuclei responsible for them.

10. Discuss the differences observed in the IR and NMR spectra of 3-nitrophthalic acid and 3-nitrophthalhydrazide that are consistent with replacement of the carboxylic acid functions with the hydrazide moiety in this experiment.

11. Discuss the differences observed in the IR and NMR spectra of 3-nitrophthalhydrazide and luminol that are consistent with reduction of the nitro function to an amino group in this experiment.

SPECTRA

Starting Material and Products

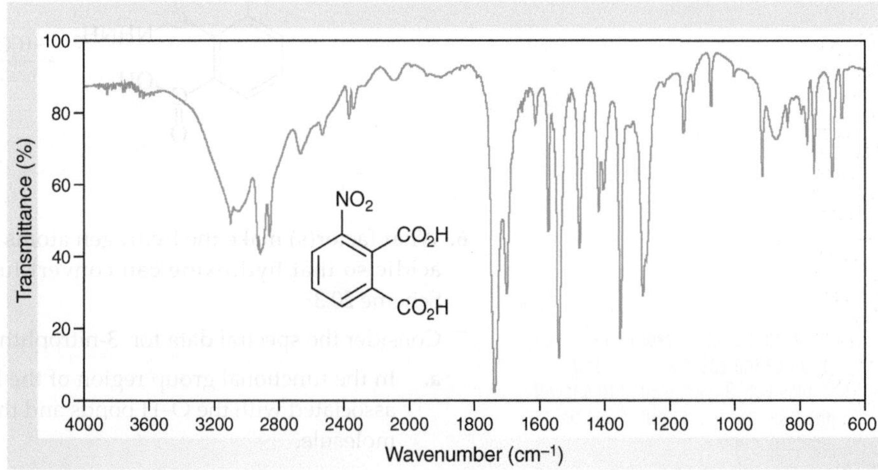

Figure 20.15
IR spectrum of 3-nitrophthalic acid (IR card).

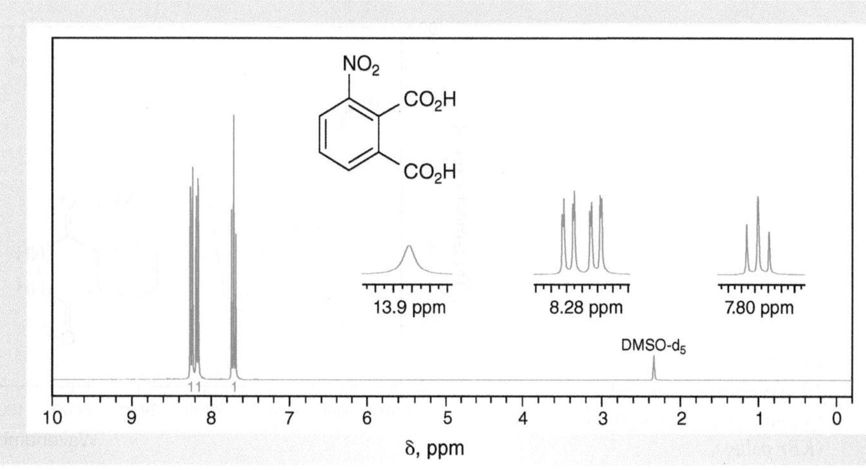

Figure 20.16
NMR data for 3-nitrophthalic acid ($DMSO$-d_6).

(a) ^1H NMR spectrum (300 MHz).
(b) ^{13}C NMR data: δ127.4, 130.4, 130.7, 131.3, 134.9, 146.5, 165.7, 165.8.

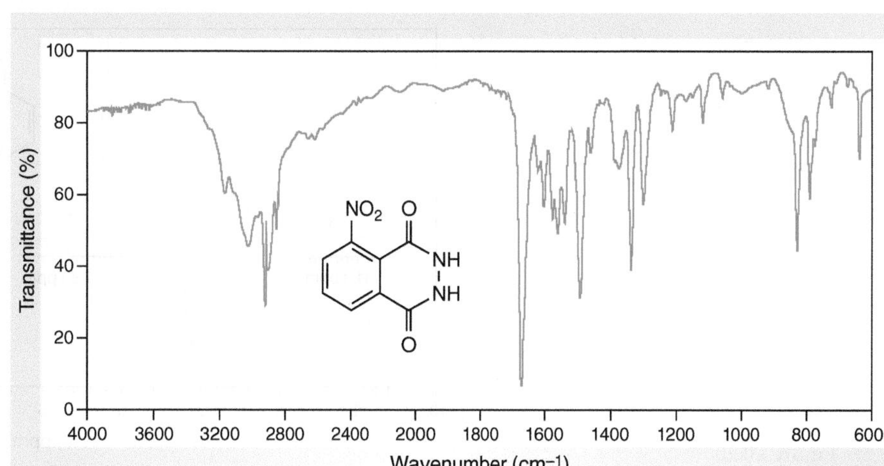

Figure 20.17
IR spectrum of 3-nitrophthalhydrazide (IR card).

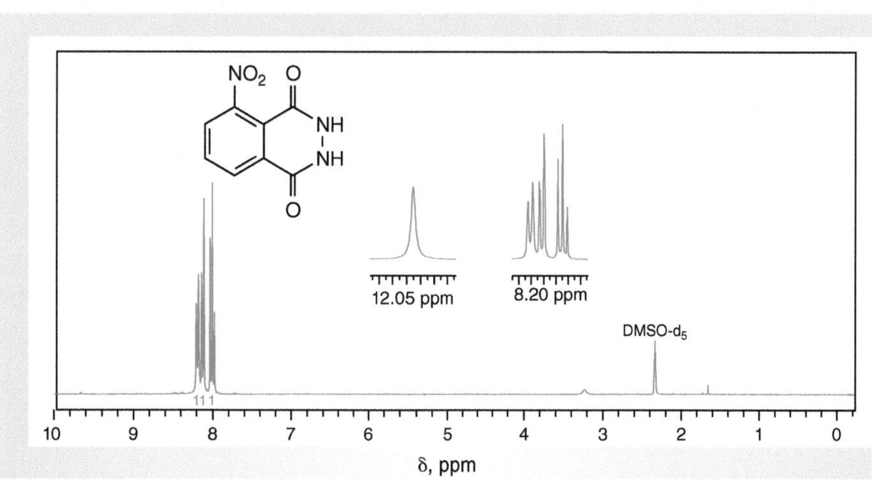

Figure 20.18
NMR data for 3-nitrophthalhydrazide ($DMSO$-d_6).

(a) ^1H NMR spectrum (300 MHz).
(b) ^{13}C NMR data: δ 118.4, 126.1, 127.6, 127.8, 133.9, 147.7, 151.9, 152.7.

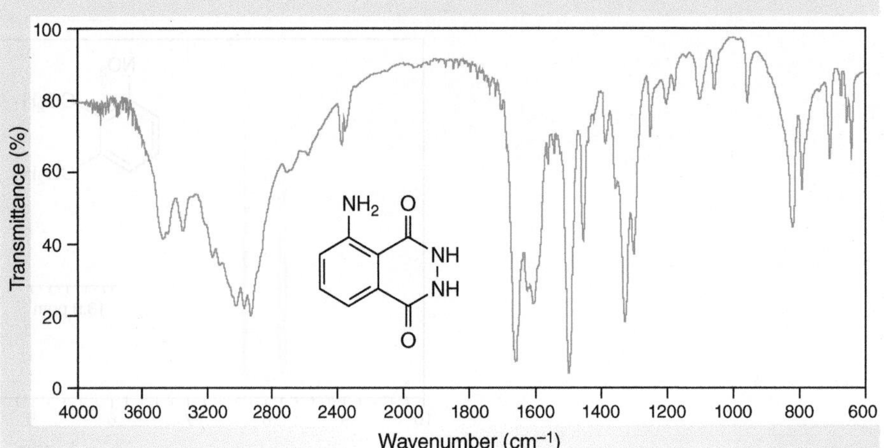

Figure 20.19
IR spectrum of luminol (3-aminophthalhydrazide) (KBr pellet).

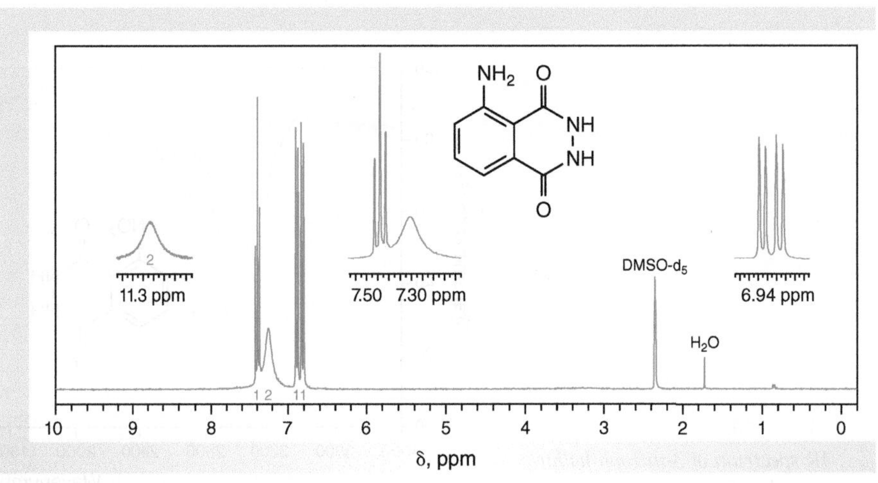

Figure 20.20
NMR data for luminol (3-aminophthalhydrazide) (DMSO-d_6).

(a) ^{1}H NMR spectrum (300 MHz).
(b) ^{13}C NMR data: δ 109.8, 110.6, 116.7, 126.5, 133.9, 150.2, 151.5, 161.2.

EXPERIMENTAL PROCEDURES

Preparation of Nylon-6,10

Discovery Experiment **Purpose** To demonstrate step-growth polymerization by the synthesis of Nylon-6,10.

SAFETY ALERT

1. **Wear safety glasses or goggles and suitable protective gloves while performing the experiment.**
2. **If Pasteur pipets are used instead of syringes to measure the reactants, use a rubber bulb to draw up the liquid.**
3. **Do not handle the polymer rope with your bare hands more than is necessary until it has been washed free of solvent and reagents. Use tongs or forceps to manipulate it. If the crude polymer comes in contact with your skin, immediately wash the area with soap and warm water.**
4. **If you use formic acid to form a film, do not let it get on your skin, because it causes deep skin burns that are not immediately obvious. If the acid does accidentally come in contact with your skin, wash the affected area immediately with 5% sodium bicarbonate solution and then with copious amounts of water.**

MINISCALE PROCEDURE

Preparation Refer to the online resources to answer Pre-Lab Exercises, access videos, and read the MSDSs for the chemicals used or produced in this procedure. Discuss the experiment with your lab partner.

Apparatus A 250-mL beaker, a 5-mL syringe, separatory funnel, apparatus for the "Nylon Rope Trick."

Setting Up Measure 2 mL of decanedioyl dichloride into a 250-mL beaker using the syringe. *The size of the beaker is important:* In smaller beakers, the polymer tends to stick to the walls, whereas in larger beakers, poor "ropes" are obtained unless larger amounts of reagents are used. Dissolve the decanedioyl dichloride in 100 mL of dichloromethane. Place 1.1 g of crystalline 1,6-hexanediamine or 1.3 mL of its commercially available 80–95% aqueous solution in a separatory funnel, and add 2.0 g of sodium carbonate and 50 mL of water. Gently shake the mixture to dissolve both reactants. Arrange the drum onto which the polymer is to be wound at a height such that the beaker containing the decanedioyl dichloride solution can be placed on the lab bench about 40 cm beneath and slightly in front of the drum (Fig. 22.3). Support the separatory funnel containing the other reagents so the lower tip of the funnel is centered no more than a centimeter above the surface of the dichloromethane solution of the decanedioyl dichloride.

Reaction Open the stopcock of the separatory funnel slightly so the aqueous solution runs *slowly and gently* onto the surface of the organic solution. A film of polymer will form immediately at the interface of the two solutions. Use long forceps or tongs to grasp the *center* of the polymer film and pull the rope that forms up to the front of the drum, loop it over the drum, and rotate the drum so as to wind the rope onto the drum. For the first turn or two it may be necessary to use your fingers to secure the rope to the drum. Continue to rotate the drum and rapidly wind the nylon rope onto the drum until the reactants are consumed, remembering to count the revolutions of the drum as you wind.

Work-Up and Isolation Replace the beaker with a large dish or pan containing about 200 mL of 50% aqueous ethanol and unwind the nylon rope into the wash solution. After stirring the mixture gently, decant the wash solution, and transfer the polymer to a filter on a Büchner funnel. Press the polymer as dry as possible, and then place it in your desk until the next laboratory period. When the nylon is thoroughly dry, weigh it and calculate the yield. Note how the bulk of polymer is affected upon drying.

Film Formation To produce a film of Nylon-6,10, dissolve the dry polymer in about 10 times its weight of 90–100% formic acid (*Caution:* See entry 4 of the Safety Alert) by stirring the mixture at *room temperature;* heating to achieve dissolution degrades the polymer. Spread the viscous solution on a glass plate. Leave the plate *in a hood* until the next laboratory period to allow evaporation of the formic acid.

Alternative Procedure

Apparatus A 100-mL beaker, 10-mL graduated cylinder, Pasteur pipet, glass rod or 15-cm length of copper wire.

Setting Up Pour 10 mL of a 5% aqueous solution of 1,6-hexanediamine into the beaker and add 10 drops of 20% aqueous sodium hydroxide solution. Stir the solution to ensure homogeneity.

Reaction Carefully pour 10 mL of a 5% solution of decanedioyl dichloride into the beaker to produce a biphasic mixture. Touch the tip of the glass rod or end of the copper wire to the interface between the two layers and gently remove the rod or wire from the mixture, pulling the fiber of polymer along with it. Twist the rod or wire to spin the fiber around it.

Work-Up and Isolation Follow the procedure described for the "Nylon Rope Trick."

Fiber Formation Form fibers by carefully melting the dry polymer in a metal spoon or spatula with gentle heating over a very small burner flame or a hot plate, and then drawing fibers from the melt with a small glass rod. If necessary, combine your polymer with that of several students to provide enough material to be melted and drawn successfully. Do not heat the polymer much above the melting temperature because it becomes discolored and charred.

Obtain IR and NMR spectra of your starting materials and compare them to those of authentic specimens (Figs. 22.4–22.7).

WRAPPING IT UP

After the rope has been drawn, stir the remaining reaction mixture thoroughly until no more *polymer* forms. Isolate any additional polymer and, after thoroughly washing it with water, put it in the container for nonhazardous organic solids. Separate the *dichloromethane and aqueous layers* of the reaction mixture. Pour the *dichloromethane* into the container for halogenated organic liquids. Flush the *aqueous layer and all aqueous solutions* down the drain.

EXERCISES

1. Explain why the preparation of Nylon-6,10 occurs under milder conditions when decanedioyl dichloride is used instead of decanedioic acid.
2. Using curved arrows to symbolize the flow of electrons, write the stepwise mechanism for the condensation reaction between decandioyl dichloride and 1,6-hexanediamine.
3. Write an equation for the formation of the salt produced from one molecule of hexanedioic acid and two molecules of 1,6-hexanediamine.
4. Why is sodium carbonate used in the reaction to prepare Nylon-6,10?
5. Explain the large decrease in the bulk of the rope of Nylon-6,10 upon drying.
6. Using full structural formulas, draw a typical portion of a Nylon-6,6 molecule; that is, expand a portion of the formula given in Equation 22.15. Show at least two hexanedioic acid units and two 1,6-hexanediamine units.
7. Draw formulas that illustrate the hydrogen bonding that may exist between two polyamide molecules after fibers have been "cold-drawn."
8. Nylons undergo *de*polymerization when heated in aqueous acid. Propose a reaction mechanism that accounts for this fact, using curved arrows to symbolize the flow of electrons.
9. Nylon-6 is produced from caprolactam by adding a small amount of aqueous base and then heating the mixture to about 270 °C.

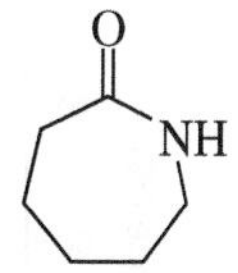

O
NH

Caprolactam

   a. Draw a representative portion of the polyamide molecule.
   b. Suggest a mechanism for the polymerization, using curved arrows to symbolize the flow of electrons, and indicate whether it is of the chain-reaction or step-growth type.

10. Would you expect polyesters to be stabilized by hydrogen bonding? Explain.

11. Proteins are polyamides formed from α-amino acids.

An α-amino acid

a. Write a partial structure of a protein by drawing three monomeric units of it.

b. Are proteins *chain-reaction* or *step-growth* polymers?

Refer to the online resources and use the spectra viewer and Tables 8.1-8.8 as needed to answer the blue-numbered questions on spectroscopy

12. Consider the spectral data for decanedioyl dichloride (Figs. 22.4 and 22.5).

a. In the functional group region of the IR spectrum, specify the absorptions associated with the carbonyl component of the acid chloride.

b. In the ^{1}H NMR spectrum, assign the various resonances to the hydrogen nuclei responsible for them.

c. For the ^{13}C NMR data, assign the various resonances to the carbon nuclei responsible for them.

13. Consider the spectral data for 1,6-hexanediamine (Figs. 22.6 and 22.7).

a. In the IR spectrum, specify the absorptions associated with the amino group.

b. In the ^{1}H NMR spectrum, assign the various resonances to the hydrogen nuclei responsible for them.

c. For the ^{13}C NMR data, assign the various resonances to the carbon nuclei responsible for them.

SPECTRA

Starting Materials

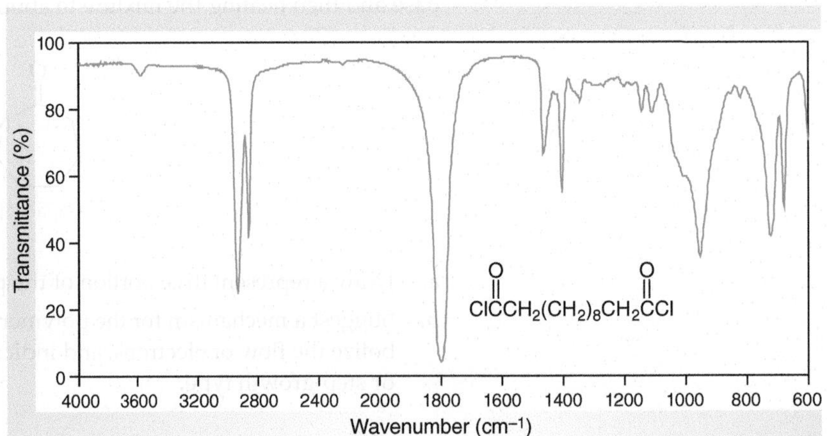

Figure 22.4
IR spectrum of decanedioyl dichloride (neat).

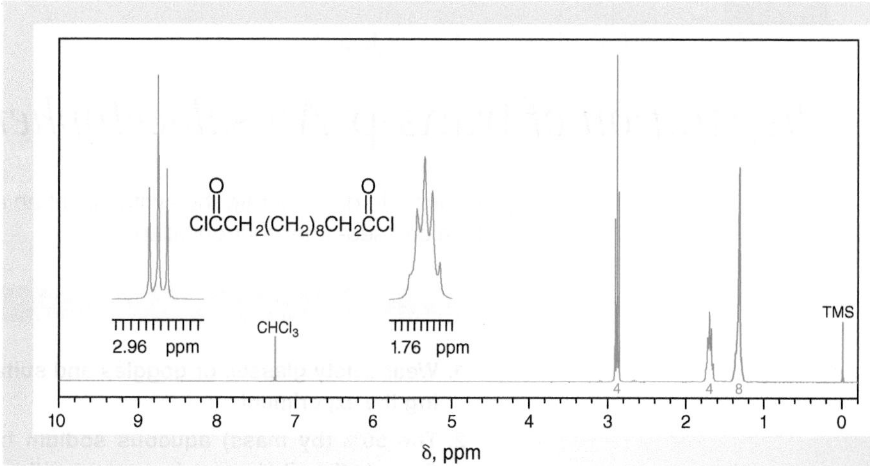

Figure 22.5
NMR data for decanedioyl dichloride ($CDCl_3$).

(a) ^{1}H NMR spectrum (300 MHz).
(b) ^{13}C NMR data: δ 24.7, 27.9, 28.4, 46.7, 173.2.

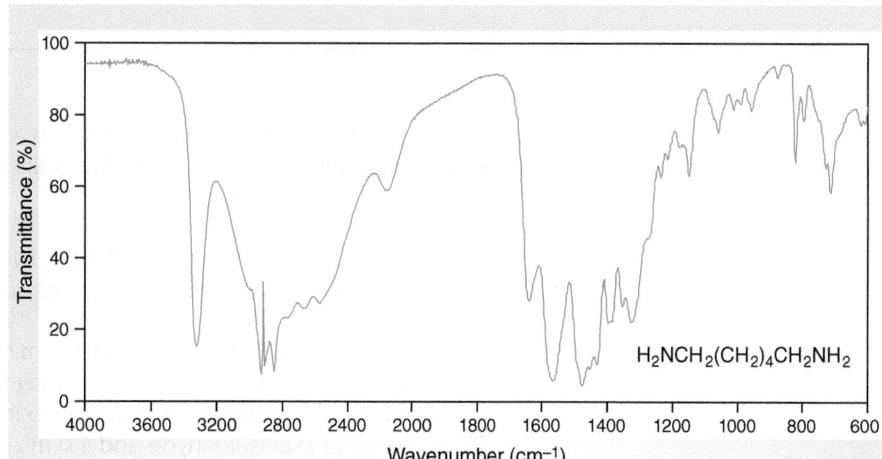

Figure 22.6
IR spectrum of 1,6-hexanediamine (neat).

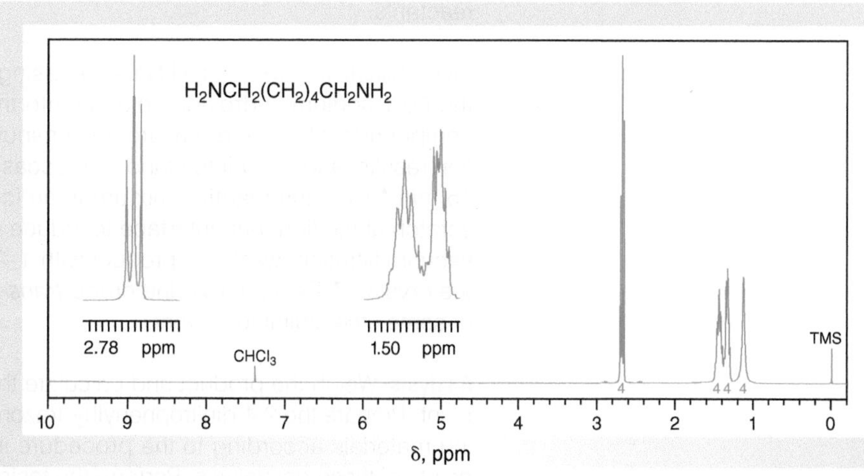

Figure 22.7
NMR data for 1,6-hexanediamine ($CDCl_3$).

(a) ^{1}H NMR spectrum (300 MHz).
(b) ^{13}C NMR data: δ 26.0, 33.0, 41.4.

EXPERIMENTAL PROCEDURES

Preparation of trans-p-*Anisalacetophenone*

Purpose To demonstrate the synthesis of an α,β-unsaturated carbonyl compound by a crossed-aldol condensation.

SAFETY ALERT

1. **Wear safety glasses or goggles and suitable protective gloves while performing the experiment.**
2. **The 50% (by mass) aqueous sodium hydroxide solution is *highly* caustic. *Do not allow it to come in contact with your skin.* If this should happen, wash the affected area with dilute acetic acid and then copious amounts of water.**

MINISCALE PROCEDURE

Preparation Refer to the online resources to answer Pre-Lab Exercises, access videos, and read the MSDSs for the chemicals used or produced in this procedure. Review Sections 2.9, 2.10, 2.11, and 2.17.

Apparatus A 13-mm × 100-mm test tube, two 1-mL syringes, ice-water bath, apparatus for vacuum filtration and *flameless* heating.

Setting Up Prepare a 50% (by mass) sodium hydroxide solution by dissolving 1.0 g sodium hydroxide in 1 mL of water. You may heat the mixture gently to hasten dissolution, but be sure to cool the solution to room temperature before proceeding. Place 1.0 mL of *p*-anisaldehyde and 1.0 mL of acetophenone in the test tube and add 3.0 mL of 95% ethanol. Shake the test tube gently to mix and dissolve the reactants.

Aldol Reaction, Work-Up, and Isolation Using a Pasteur pipet, transfer 5 drops of the 50% sodium hydroxide solution into the ethanolic solution of the carbonyl compounds, shake the mixture for a minute or two until a homogeneous solution results, and allow it to stand with occasional shaking at room temperature for 15 min.★ Cool the reaction mixture in an ice-water bath. If crystals do not form, scratch at the liquid-air interface to induce crystallization. Collect the product by vacuum filtration, wash the product with 1–2 mL of *cold* 95% ethanol, and air-dry the crystals.★ Recrystallize the crude *trans-p*-anisalacetophenone from methanol or some other suitable solvent.

Analysis Weigh the product and calculate the percent yield; determine its melting point. Prepare the 2,4-dinitrophenylhydrazones of the product and of the two starting materials according to the procedure in Section 7.4B; compare the melting points of these derivatives. Perform the tests for unsaturation on the product using

See *Who was Baeyer?*

the bromine and Baeyer tests provided in Section 4.7A. Obtain IR and ^{1}H NMR spectra of your starting materials and product and compare them with those of authentic samples (Figs. 18.9–18.14).

Discovery Experiment

Synthesis of trans,trans-*Dibenzylideneacetone*

Consult with your instructor before performing this experiment, in which you will prepare *trans,trans*-dibenzylideneacetone by the crossed-aldol condensation of benzaldehyde with acetone. Design an experiment using either a miniscale or microscale procedure to produce the product. Determine the relative amounts of benzaldehyde and acetone that should be used by considering the stoichiometry of the reaction and the potential problems that might be associated with side reactions and the use of large excesses of reactants. Freshly distilled benzaldehyde should be used. The product may be recrystallized from an 85% (*v:v*) ethanol-water mixture. Perform the tests for unsaturation on the product using the bromine and Baeyer tests provided in Section 4.7A. Obtain the melting point and the IR, ^{1}H, and ^{13}C NMR spectra of the purified product for purposes of characterization, and compare these with the literature data. Determine the λ_{max} and ε_{max} in the UV spectrum for the product, and compare to the literature values.

Discovery Experiment

Solvent-Free Aldol Condensation

Some but not all organic reactions proceed well in the absence of solvent(s). Develop a solvent-free protocol for the aldol reaction using solid sodium or potassium hydroxide as the base. The reaction can be successfully performed on a 5–10 mmol scale, using an equivalent of base. Bear in mind that the base should be finely divided, so it should first be crushed with a mortar and pestle. In addition, the condensation partners should be mixed thoroughly before the base is added. The reaction should take no more than 20–25 min, and the mixture should be acidified to pH ~5 with 10% HCl prior to isolation of the product. Characterize the product by its melting point and using spectroscopic techniques.

Possible combinations that you might use include acetophenone with either 4-methylbenzaldehyde or 4-chlorobenzaldehyde, 1-indanone with either 4-phenylcyclohexanone or 3,4-dimethoxybenzaldehyde, 4-phenylcyclohexanone with 3,4-dimethoxybenzaldehyde, and 3,4-dimethoxybenzaldehyde with 3,4-dimethoxyacetophenone. Self-condensation of 4-methylbenzaldehyde is also a possibility. Consult with your instructor before undertaking any experiments.

WRAPPING IT UP

Neutralize the *ethanolic filtrates* with dilute hydrochloric acid, and flush them down the drain. Place the *dichloromethane solution* from the bromine test for unsaturation in a container for halogenated organic liquids.

EXERCISES

1. Compute the equilibrium constant, K_{eq}, for the reaction of equimolar amounts of acetophenone, $C_6H_5COCH_3$, and hydroxide ion to generate the enolate ion. The pK_a values of the ketone and of water are 19.0 and 15.7, respectively.
2. Explain why the main reaction between acetophenone and *p*-anisaldehyde is the mixed-aldol reaction rather than (a) self-condensation of acetophenone or (b) the Cannizzaro reaction (Sec. 16.3) of *p*-anisaldehyde.
3. Identify the nucleophile and electrophile involved in the rate-determining step of the synthesis of *trans-p*-anisalacetophenone.
4. Explain why *trans-p*-anisalacetophenone would be expected to be more stable than the corresponding *cis* isomer.
5. Propose a synthesis of cinnamaldehyde using a mixed-aldol condensation reaction.

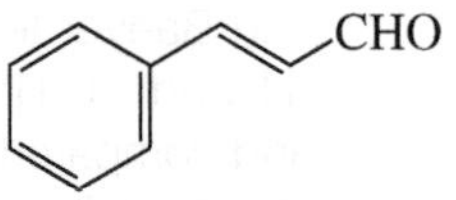

CHO

Cinnamaldehyde

6. Write structures for the various aldol condensation products you expect from the aldol self-condensation of 2-butanone, $CH_3C(=O)CH_2CH_3$.
7. Predict the product of the *intramolecular* aldol reaction of the diketone shown below.

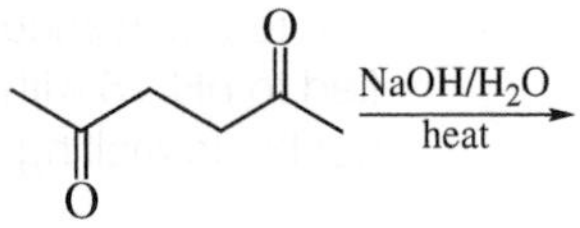

O

O

NaOH/H_2O
heat

2,4-Pentanedione

8. α,β-Unsaturated carbonyl compounds such as *trans-p*-anisalacetophenone (**25**) undergo reactions that are typical of both carbonyl compounds and alkenes. Illustrate this by showing the reaction of **25** with bromine (Sec. 10.6) and 2,4-dinitrophenylhydrazine (Sec. 7.4B) to give the corresponding products.
9. The addition of bromine to *trans-p*-anisalacetophenone (**25**) gives a single diastereomer.
   a. Using curved arrows to symbolize the flow of electrons and suitable stereochemical drawings, show the mechanism of this reaction (*Hint:* See Sec. 10.6).
   b. How does the mechanism you proposed in Part **a** support the formation of the racemic form of a single diastereomer?

Refer to the online resources and use the spectra viewer and Tables 8.1–8.8 as needed to answer the blue-numbered questions on spectroscopy.

10. Consider the spectral data for acetophenone (Figs. 18.9 and 18.10).
    a. In the functional group region of the IR spectrum, specify the absorptions associated with the carbonyl group and the aromatic ring.
    b. In the ^{1}H NMR spectrum, assign the various resonances to the hydrogen nuclei responsible for them.
    c. For the ^{13}C NMR data, assign the various resonances to the carbon nuclei responsible for them.
11. Consider the spectral data for *p*-anisaldehyde (Figs. 18.11 and 18.12).
    a. In the functional group region of the IR spectrum, specify the absorptions associated with the carbonyl group and the aromatic ring. Also specify the absorption in the fingerprint region that is associated with the *para* substitution on the aromatic ring.
    b. In the ^{1}H NMR spectrum, assign the various resonances to the hydrogen nuclei responsible for them.
    c. For the ^{13}C NMR data, assign the various resonances to the carbon nuclei responsible for them.
12. Consider the spectral data for *trans-p*-anisalacetophenone (Figs. 18.13 and 18.14).
    a. In the functional group region of the IR spectrum, specify the absorptions associated with the unsaturated ketone group and the aromatic rings. Also specify the absorptions in the fingerprint region that are associated with the *para* substitution on the aromatic ring and the *trans* carbon-carbon double bond.
    b. In the ^{1}H NMR spectrum, assign the various resonances to the hydrogen nuclei responsible for them.
    c. For the ^{13}C NMR data, assign the various resonances to the carbon nuclei responsible for them.
13. Discuss the differences observed in the IR and NMR spectra of acetophenone, *p*-anisaldehyde, and *trans-p*-anisalacetophenone that are consistent with the crossed-aldol condensation occurring in this experiment.

SPECTRA

Starting Materials and Products

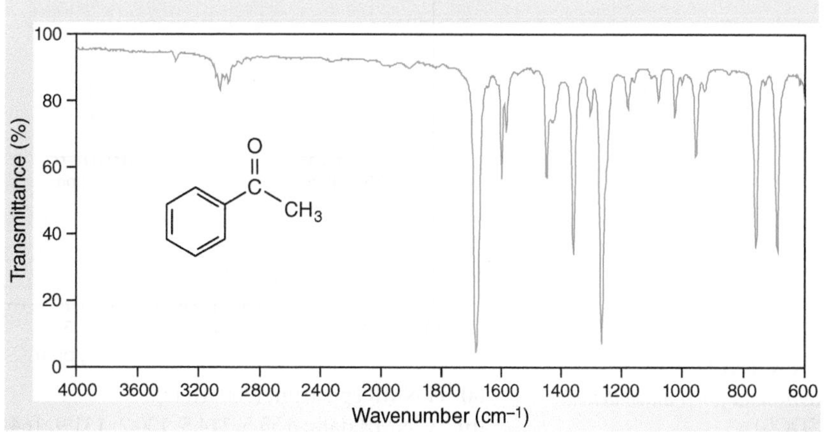

Figure 18.9
IR spectrum of acetophenone (neat).

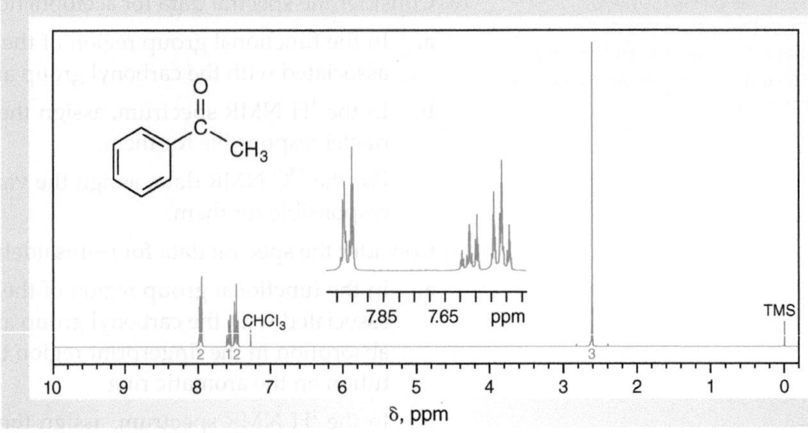

Figure 18.10
NMR data for acetophenone ($CDCl_3$).

(a) ^{1}H NMR spectrum (300 MHz).
(b) ^{13}C NMR data: δ 26.3, 128.3, 128.8, 133.0, 137.3, 197.4.

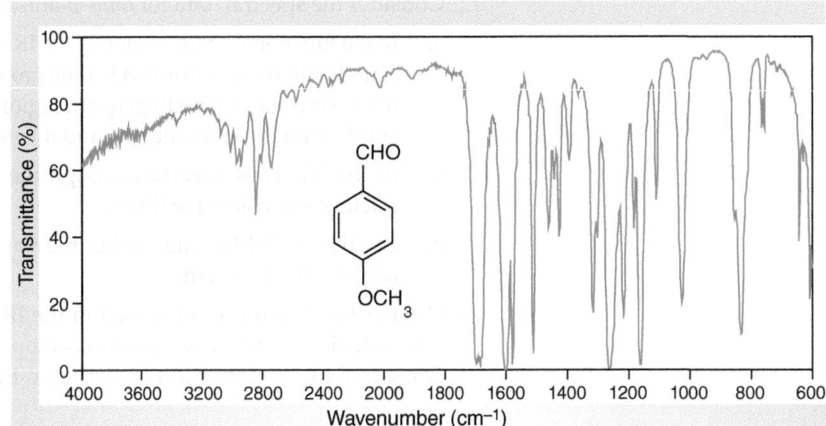

Figure 18.11
IR spectrum of p*-anisaldehyde (neat).*

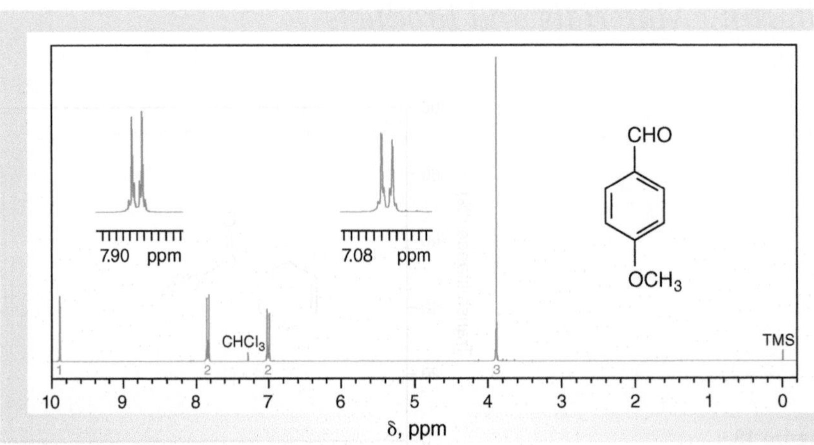

Figure 18.12
NMR data for p*-anisaldehyde ($CDCl_3$).*

(a) ^{1}H NMR spectrum (300 MHz).
(b) ^{13}C NMR data: δ 55.5, 114.5, 130.2, 131.9, 164.6, 190.5.

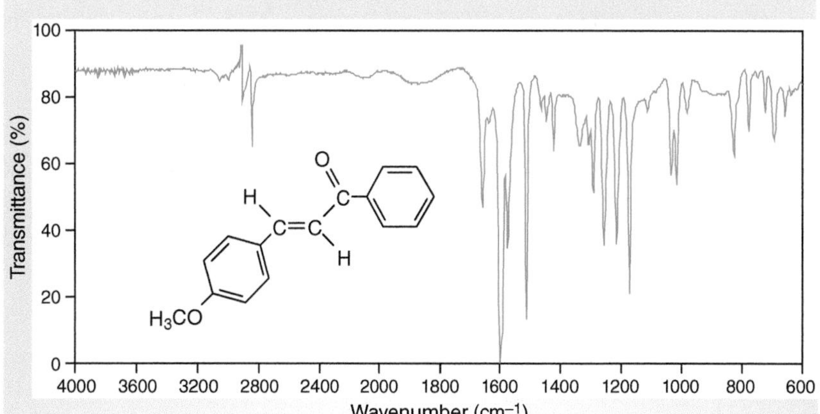

Figure 18.13
IR spectrum of trans-p-anisalacetophenone (IR card).

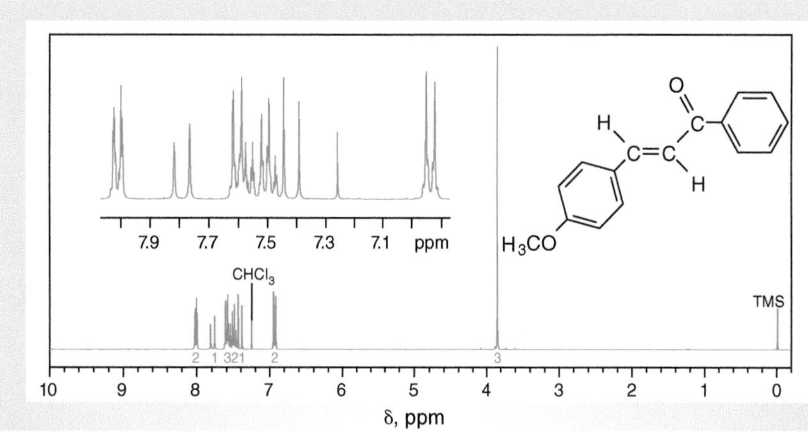

Figure 18.14
NMR data for trans-p-anisalacetophenone ($CDCl_3$).

(a) ^{1}H NMR spectrum (300 MHz).

(b) ^{13}C NMR data: δ 55.3, 114.4, 119.7, 127.6, 128.4, 128.5, 130.2, 132.5, 138.5, 144.6, 161.7, 190.4.

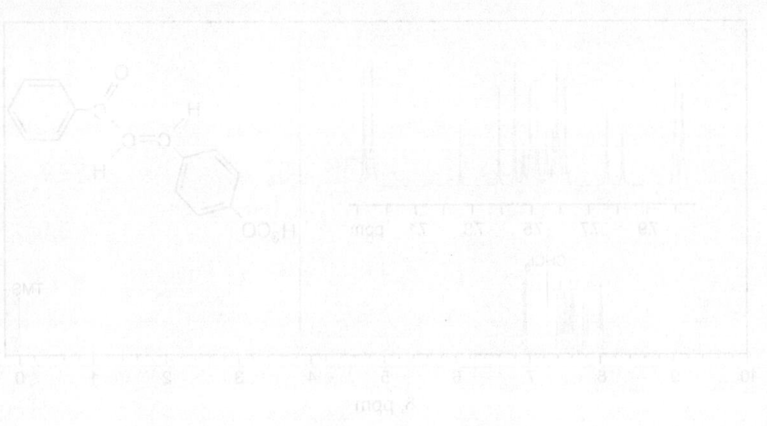